D1452133

Gardening
for the Birds

Gardening
for the Birds

Thomas G. Barnes

THE UNIVERSITY PRESS OF KENTUCKY

Publication of this volume was made possible in part by grants from the Kentucky Department of Fish and Wildlife Resources and the National Endowment for the Humanities.

Scholarly publisher for the Commonwealth,
serving Bellarmine College, Berea College, Centre
College of Kentucky, Eastern Kentucky University,
The Filson Club Historical Society, Georgetown College,
Kentucky Historical Society, Kentucky State University,
Morehead State University, Murray State University,
Northern Kentucky University, Transylvania University,
University of Kentucky, University of Louisville,
and Western Kentucky University.

Editorial and Sales Offices: The University Press of Kentucky
663 South Limestone Street, Lexington, Kentucky 40508-4008

03 02 01 00 99   5 4 3 2 1

Library of Congress Cataloging-in-Publication Data

Barnes, Thomas G., 1957-
    Gardening for the birds / Thomas G. Barnes
       p.   cm.
    Includes bibliographical references and index.
    ISBN 0-8131-2071-3 (alk. paper)
    1. Gardening to attract birds.   I. Title.
  QL676.5.B26   1998
  635.9'67—dc21   98-6128

Manufactured in South Korea

Contents

Acknowledgments

Writing this book has been a wonderful and educational experience for me. This project would not have been possible without the assistance of numerous individuals. The book was written with the assistance of the following individuals, who wrote or provided information for these chapters: Karen Bess, landscape designer, Louisville, Kentucky, for chapter 3; Sherri Evans, native plantscaper, Kentucky Department of Fish and Wildlife Resources, for chapter 4; Michael Masser, aquaculture specialist, Auburn University, for chapter 6; Scott Craven, Extension wildlife specialist, University of Wisconsin, for chapter 7.

The following individuals provided professional and thoughtful comments on early drafts: Paul Barnes, plant ecologist, Southwest Texas State University; Carroll Henderson, urban wildlife biologist, Minnesota Department of Natural Resources; Jeff Jackson, Extension wildlife specialist, University of Georgia; Julian Campbell, botanist, Kentucky Chapter of the Nature Conservancy; Lynn Garrison, wildlife biologist, Kentucky Department of Fish and Wildlife Resources; Del Benson, Extension wildlife specialist, Colorado State University; Wayne Davis, retired biology professor, University of Kentucky; Dean Stewart, Extension wildlife specialist, Mississippi State University; Lowell Adams, urban wildlife biologist, Columbia, Maryland; Mary Witt, horticulture professor, University of Kentucky; Ken Hiday, owner of Wild Birds Unlimited, Lexington, Kentucky; and several anonymous reviewers for the University Press of Kentucky.

I am indebted to copyeditor Linda Gregonis for her assistance. Debbie

Allen, formerly of the University of Kentucky Agricultural Extension Service, provided initial editing of the manuscript.

Ryan Gugler, Kentucky Agricultural Extension Service, created all the original watercolors for the book and redrew all the black-and-white drawings. I appreciate the Cooperative Extension Services of the University of Kentucky, the University of Nebraska, the University of Wisconsin, West Virginia University, and the University of South Carolina for use and reproduction of various drawings in the book. The photographs were all taken by me with the exception of the bluebird on page 260, taken by Philippe Roca.

I would like to extend a special thank you to all the individuals and organizations that allowed me to intrude into their homes or yards to photograph birds: Patty Hornback, Mark and Cathy Morgan, Dean and Mildred Schryer, Charlie Smith, Marie Sutton, the staff at North Central 4-H Camp, the Living Arts & Sciences Center, Mike Lorton and the staff of Raven Run Nature Sanctuary, and numerous other individuals I have failed to mention and who assisted in this project.

I extend deep appreciation to my chair, Dr. Robert Muller, and the deans in the College of Agriculture, Oran Little and Walter Walla, for their support of my programs and this book.

Finally, I would like to thank my wife, Linda, and son, Jeremiah, for their support throughout this project. They endured my long days away from home and the open window on winter days as I photographed birds in my backyard. I love you both.

I would like to extend my sincere appreciation to the Kentucky Department of Fish and Wildlife Resources, the Kentucky Division of Forestry, and the Cooperative Extension Service Renewable Resources Extension Act (RREA) for partial funding of this book.

Introduction

THE BOOK MARKET has been inundated in the past several years with books on attracting birds, feeding birds, landscaping with wildflowers, and so on. I believe this development indicates great interest in wildlife management, use of native plants, and landscaping for wildlife. A primary mission of the Cooperative Extension Service is to provide the people of Kentucky with information to help them become better stewards of their resources, including specific information pertaining to natural resources. One purpose of this book is to satisfy the great demand on county extension agents for this information. Various statewide programs, including master gardeners, Color Me Beautiful with Wildflowers (the home economics landscape program), and 4-H programs on urban wildlife and bird feeding, have swelled in the past several years.

Although Kentucky could be considered a rural state, in actuality more than 75 percent of our population lives in the five largest urban counties. In fact, fewer than 3 percent of United States residents are farmers. One study predicted that more than 75 percent of America's population will live in cities by the year 2000. When I examined the number of people interested in wildlife, factored in the urban population numbers, and realized that most people do not comprehend the idea of managing for wildlife, it seemed that a book explaining step-by-step how to create a wildlife-friendly urban environment—a habitat—using native plants would be useful. Creating habitat is nothing more than providing cover or shelter, food, and water, and a space in which wildlife can use these elements.

Before the topic of habitat development is considered, it is important to understand that planting vegetation in urban environments provides not only wildlife habitat but other important values as well. Del Benson, Extension Wildlife Specialist at Colorado State University, writes, "Vegetation provides beauty, reduces noise, controls erosion, absorbs airborne and waterborne wastes, cools and filters air, reduces wind, absorbs carbon dioxide, processes ozone and sulfur dioxide, produces oxygen, and improves property values. It can also help buffer conflicting recreational activities and serve to direct traffic and movements within urban parks."

This book was written for anyone interested in wildlife and urban green space, or in protecting Kentucky's biodiversity—the variety of life and its processes. Urban wildlife management is everyone's job—that of homeowners, urban planners, landscape architects, builders, politicians, developers, garden clubs, civic organizations, schools, neighborhood associations, wildlife managers, or anyone with open space. Everyone has the *potential* to provide the necessary ingredients of wildlife habitat. Horticulturists, teachers and other educators, nursery people, and county extension agents also can use the information provided in this book.

Urban landscaping for wildlife can be as simple or complex as you want it to be. For the most part, it is not difficult and only requires some considerations for habitat during the planning or design process. The primary focus of this book is a landscape architecture concept defined as "the manipulation, modification, and management of outdoor environments to bring about a peaceful coexistence between the human population, wildlife resources, and plant communities that support various animal groups (including humans)." Janice Schach addressed the concept of landscape design as "using plants as architectural, engineering, and aesthetic tools which build an enjoyable outdoor environment." Thus, ideas are presented on planning, designing, creating, enhancing, and managing urban landscapes for wildlife and humans. Urban landscapes include backyards, parks, road rights-of-way, green spaces, and other open lands. Although the information is specific to Kentucky's environment, many of the plants recommended also are native to Illinois, Ohio, Indiana, West Virginia, Virginia, Tennessee, Missouri, and other states. Because Kentucky lies at the crossroads between north and south and east and west, we have habitats similar to prairie states, coastal plains states, and eastern mountain states.

Although the book is geared toward making urban environments more wildlife-friendly and emphasizes the positive aspects of wildlife, it also discusses ways to deal with problem wildlife. Sometimes wildlife is in the wrong place at the wrong time, causing homeowners aggravation or economic damage. The final chapter provides a common-sense approach to predicting where animal problems might occur and to finding solutions before problems arise.

Finally, the appendixes of this book contain a wealth of valuable information, such as how to build birdhouses and which nurseries supply the planting stocks you need.

This book is a component of the Kentucky Department of Fish and Wildlife Resources' Backyard Wildlife: A Habitat Improvement Program. The program was developed in 1996 to promote the development of urban wildlife management in Kentucky. To participate in the program, you may write to the Department of Fish and Wildlife Resources, #1 Game Farm Road, Frankfort, KY 40601. The department will send you an application for certification of your property as wildlife-friendly. If your habitat is certified, the Department of Fish and Wildlife Resources will send you an attractive certificate suitable for framing and a "Going Wild in My Backyard" sign to display. Outstanding examples of backyard habitats will be featured in a revolving exhibit at the Salato Wildlife Center, and creators will receive their certificates in special ceremonies. Schools interested in participating can receive technical assistance from a wildlife biologist, as well as reimbursement for costs associated with development and maintenance of outdoor classrooms.

References

Henderson, C.L. 1987. *Landscaping for Wildlife*. Minneapolis: Minnesota Department of Natural Resources, 144 pp.

Cervelli-Schach, J. 1985. *Landscape Design with Plants: Creating Outdoor Rooms*. University of Kentucky Cooperative Extension Publication H062.

Urban Wildlife Conservation

1

> There are some who can live with wild things, and
> some who cannot. These essays are the delights and dilemmas
> of one who cannot.
>
> —Aldo Leopold, 1949, *A Sand County Almanac*

I ADMIT IT, I live in the city. But I still enjoy wildlife at my home in the center of Lexington, Kentucky. Like clockwork every June, I am visited by and take tremendous enjoyment in the flock of cedar waxwings that ravage the cherry tree. In August and September, I sit in my lawn chair at dusk, amazed by the high-flying acrobatics of common nighthawks, chimney swifts, and big brown bats. I tolerate the gray squirrels raiding the bird feeder every morning and watch my son marvel at blue jays eating large peanuts in the shell. Through my office window at the University of Kentucky, I am greeted by the Northern mockingbird that resides in the nearby American holly tree and am distracted by the red-tailed hawk that glides above campus. As you can see, even though I live and work in the city, I have many opportunities to view wildlife. You, too, can enjoy such opportunities.

The main goal of this book is to help you enjoy, understand, and manage wildlife in an urban environment. Plants are the foundation in creating habitat for wildlife, and habitat is the key to bringing wildlife into your backyard. This book focuses on using native plants in landscaping. Why? There are numerous reasons, but the most important is that various forms of wildlife have adapted over thousands of years to using native plants. Kentucky's butterflies prefer milkweed, blazing stars, and coneflowers to petunias, zinnias, and butterfly bush. The region's birds like seed of native sunflowers, silphium, and coreopsis over wheat, oats, and corn. A dozen species of butterflies have been observed using the native wildflower garden at the Living Arts & Science Center in downtown Lexington. All of these butterflies were seen using native flowers; not once during the garden's three years of existence has a butterfly been seen feeding on the exotic butterfly bush immediately adjacent to the garden.

Native plants are naturally hardy and can withstand some neglect once established, as well as being able to withstand severe drought, excessive rainfall, aphid and Japanese beetle attacks, and other natural calamities. Why? Again, over thousands of years these plants have become adapted to our soils, climate, insect pests, and pathogens. Why choose a native plant over a readily available, cheap or inexpensive flower like a petunia? How about low maintenance. Only the best and strongest survive in nature's grand plan, so once a native is firmly established it doesn't need watering, fertilizing, or pesticides to survive. This means that you save money in the long run. Native plants are more expensive to establish (most cost between $3.00 and $6.00 per plant), but many are long-lived perennials and you save money by not purchasing plants annually and by reducing maintenance costs.

Native plants can be used in every garden situation, even those that are difficult or extreme. More than 3,500 species of plants call Kentucky home. Our native species come in all sizes, shapes, textures, and colors. This wide selection provides you with opportunities to provide visual interest in your yard all year long. There are plants adapted to full sun (prairie plants like purple coneflowers, butterfly weed, or black-eyed Susans) or full shade (woodland plants like wild ginger, foamflower, or wild geranium, for example, actually will grow under that old walnut tree in your yard). There are plants adapted to wet or dry conditions. Kentucky's native prickly pear cactus, side oats grama grass, agave, flower-of-an-hour, and pale purple coneflower almost grow out of rock. At the other extreme, southern blue flag iris, copper iris, arrowhead, river birch, and bald cypress grow in damp soil or even in standing water.

Native wildflowers create a garden full of wonderful plants unlike anyone else's in the neighborhood. Their stunning beauty rivals any exotic you can imagine planting. Natives are part of our biological and historical heritage. Why can't we create neighborhoods that represent how the area looked before our houses or subdivisions were built? A stroll down the street could be an educational experience in which we could talk about plants that sustained Native Americans, plants that provided food and fiber for the early settlers, or interesting plants that have mystified botanists for years? As Lady Bird Johnson said, "I want places to look like where they are. I want Alabama to look like Alabama, and Texas to look like Texas."

As I travel around Kentucky giving lectures on using native plants and wildflowers to attract wildlife, horticulturalists inform me that native species are too difficult to grow, they aren't "showy" enough, don't bloom long enough, and are difficult to obtain. At a cursory, uninformed level you might be inclined to agree; but growing native perennials from good nursery stock is no different from, and no more difficult than, growing hostas or other cultivated plants. If you create a good, weed-free seed bed, place the plant in the proper habitat (sun, shade, and so on), provide water and eliminate weeds they do fine. Creating prairie from seed can be a different story. Techniques for prairie or meadow establishment are covered in chapter 4.

As I mentioned, one potential disadvantage is that the plants aren't "showy" enough or don't bloom long enough. Many woodland species of wildflowers do not have large, showy blooms and they bloom for a very short period of the year. This can be compensated for by planting a variety of species in drifts, masses, or clusters. The open sun or prairie species are definitely showy and their blooms can last for weeks. Think about natives that have been cultivated by horticulturalists: spiked blazing star, purple coneflower, black-eyed Susan, "purple dome" New England aster—the list goes on and on.

Native plants *can* be difficult to find from your "traditional" nursery or garden center. This has been a big barrier to landscaping with native plants. In response to growing demand, however, nurseries specializing in native plants have sprung up across the nation. There are now a few of these nurseries in Kentucky and adjacent states. To find one close to you, check the list in Appendix D. Be sure to order early, as many native plant nurseries sell out of popular plants before the planting season even begins.

Do not collect plants from the wild unless you are transplanting them from areas slated for development. Do collect seeds from wild plants to propagate native plants. Look for native plants along country roads. Be sure to obtain the landowner's permission before collecting seeds from plants on private land.

Where We've Been and Where We're Going

The faces of the United States and Kentucky have changed since Europeans arrived in this country. Forestry, agriculture, mining, industrial development, and urbanization have reduced the amount of undeveloped land, which wildlife needs to survive. History tells the story of how past land uses have changed the landscape and wildlife of Kentucky. Actions in the past were largely reflective of people's attitudes, resource availability, and environmental, social, and economic conditions. When European settlers arrived in the New World, they gave little thought to increasing wildlife populations because many species were in abundant supply. When those supplies began to dwindle, efforts were initiated to regulate the killing of some wildlife species. It wasn't until the 1930s that dwindling wildlife populations became important enough in the public's consciousness that Congress passed legislation to provide for the conservation and restoration of numerous wildlife species. Historical changes in land-use patterns never were intentionally meant to harm wildlife. They were an unavoidable circumstance of developing and creating a society for the future.

So, what greeted the Europeans? A vast forest reached from the Atlantic Ocean to the Mississippi River. As Daniel Boone, Simon Kenton, and other early settlers moved through Kentucky in the last quarter of the 1700s, they found that about 90 percent (23 million acres) of Kentucky was forested. The forests were considered to be some of the most luxuriant hardwood stands in North America. The central bluegrass and barrens (prairies) were the only regions of the state without large acreages of forest land. Tall grass prairie covered nearly 3 million acres in central and western Kentucky. Miles of rivers and streams, numerous sinkhole ponds and springs, and more than 1.6 million acres of floodplain wetlands provided a rich and varied aquatic habitat. Thousands of caves and underground passages added to the complex biological heritage of Kentucky.

Settlement of the unspoiled wilderness and a growing Anglo-American population exacted a heavy toll on our natural resources. Early settlers used great amounts of wood in building and as a source of heat. In addition, open land in most of the state was scarce, and the settlers needed treeless acreage to produce food. The transformation, or conversion, of the land from forests to other uses began in earnest in the 1800s. During the early settlement period, forests were cut and burned to provide for the needs of society. Such disturbances to the forests were undoubtedly localized and probably did not affect wildlife populations on a broad scale.

The next stage of land transformation began in the late 1800s and early 1900s, at the beginning of the industrial age. Our society was becoming more urbanized. As the industrial society developed, it had a ravenous need for iron and steel. Wood products were also in demand. The heaviest assault on the forests came during this period. Large acreages were cut for the iron furnace and charcoal industries. As these forests were cleared, large tracts were converted to permanent agricultural land. Populations of wildlife species that required vast forested acreages—red wolves, mountain lions, Carolina parakeets, wild turkeys, gray squirrels, and others—were eliminated or greatly reduced in numbers. Other species, the Northern bobwhite quail and cottontail rabbit, for example, increased with the presence of crop fields and brushy hedgerows.

In the Kentucky we know today, fewer than 5,000 of the original 23 million forested acres remain uncut. The amount of forested habitat in the state has been reduced from 90 percent to 53 percent. As forested habitat was impacted, so was the wildlife that depended on that habitat. The tall grass prairie, where a man could get lost in a sea of grass grazed by bison and elk, has been reduced to fewer than 200 acres. Bison, elk, and prairie chickens are gone from Kentucky. Eighty percent of our state's precious wetlands, swamps, and marshes have been destroyed. As these habitats were destroyed, their vast diversity of water birds and millions of waterfowl were forced to seek habitat elsewhere or perish. You rarely can enter a cave without seeing some sign of human disturbance such as trash or graffiti. It is not surprising that more than 50 percent of our bats that live in caves are considered rare, threatened, or endangered. Not one acre of the stately bluegrass savanna, an ecosystem unique to North America, is left in central Kentucky. These changes were probably inevitable and certainly were not done to harm Kentucky's native wildlife. Rather, they are the cost of people attempting to survive and make a living in a wild new land. The human pressures on natural resources in Kentucky have multiplied thousands of times over since Boone and Kenton explored this beautiful and wonderful state.

As time passed, the forests regenerated in sections of eastern Kentucky that had been cleared and once again provided habitat for squirrels, turkeys, and other forest-dwelling wildlife. Today, between 70 and 80 percent of eastern Kentucky is forested. The only large-scale destruction of forest habitat is strip-mining for coal. The story is different in western Kentucky, where only 40 percent of the land regenerated to forests. Because of the topography and more fertile soils, the remaining lands were converted for permanent agricultural uses. As for central Kentucky, with the growth of Lexington and the urban forest created in the city, there is probably more forested land in the bluegrass today than at any other time in history.

The face of Kentucky has changed and continues to change. As our population expands and our economy and society shift to an industrially based society, citizens abandon farm life and move to the city or suburbs. One of the greatest threats to some wildlife populations today is development and suburbanization. One need only fly on a clear night from Lexington to Louisville to northern Kentucky to see the clusters of lights indicating suburban developments that have fragmented remaining forest lands. People enjoy and appreciate the amenities of the city but they can feel "isolated" on a 1- to 10-acre tract of land. As suburbs develop, the forest canopy is broken apart; green, weed-free lawns are established, and exotic, or nonnative, plants are introduced into the environment. Some wildlife, particularly generalists such as the white-tailed deer or robin, flourish with these changes. Others, including some amphibians and neotropical migrant songbirds, cannot accommodate the change and disappear.

This gives people the impression that as wild land is converted to urban or suburban uses, it loses its value to wildlife. The habitat value is altered, but development does not have to destroy *all* the wildlife habitat value of the land. With proper knowledge in hand, creative planning, and proper management of the remaining resources, some species of wildlife can thrive in the urban environment.

There can be little doubt that people enjoy wildlife in parks and other urban environments. Pass the pond in front of Lexington Mall during daylight hours and you are likely to see someone feeding the ducks or geese. The success of the peregrine falcon project in Lexington was largely due to countless hours that volunteers spent watching the birds. On my way to work, I pass the Gluck Equine Research Center and watch people carrying five-gallon pails of corn to feed the mallards that roost on its pond. A study conducted in Massachusetts in the early 1970s found that 67 percent of people who visit urban parks do so to feed ducks and another 32 percent come to view birds.

The public is willing to support urban wildlife management by paying higher taxes. A recent survey of Lexington residents found that 49 percent of the people would be willing to pay higher taxes for more green space and parks. A study in Guelph, Ontario, found that more than 50 percent of the residents are willing to pay higher taxes for wildlife conservation. Fifty-five percent of Kentucky residents favor protecting biodiversity over economic development.

Why is preserving, enhancing, and creating vegetation or wildlife

Urban mallard populations are thriving throughout Kentucky. Feeding ducks is one of the most popular wildlife activities in urban environments.

habitats in urban environments important? One reason may be that wildlife and natural resources management in urban environments might be the only links city dwellers have to the natural world. Another compelling reason may be that the American public has an extremely limited knowledge of wildlife and the benefits of landscaping for wildlife. One survey conducted in Guelph, Ontario, found that most urban residents could neither identify individual wildlife species nor relate habitat conditions to the wildlife they observed. Several examples illustrate this point at the local level.

A Tale of Two Cities: Lexington and Louisville

Development on the south side of Lexington is running rampant. It seems that new subdivisions are planned and built almost daily. A recent development on Tates Creek Road eliminated the vegetation along Hickman Creek, just north of the Man O' War intersection. After the vegetation was cleared, a massive earthen flood wall was created to prevent flooding. This high-density housing development was built, lawns were seeded to tall fescue, a few ornamental landscape trees were put in lawns, and Scotch pine trees were planted as a buffer along the earthen wall. Little thought was given to preserving the streamside forest and the valuable functions of that forest such as filtering pollutants, improving water quality, and providing wildlife habitat.

A mile south of that development is the Waterford subdivision. This development is also along Hickman Creek, where upscale houses were built above the creek on the hillside. During construction, significant amounts of forest were destroyed. Before the development was completed, I would walk by the area and see white-tailed deer and an occasional wild turkey in the woods. I probably will never again see those animals (both uncommon in Fayette County) at that location because most of their significant habitat was destroyed. In the developer's favor, a pond with a fountain was developed at the entrance to the subdivision. Unfortunately, its perimeter is being mowed, and no vegetation has been planted around or in the pond to make it attractive to wildlife.

Why was existing habitat not preserved in these examples? Why weren't clustered developments considered in these examples? Why, despite overwhelming evidence that the public desires urban green spaces and wildlife habitat development, isn't wildlife habitat considered in the planning of most new developments?

But all is not as bleak as it may seem; Lexington does make some effort to preserve wild places. The city has acquired McConnell Springs and is working to restore the 25 acres to a more natural condition. Perhaps the greatest strides are being achieved by individual schools in Lexington. I have had numerous calls from schools seeking information on planting a butterfly garden or landscaping to attract wildlife.

Louisville and Jefferson County are at the other end of the development-versus-conservation spectrum. A strong corps of highly motivated individuals is making Louisville more wildlife-friendly. The city established and maintains two exceptional parks, Iroquois and Cherokee, and the parks department is working on a small barrens restoration in one of the parks. The city is attempting to protect Floyds Fork Creek and is restoring parts of Beargrass Creek. The zoological garden is restoring and rehabilitating a wetland. The county also has protected the 5,000-acre Jefferson Forest. The city is now mandating the use of native plant materials whenever possible for streambank restorations and other park uses.

Where does this leave us when discussing urban wildlife management and biodiversity? I believe it indicates that great strides can be made when an educated and enlightened public makes its wishes and desires known to elected officials. I also think it is a matter of community pride. I am encouraged by the active work being done in Louisville and at schools throughout the commonwealth. Since passage of the Kentucky Education Reform Act, numerous schools have initiated outdoor classroom projects that include some aspects of landscaping for wildlife. Finally, I am encouraged that the Kentucky Department of Fish and Wildlife Resources has completed the Salato Education Center in Frankfort and landscaped it with native plants. They hired a staff person who has developed a nursery to provide schools and other groups with native plant material and provide educational opportunities for those interested in landscaping for wildlife. They have initiated a new "backyard wildlife" habitat improvement program that will certify schools and any property less than 5 acres in size as "going wild in my backyard." That program provided a major portion of the funding for this book. (Contact the Department at #1 Game Farm Road, Frankfort, KY 40601, phone: 502-564-3400, for more information about their backyard wildlife habitat program.)

Why is it important to create wildlife habitat in the city? It might seem counterintuitive to spend time and effort managing urban wildlife when so many other habitats are in jeopardy and species imperiled. My opinion is that informed citizens are more likely to work to protect other rural habitats once they understand the importance of these habitats for wildlife. The best way to learn this is to create habitat in their own backyards. Wildlife conservation begins at home.

Benefits of Landscaping for Wildlife

Economics

One of the most compelling reasons to landscape is economic. One study showed that the property value of "aesthetically pleasing landscaped" yards increased by as much as 20 percent. In addition, at selling time these properties sell faster than yards without landscaping. We also know, all factors being equal, that houses next to parks and green spaces are more valuable than other houses. Additional economic benefits can be obtained as a result of decreased energy usage, decreased usage of chemicals and lawn services required to maintain "green carpets" (it can cost up to $2,000 per year to maintain an average weed-free lawn), and decreased water and sewer costs. Finally, if you own more than a few acres with trees, you can harvest firewood.

Energy Conservation

One economic advantage to landscaping for wildlife is the opportunity to save on heating and cooling costs. As petroleum supplies dwindle and energy costs rise, you can save money by planting conifers along the north

To achieve maximum energy conservation benefits, conifers should be placed on the north and west sides of a property and hardwood trees should be placed on the south and east sides of the property.

POOR ARRANGEMENT

GOOD ARRANGEMENT

and west sides of your property. Temperatures on the leeward side of these windbreaks can be up to 5 degrees Fahrenheit warmer, and wind velocity may be reduced 10 to 15 times the height of the plantings on the leeward side. These plantings help block the harsh winter wind from your house and provide excellent nesting sites and winter cover for a variety of birds. They provide wildlife with an area to "get out of the elements."

By planting hardwood trees on the south and east sides you will shade the house during the hot summer. As much as 90 percent of the sunlight during summer months can be blocked by certain trees. Studies have shown that temperatures under beech trees can be 8 degrees Fahrenheit lower than in surrounding areas. When winter arrives and these trees drop their leaves, it will allow the warm rays of the winter sun to partially heat the house.

Another method of reducing energy costs is to plant dense evergreen massing or to construct raised beds around the foundation of the house.

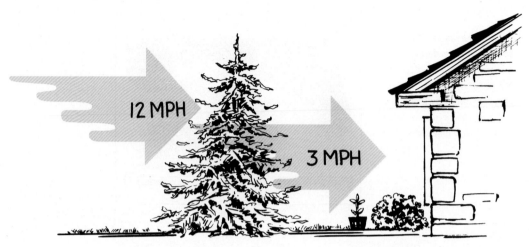

Wind velocity is generally reduced for a distance two to five times the height of a wind barrier on the windward side and 10 to 15 times the height on the leeward side. (Redrawn from J. Cervelli-Shach, Landscape Design with Plants: Creating Outdoor Rooms.*)*

These help provide dead air insulation around the base of the house and reduce heating and cooling bills by as much as 23 percent.

Soil Conservation

Soil is nothing more than organic material and weathered bedrock (sand, silt, and clay). Plants get much of their moisture and nutrients from the soil. In addition, soil provides the foundation or structure for plants to survive in. As a general rule, the more fertile the soil, the more abundant

Hardwood trees on the south side of a house will help shade the house from the summer sun.

Native warm-season grasses, like this broomsedge bluestem, build soil and provide excellent winter color in the landscape.

and healthy the plants and animals. Soil is building block for everything you are trying to accomplish.

As a result of the disruption and disturbance caused by heavy machinery during the development process, urban soils are generally compacted, poorly drained and aerated, and have little space for roots. Compaction reduces the space between soil particles and can lead to oxygen depletion in the soil. It also makes it hard for roots to penetrate the soil and increases water runoff into storm sewers (this results in less water going to the plants in the soil). This is not good for growing plants! Sometimes brick, mortar, concrete, asphalt, and other debris may be found in the soil, which further diminishes its ability to support plants. Finally, soil fertility (particularly nitrogen) is decreased because we remove organic material, such as leaves and lawn clippings, from our urban green spaces.

The great thing about landscaping with native plants is that many native prairie or meadow plants actually build soil. Native warm-season grasses, for example, have root systems that can penetrate compacted or clay soils and send roots 15 feet into the earth. Many native grasses and shrubs planted on erosion-prone slopes reduce the amount of soil lost. Native legumes can be planted to increase soil fertility because artificial fertilizers are not adequate in building soil.

Reduced Yard Maintenance

I hate mowing the grass. Consequently, I am always looking for ways to reduce the time spent clipping grass into miniature pieces. Craig Tufts, author of *The Backyard Naturalist* and the urban wildlife specialist for the National Wildlife Federation, coined the phrase "a little less lawn, please," to describe techniques for growing less lawn. He states that you can reduce the amount of lawn you have to mow by including a raised bed vegetable

Xeriscaping is an official term of the National Xeriscaping Council, Inc. Literally translated from Greek it means "dry landscaping." Xeriscaping does not mean rock gardens, cacti, and yuccas; rather it is a philosophy that incorporates good gardening principles that can be used any place. The National Xeriscaping Council recommends seven basic principles:

1. Start with a good master plan.
2. Improve your soil.
3. Use mulch.
4. Reduce the amount of lawn.
5. Water your plantings efficiently.
6. Practice good maintenance.
7. Choose native plants adapted to your ecological region.

garden, mini-orchard, wildlife-attracting pool, or new deck to view wildlife and by creating clumps of shrubs and flowers. Sherri Evans, of Shooting Star Nursery in Frankfort, recommends planting "prairie patches and woodland niches" in addition to perennial ground covers to create a "freedom lawn"—a new landscape notion that is more environmentally friendly and views the lawn as green space in an interconnected ecological system.

By combining water conservation techniques with landscaping (a concept known as xeriscaping), you can reduce lawn maintenance by as much as 50 percent. How? You reduce mowing by limiting lawn areas and using proper fertilization techniques, reduce pruning of trees and shrubs by selecting appropriate plant species, reduce replacement plantings by proper watering and soil preparation, reduce weeding by proper mulching, reduce disease and pest problems by maintaining healthy plants, and reduce potential damage (and repair) to houses or buildings by proper plant species selection, placement, and watering. Once established, native vegetation often becomes almost maintenance free.

Reduced Dependency on Water

Worry about water in Kentucky? Are you kidding? Although water is one of the most abundant resources on earth, approximately 97 percent is saltwater in the oceans and the other 3 percent (freshwater) is locked up in the polar ice sheets. Thus, less than 1 percent of global water is available for human use. The average middle-class person in the United States uses 80 gallons of water every day! This means that the country uses approximately 82 billion gallons of groundwater daily. Remember the 1980s? Five of the driest years on record occurred during that decade, leading to lawn watering restrictions, water rationing, and outright bans on watering landscapes.

Water is not an unlimited resource and must be used wisely. A recent South Carolina study found that residential consumers use 566 million gallons of water daily. This was projected to increase to 743 million gallons by the year 2005. Much of this water goes to create lush, weed-free "green carpet" lawns. Americans are dependent on cheap, abundant water. If we are to enjoy that inexpensive, abundant water in the future, we must implement water conservation measures today. Because much residential water is used for irrigating landscapes, the first step in relieving pressures on the water supply is to use native plant species that are drought tolerant. By using native plants in conjunction with a properly planned and implemented xeriscape design and irrigation system, water is conserved because plants are grouped according to their water needs and are not overwatered. Water requirements can also be lowered because plant root systems are healthier and penetrate the soil more deeply.

Chemical Reduction:
Pesticides, Herbicides, and Fertilizers

Another valuable benefit to landscaping for wildlife is a reduction in the amount of pesticides, herbicides, and fertilizers used in the urban environment. If plants are not stressed, you have fewer disease and pest problems, which means you use fewer chemicals to control those organisms. And remember, butterflies are insects—it makes no sense to use commercial insecticides and kill the very organisms you are trying to attract. Using fewer chemicals on our yards means that those chemicals don't make their way into our water supply; children and pets are not exposed to potentially dangerous compounds; and you do not kill beneficial insects or plants. This also has wildlife benefits for species you might not think about: bats. A national authority on bats, Dr. Wayne Davis, has observed a decline in bats in suburban Lexington but not downtown. He attributes the decline in the suburbs to the lawn care industry's extensive use of pesticides, which reduces the numbers of insects available for bats.

By taking soil samples to your local extension office and asking them to do a soil test (for a minimum fee), you may reduce the amount and types of fertilizers used in your lawn. Extension agents will provide specific recommendations on adding the proper type and amount of fertilizer and other soil amendments. You can also reduce the amount of fertilizer required by composting leaves, grass clippings, and other organic materials. Proper timing of fertilization also decreases mowing and irrigation needs. Today, most landscape plants and lawns are overfertilized, creating excessive growth that requires more water. You only need to fertilize your lawn in the fall. By using proper planning and design of shrub and flower bed

Attracting wildlife, like this red bat, can provide a source of natural insect control.

plantings around the perimeter of the property, you allow fertilizer runoff to fertilize these plantings as well.

Natural Insect Control

Sometimes insects like mosquitoes, aphids, or grasshoppers can become pests. Because you are not using chemicals to control the populations of these species, one of the benefits of having bats, purple martins, tree swallows, toads, and dragonflies around is that they provide natural control of these pests. Martins, swallows, and dragonflies eat insects during the day, and bats munch away at night. A colony of 100 little brown bats may eat more than a quarter of a million mosquitoes and other small insects each night. Big brown bats, which live primarily in agricultural areas, feed on June bugs, cucumber beetles, green and brown stinkbugs, and leafhoppers. Over the course of a summer, a colony of 150 big brown bats can eat 38,000 cucumber beetles, 16,000 June bugs, 19,000 stinkbugs, and 50,000 leafhoppers and can prevent the hatching of 18 million corn rootworms by devouring the adult beetles. All Kentucky bats (13 species) eat insects and capture flying insects at night. They are the only major predator of night-flying insects, and some bat species can eat between 3,000 and 7,000 insects in a single night.

New research has helped create bat houses that have a better chance of attracting these winged wonders, particularly if they are placed near water. Nest box plans for bats and other insect-eating species are included in Appendix F. Accommodating insect eaters is economically better for you and ecologically better for the environment than using insecticides or "bug zappers."

Food Production

Most people like cherries, strawberries, raspberries, grapes, and other kinds of fruits or vegetables. Wildlife is no different. Many plants that are good people food also provide excellent wildlife food. For example, the black swallowtail caterpillar prefers to feed on dill, parsley, and fennel. Anise, spearmint, and thyme also provide food for butterfly caterpillars. Woodchucks and rabbits like to eat beans, peas, and other legumes. Birds love chokecherries, grapes, strawberries, raspberries, plums, blueberries, and other fruits. Keep this old adage in mind when planting food crops: "Plant one for the mold, one for the crow, and one to grow." This means planting a surplus so you can *share* the harvest with wildlife rather than compete for it.

Pollution Control and Climate Moderation

Because plants are everywhere, we tend to overlook their ability to moderate climate and filter pollutants in urban environments. What you do in your yard throughout the year, such as sitting, reading, or playing, is often limited by climatic factors like temperature and wind. Landscape plants can be used as natural air conditioners, heaters, and humidifiers to alter the climate around you. For example, a house on a prominent hill is exposed to stronger winds than a house located in a depression or valley. Similarly, temperatures around houses in cities are higher than those in suburban or rural areas. I have already discussed how energy can be saved with landscaping, but you also can moderate the climate by altering wind patterns. Wind speed increases as it passes under a tree canopy, so it can be used to help cool a building or yard. Developing a layered vegetation structure further increases the ability of plants to moderate the climate around your yard.

Plants also serve to control pollution in congested urban settings. They purify the air by removing carbon dioxide and sulfur dioxide and

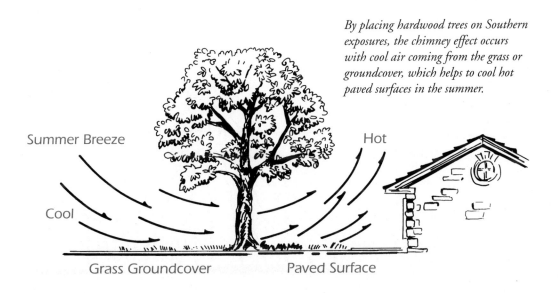

By placing hardwood trees on Southern exposures, the chimney effect occurs with cool air coming from the grass or groundcover, which helps to cool hot paved surfaces in the summer.

Summer Breeze

Hot

Cool

Grass Groundcover

Paved Surface

Plants can be used to direct wind movement through or around buildings. Air movement speeds up under deciduous trees and can be used to cool a building. (Redrawn from J. Cervelli-Schach, Landscape Design with Plants: Creating Outdoor Rooms.)

replacing those compounds with oxygen. Studies have shown that plants can remove as much as 75 percent of the coarse dust fraction in the air. Not all plants are viable options in polluted areas, however. For example, serviceberry and red ash are not tolerant of pollution, but sugar maple, red oak, and basswood can withstand exposure to sulfur dioxide and ozone. Trees that resist injury from salt (from winter road clearing activities) include serviceberry, red cedar, white oak, and red oak, but white pine, American beech, and Eastern hemlock cannot withstand salty conditions.

Cities are noisy places. We are besieged by and perhaps somewhat immune to the sounds of busy traffic, construction, fire trucks, and police cars. To a certain extent, plants can act as buffers to reduce sound pollution. Research has found that a 100-foot-wide planting reduces noise by seven decibels. Plants are most effective at screening higher, more annoying

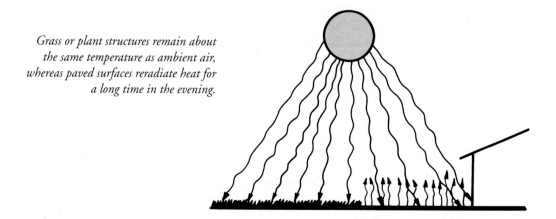

Grass or plant structures remain about the same temperature as ambient air, whereas paved surfaces reradiate heat for a long time in the evening.

Evergreens are essential screening elements on a west facing exposure because of the direction from the summer heat. Long, late summer afternoons deliver unwanted heat to the exterior space exposed to western directions. Evergreens are suited to blunt the severity of this effect.

frequencies of unwanted sound. Deciduous plants with thick, fleshy leaves are the most effective in absorbing, deflecting, and reflecting noise.

Aesthetics

As a society, we spend billions of dollars acquiring, protecting, and enjoying beautiful works of art, music, or architecture. We are outraged when vandals attack precious paintings or sculptures. But have you ever looked closely at a monarch butterfly, a lady-slipper orchid, a Kentucky warbler? Their beauty and intricacy rival the finest works of art.

Painters, sculptors, poets, philosophers, and scientists throughout the ages have used the endearing beauty of landscape plants in their work. People of all races, religions, and nationalities devote countless hours to gardening and landscaping simply for the aesthetics. Some of the most desirable and beautiful plants used for landscaping are natives that are beneficial to wildlife.

In the opening paragraph of *The Backyard Naturalist,* Craig Tufts states, "If you're a gardener, you've experienced that love-hate relationship with your lawn. There's almost nothing that sets off your landscape like a well maintained lawn. And nothing feels better than stepping out shoeless on a summer morning to wander among the flowers and shrubs." The

Many photographic and educational opportunities exist when a yard is full of wildlife like this monarch feeding on a tall goldenrod.

beauty of the many life forms with which we share the earth is another reason for landscaping for wildlife.

Education for Kids and Kids at Heart

I'll never forget the day the monarch emerged from its chrysalis in the pickle jar. I had placed a caterpillar, picked from a milkweed plant in my garden, into that jar so my son could observe the wonder of a biological miracle: the transformation from caterpillar to butterfly. I'll never forget the look of fascination and excitement in his eyes when we let the butterfly go free.

Many of us have forgotten how to look at the world with the eyes of a child. Imagine what opportunities exist for a young and growing mind in a yard full of native plants and wildlife. Landscaping for wildlife offers one of the best opportunities to expose your children, grandchildren, or neighbors' children to the wonders of the natural world. It even offers the chance for those of us who are young at heart to rejuvenate ourselves and get back to nature without leaving our backyards. In his famous poem *Thanatopsis,* William Cullen Bryant says, "To him who in the love of Nature holds / Communion with her visible forms, she speaks / A various language."

Photography and Birdwatching

I love nature, and my hobbies—photography, birdwatching, and hunting—involve nature-related activities. As a photographer, imagine what opportunities exist if your own yard is visited by butterflies, chipmunks, squirrels, hummingbirds, and colorful songbirds. If you develop adequate habitat, you might be able to see more than 100 different bird species in your backyard over the years.

I added a bird to my list of sightings last spring when I spotted a chestnut-sided warbler eating blossoms off the Washington hawthorn outside my front window. This bird is often found in urban and suburban

Birdwatching is the number two hobby in the United States after gardening. What a wonderful marriage of hobbies by landscaping for wildlife.

areas as it migrates through Kentucky. I have seen indigo buntings, yellow-breasted chats, goldfinches, rose-breasted grosbeaks, cardinals, scarlet tanagers, and many other species at a local nature sanctuary. Tree swallows and house wrens live in nest boxes throughout Lexington. It is fun to document the different birds that use various plants in your yard, or you might pick up birdwatching as a hobby. There will be numerous bird- and wildlife-watching opportunities if you make your yard wildlife-friendly.

Protecting Biodiversity

Biodiversity is the variety of life and its processes. It occurs at many levels, from the genetic, to the species, the community, and the ecosystem. By landscaping with native plants you can help protect the genetic diversity of plant species. A perfect example is the royal catchfly. Hummingbirds love this plant, which has become rare in nature. Fortunately, seeds were collected by a native nurseryman from a remnant population in Hardin County. They were propagated at his nursery. You can now purchase seeds or plants from this population for use in your hummingbird garden.

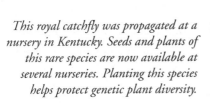

This royal catchfly was propagated at a nursery in Kentucky. Seeds and plants of this rare species are now available at several nurseries. Planting this species helps protect genetic plant diversity.

Disadvantages of Landscaping for Wildlife

As with other things in life, there are some pitfalls to landscaping for wild-life. First, if you build it they will come. All kinds of creatures will visit your yard and, potentially, your neighbors' yards. Your neighbors might not appreciate bats, snakes, or other creatures, and they might not share your enthusiasm for reducing lawn. Be sure to follow good design principles to avoid hassles from neighbors. One way to alleviate this concern is to become certified as "Going Wild in My Backyard." If you are certified, the Kentucky Department of Fish and Wildlife Resources will provide you with a nifty sign to make everyone aware of what you are doing.

Second, you will need to do your homework to understand the basic ecology of when and how to plant natives. Some species may not like your soils even though other conditions are ideal. We don't know everything about gardening with natives. You may have some trial-and-error projects that could be expensive nightmares! Talk to anyone and everyone knowledgeable so you minimize mistakes. Be prepared for the expense in general. The initial costs of plants may scare you, but you will save money in the long run.

Third, patience is a necessary virtue for landscaping with native plants. It may take years for your plantings to develop. It can take up to three years to establish prairie from seed. Even filling in a garden with plants takes time. Many of the seeds of woodland plants are dispersed by ants so it takes them longer to fill in vacant areas. Be patient; it will happen.

Finally, you must get used to using scientific names. Unfortunately botanists can't agree on standardized common names and are constantly changing the names of plants. As Jim Wilson writes in *Landscaping with Wildflowers*, "You might as well bite the bullet and begin learning botanical names. Often a common name is shared by two or more species, so the only way . . . . to communicate clearly is by using . . . botanical names. Use these names when ordering plants and seeds." To standardize the botanical names in this book, I used the following reference published in 1994 from Timber Press of Portland, Oregon: *A Synonymized Checklist of the Vascular Flora of the United States, Canada, and Greenland* (second edition) by John T. Kartesz. I have not used botanical names in the text because those plants are listed along with their scientific names in various appendix tables. To further simplify the text and make it readable, bird and mammal scientific names are not used but follow the nomenclature of the American Ornithologists Union (AOU) for birds and *Wild Mammals of North America* by J.A. Chapman and G.A. Feldhammer for mammals.

References

Adams, L.W. 1994. *Urban Wildlife Habitats: A Landscape Perspective.* Minneapolis: Univ. of Minnesota Press. 186 pp.

American Ornithologists Union. 1983. *Check-list of North American Birds.* 6th ed. Lawrence, Kans.: Allen Press. n.p.

Arms, K. 1992. *Environmental Gardening.* Savannah, Ga.: Halfmoon Publishing. 308 pp.

Beatley, T. 1994. *Habitat Conservation Planning: Endangered Species and Urban Growth.* Austin: Univ. of Texas Press. 234 pp.

Borman, R.H., D. Balmori, and G.T. Beballe. 1993. *Redesigning the American Lawn: A Search for Environmental Harmony.* New Haven: Yale Univ. Press. 166 pp.

Cervelli-Schach, J. 1985. *Landscape Design with Plants: Creating Outdoor Rooms.* Univ. of Kentucky Cooperative Extension Publication HO-62.

The Basics

This we know: All things are connected. Like the blood
which unites one family. All things are connected. Whatever
befalls the earth befalls the sons of Earth. Man did not weave
the web of life. He is merely a strand in it.
Whatever he does to the web, he does to himself.

—Chief Seattle, 1856

To ASSIST YOU in transforming your yard into a naturalized landscape attractive to wildlife, here is a list and short description of
some basic landscaping-for-wildlife principles. Don't let the list
intimidate or overwhelm you. Remember, the idea is to have some fun and
to enjoy your project.

Have Realistic Expectations about Wildlife Visitation

Many homeowners think that if they plant a dogwood tree they will have
all sorts of wonderful birds visiting them. Most homeowners have unrealistic expectations about the number and type of wildlife that come into an
urban environment. This idea is fostered by many popular books. For example, Carroll Henderson, of the Minnesota Department of Natural Resources, writes in his book *Landscaping for Wildlife* about a couple who
observed more than 190 different birds in their backyard. That number
would certainly be possible in a large urban forest like the Lexington Cemetery, Shady Lane Woods, or Jefferson County Memorial Forest over a
period of time. But the typical homeowner will probably see only a dozen
to two dozen birds on a regular basis. Why? There are several reasons. The
most significant is that cities do not provide the appropriate type of habitat
for many species. The specific type of habitat required by the species deter-
mines how well they will do in an urban environment. For example, because cities are mostly early plant successional communities with large
amounts of edge, most of the wildlife that live in cities are early plant

successional species, such as American robins, northern mockingbirds, and white-tailed deer.

Furthermore, each animal requires a certain amount of space to move about, avoid or escape predators, locate a mate, and find food and water. Wildlife space requirements vary by species, but generally the amount of space required is determined by the quantity and quality of food, cover, and water (habitat in general).

Other factors affecting spatial needs of wildlife include the fact that larger animals require more space than smaller animals and carnivores require more space than herbivores. Individual animals living in groups need less space than solitary animals, but the group naturally requires more territory.

Putting all this information together helps you develop reasonable expectations of what and how much wildlife will visit your backyard. For instance, the home range (the amount of space required by an animal) of a chipmunk is about 100 square yards. On the other hand, a pair of eastern bluebird needs about 5 acres, and the hairy woodpecker needs 40 acres of land. It should become apparent that you are more likely to see chipmunks in the yard than hairy woodpeckers. This isn't to say you will not see the woodpeckers; it only means that, if your yard is part of their home range, you will see them at a feeder or, if you're lucky, nesting in a tree in your yard. Some neotropical migrant songbirds (birds that breed in Kentucky and winter in Mexico and Central and South America), for instance, need thousands of acres of mature, unfragmented forest land to succeed at reproduction. You usually cannot create the type of habitat these creatures need in an urban environment but you can often see them during migration at places like the Lexington Cemetery and Shady Lane Woods.

Don't become discouraged and think that few animals will visit your yard. You just need to develop realistic expectations. For instance, 18 of the 144 butterfly species found in Kentucky are common urban residents. The birds most frequently observed in a typical Kentucky yard include the American robin, northern cardinal, northern mockingbird, house sparrow, house finch, European starling, common grackle, mourning dove, and blue jay. Others that visit on a regular basis include the northern flicker, brown thrasher, cedar waxwing, American goldfinch, tufted titmouse, Carolina chickadee, Carolina wren, and downy woodpecker.

You'll certainly delight in seeing something unusual coming into a feeder, such as an evening grosbeak or those songbirds that drop in during

Predicted Number of Bird Species for Urban Habitats

Showing how the size of habitat affects the number of birds found. The larger the habitat, the more species will be found.

Patch Size (acres)	Woodland Bird Species (Number)		
	Luniak[1]	Tilghman[2]	Vizyova[3]
2.5	0	0	6.4
5	0	24	13.8
10	13	27	21.2
20	21	31	28.6
30	27	33	32.9
60	31.5	39	40.3
105	33.5	43	46.2

Sources: [1] M. Luniak, "The Avifauna of Urban Green Areas in Poland and Possibilities of Managing It," *Acta Ornithologica* 19 (1983): 3-6; [2] N.G. Tilghman, "Characteristics of Urban Woodlands Affecting Breeding Bird Diversity and Abundance," *Landscape and Urban Planning* 14 (1987): 481-95; and [3] A. Vizyova, "Urban Woodlots as Islands for Land Vertebrates: A Preliminary Attempt on Estimating the Barrier Effects of Urban Structural Units," *Ecology* (CSSR) 5 (1986): 407-19.

migration. I will never forget spotting my first male blackburnian warblers picking bugs out of a hackberry tree last spring. I was thrilled and delighted. And I still have vivid memories of the Cape May warbler eating Washington hawthorn berries on its migration northward. Every August I enjoy watching the common nighthawks as they perform their aerobatic flights catching insects at dusk on their way south. I also enjoy visiting small ponds and reservoirs and am particularly thrilled when the belted kingfisher sits on the wire while taking a break from fishing, or when the green-backed heron darts away when I approach too closely.

The size and location of habitat development will also affect the abundance and diversity of wildlife that visits. A general scheme of wildlife abundance, from highest to lowest, might be moving from a rural environment to the suburbs to the city to a high-rise apartment (for instance, from 1000 acres to to 100 acres to 5 acres to 1/4 acre). The same decrease in abundance might be found in going from undeveloped land to a park to a backyard to an industrial or business site.

No matter what the size of your yard, it takes time for habitat to develop, for plants to mature and produce flowers and fruit, and for wildlife to find the space. Be patient. As your personal wildlife management area (your yard) develops and matures, wildlife will begin to use it.

Be Tolerant of Values Other than Yours

Unfortunately not everyone will share your enthusiasm for attracting wild-life to your yard. It may not take much to upset your neighbors, even something simple like having chipmunks moving from your yard to their yard and destroying a prized flower bed. Or some people may not like the vast profusion of flowers that attract bees (in addition to butterflies). What-ever the reason, make sure you talk with your neighbors, particularly dur-ing the planning stage. Early communication will prevent many future problems.

You should also pay close attention to laws and regulations regarding landscape development. Most cities have a street tree planting list. Only trees on the list can be planted along streets and boulevards. In many cases, it may not include the species you wish to plant. If this is so, contact the local government and attempt to get the ordinance changed. Many cities also have laws requiring removal of dead or dying trees, which happen to be good habitats for many animals.

Most municipalities have laws concerning weeds and grass, which state that homeowners must keep the height of herbaceous vegetation below 10 to 15 inches. A colleague of mine told of several people in Indiana suing their neighbors because they allowed grass and other flowers to grow up in the yard. These yards were certified by the National Wildlife Federation as back-yard wildlife habitat, but the courts ruled in favor of the plaintiffs. Fortu-nately, such laws are being challenged in court, and cases in Virginia and Arkansas have overturned weed and grass ordinances. The court in Fairfax County, Virginia, found one ordinance to be "an unreasonable, arbitrary and excessive exercise of the County's police powers which bears no relation to public health, safety, morals or general welfare" (Board of Supervisors of Fairfax County, Virginia).

Some subdivisions also have rules that must be adhered to. For ex-ample, one Lexington subdivision requires that at least one flowering dog-wood must be planted in the yard. Others may have rules regarding what can and cannot be planted on the property. Look at these rules closely before purchasing property in a particular subdivision because you may be restricted from landscaping the way you want.

One way to reduce these conflicts is to use common sense. For in-stance, a butterfly garden is an outstanding feature in any yard, but when it covers the entire front yard it may not be socially acceptable and many subdivisions might not allow it. Research shows that you can reduce the amount of turf by as much as 50 percent in a front lawn without causing friction from neighbors. I doubt most people would find a brush pile in the front yard acceptable. Likewise, I would not put a water garden or pond in the front yard unless there were other attractive features around it. It is best to prevent conflicts by talking with your neighbors, following good landscape design procedures, abiding by the law, and being tolerant of values other than your own.

If It Isn't Broken, Don't Fix It

This one is simple. If you have any natural features in the yard or development area, do not disturb or alter that habitat. It is hard to improve on what nature has created. Any natural habitats—trees, wetlands, or other desirable features—should be maintained.

A study in Northern Virginia compared bird use of mature forest in 1942 to bird use in 1979, after the area had become a well established community. The researchers documented an absence of wood thrushes, red-eyed vireos, ovenbirds, and scarlet tanagers. Species encountered in 1979 but not observed in 1942 included American robins, gray catbirds, and house sparrows. The authors concluded that "if we want both groups of species we must make certain that sufficiently large and undisturbed areas of the natural habitats are preserved to support the breeding of those specialized species that are dependent upon them" (Aldrich and Coffin 1980).

Planning Is the Key to Success

The most important step in any landscaping project is planning and design. Why? It will affect all your decisions, either positively or negatively. Good planning will save you time and money, it will identify where potential pest problems may arise, it will be a tool to communicate with your neighbors, and it will serve as a road map for achieving the final landscape.

As an example, many people dislike the stain black cherry fruits leave on a sidewalk, driveway, or patio. The solution in the planning process is to not plant fruit-bearing plants near those structures. Planning will alleviate neighbors' complaints about the brushpile or butterfly garden in the front yard. Planning also considers the needs of your family. How much space do you need for benches, play areas for kids or pets, paths, storage areas, and

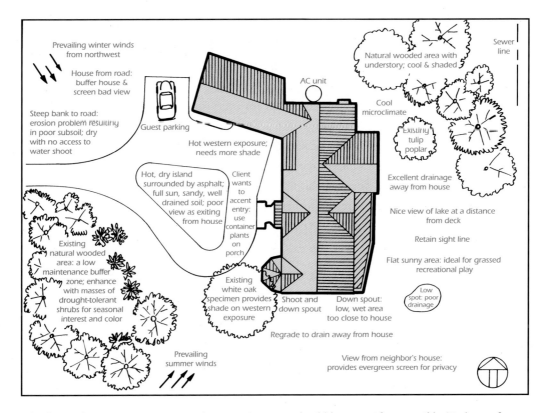

The first and most important step is planning. Drawings should be as specific as possible. (Redrawn from Kelly et al., *Xeriscape: Landscape Water Conservation in the Southeast.*)

so on? It will also help you identify views you wish to screen out, such as a road, along with vistas you wish to keep. It will help you identify natural habitats you wish to maintain, wet or dry sites, sunny or shady sites, low or poorly drained sites, or sandy, well drained sites.

Planning will also help you think about things you might not have considered. For example, plant root depth is an important planning consideration. Red maple is a shallow-rooted tree that competes with other plants for water and can cause cracking of driveways, sidewalks, and patios. Deep-rooted trees such as willow oak will accommodate understory plantings and cause less damage by roots.

Set Your Goals, Objectives, and Priorities

What animal group intrigues you the most: butterflies, birds, snakes, everything? Many people wish to attract as many different types of wildlife as possible. If this is your goal—landscaping for biodiversity—you will need to use a variety of plants to attract a variety of wildlife species. If you wish to attract only one group—butterflies, hummingbirds, reptiles, or amphibians—then you will need to intensify your planning and management based on those specific groups.

Always remember that for every species you wish to attract, others you may not want will also arrive. For instance, if you enjoy feeding birds, you may have to accept that squirrels, chipmunks, and other mammals enjoy that food source as well. Similarly, if you are feeding hummingbirds, ants and bees may also show up. This is usually not a problem, but you must be aware that other wildlife with similar habitat requirements may come to your property.

Develop a Realistic Time and Financial Budget

Develop a budget that extends over several years and coincides with your planting plan. For example, you might develop a five-year plan and budget. The same can be said for the time involved with planting and maintaining your plan. Don't try to do too much at once.

There are ways to save money on planting material: Attend season-end planting events, use smaller planting stock, use native wildflower seeds instead of plants, and so on. Remember, there are tradeoffs associated with every decision. Only you can determine which tradeoffs benefit your financial situation.

Consult with Professionals and Find Good References

If you get frustrated or overwhelmed, don't worry. Assistance is available to you. Information and assistance can be obtained from a variety of resource professionals including

Kentucky Department of Fish and Wildlife Resources
#1 Game Farm Road
Frankfort, KY 40601

Kentucky Division of Forestry
627 Comanche Trail
Frankfort, KY 40601

Kentucky Nature Preserves Commission
801 Schenkel Lane
Frankfort, KY 40601

Extension Wildlife Specialist
Department of Forestry
University of Kentucky
Lexington, KY 40546-0073

Or contact your local county office of the Cooperative Extension Service. You may also request the assistance of a landscape architect in designing the planting, a native plant nursery for plant selection, and a water garden specialist for assistance in developing a water garden.

Understand Basic Habitat Requirements

As you begin the process of landscaping, look over your yard or other potential development area and ask yourself these questions:

Are there places for wildlife to hide from potential predation by domestic cats or dogs? Predation by natural predators (hawks, owls, snakes) is a fact of life and is not a problem. In many cases you might relish a Cooper's hawk, redtailed hawk, or screech owl visiting your property. This is a sign that you have good habitat for smaller prey species.

Predation by cats and dogs is unacceptable! Ways to make a cat less harmful include declawing the animal, placing a bell around its neck, or keeping it indoors. Do not allow cats to roam at will. Dogs should also be restrained and kept under control.

Are there places for wildlife to nest? Do you have any snags (dead trees) or wolf trees (living trees with cavities) that should be saved? As long as limbs can't break and fall on a sidewalk, road, building, or power line, consider leaving them

To avoid predation at nest boxes or feeders from snakes, raccoons, house cats, and other predators, a predator guard should be constructed.

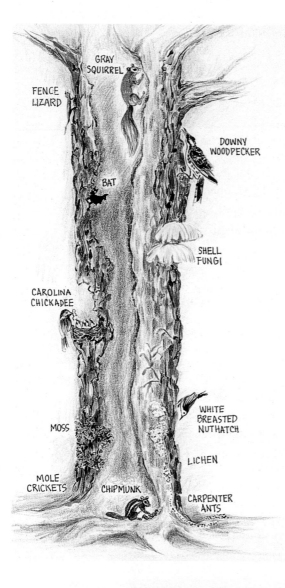

GRAY
SQUIRREL

FENCE
LIZARD

DOWNY
WOODPECKER

BAT

SHELL
FUNGI

CAROLINA
CHICKADEE

WHITE
BREASTED
NUTHATCH

MOSS

LICHEN

MOLE
CRICKETS

CHIPMUNK

CARPENTER
ANTS

Snags or dead trees provide habitat for a wide variety of living creations. (Redrawn from M. Schneck, Your Backyard Wildlife Garden: How to Attract and Identify Wildlife in Your Yard.)

for wildlife. If you can't leave snags, are there appropriate places for nest boxes? See Appendix F for information on building and placing nesting structures. Be sure your yard is suitable before erecting a particular nesting structure, as it might end up being used by an undesired species. For instance, do not erect bluebird boxes in the city as bluebirds will rarely, if ever, use the box, but starlings and sparrows will.

Are there places where wildlife can escape from the cold, wind, rain, or snow? Is there cover behind an evergreen screen? Where can you develop clumps of vegetative cover? A habitat component missing in most urban habitats is the snag or wolf tree. Not all snags are dangerous or intrinsically ugly, but many cities have laws requiring that dead or dying trees be cut and removed. Whenever possible (if they don't

Conifers provide excellent nesting habitat for birds.

Most people will not want a large brush pile in the backyard. A simple plastic five gallon pail turned upside down with two pieces of PVC pipe will provide cover for many small animals. (Redrawn from M. Schneck, *Your Backyard Wildlife Garden: How to Attract and Identify Wildlife in Your Yard.*)

pose a liability hazard), leave such trees because they provide habitat for a variety of living species from fungi, to chipmunks, to screech owls. More than 43 different kinds of birds and 26 mammals are known to use snags for nesting, perching, territory establishment, or food. Generally speaking the larger the snag (6" in diameter or greater), the greater its value for wildlife.

Other species may use structural habitat components such as a rock or brush pile. Examples of wildlife using structural cover include bats roosting in building attics, barn swallows building nests under eaves or other building overhangings, barn owls nesting in abandoned buildings, and tree swallows, house wrens, purple martins, squirrels, raccoons, and wood ducks nesting in wooden boxes. Plans for nest boxes are provided in Appendix F.

Is there adequate food? Wildlife must have food to survive. Generally, wildlife in good condition have higher reproduction rates, are more resistant to diseases, and can escape predators better than animals in poor condition. Nutrition affects birth and death rates and is important in the overall survival of any wild animal population. For example, Margaret Brittingham from Penn State found that birds that have access to feed in artificial feeders are heavier and better able to survive harsh winters.

The availability of food varies over time (season) and space (geographic location); thus, food can be abundant in one area during one sea-

Structural habitat for many species can be a nesting box for tufted titmice (left) or the top of a nest box as used by the mourning dove on the right.

son and in critically short supply in that same area during other seasons. The key to managing food supplies for wildlife is to ensure that abundant, high quality food is present every season of the year. Because food is such a powerful attractant for wildlife you can be selective in planting vegetation that provides preferred foods. The important questions to ask about food supplies are: Have I concentrated on providing native foods before developing a feeding program? If not, what can I plant to provide that food. If I decide to feed the birds, where should feeders be located? What type of feed should I use?

Are there places for birds to gather grit or dust? One type of cover that can often be missing in urban environments is dusting cover. Birds need bare ground with dry, powdery soil to "take a bath in" to control external parasites.

Another limiting factor in urban environments is grit, which is fine to coarse sand. Grit is used by birds to grind up seeds and other food in their

Dense shrubby growth provides nesting and wintering habitat for a variety of birds, including this towhee, as well as cardinals and sparrows.

PREVAILING WIND

POOR ARRANGEMENT

PREVAILING WIND

GOOD ARRANGEMENT

Proper placement of food and water will help protect wildlife from harsh weather.

gizzards. It should be a component of dusting cover. To provide this type of habitat in urban environments, create a circle of pulverized, bare ground approximately 2 feet in diameter. Add a small amount of sand in a tray directly adjacent to the dusting site and you will increase the number and variety of birds attracted to your backyard.

Is there a permanent reliable source of fresh water? Even though Kentucky receives about 40 inches of precipitation a year, water is probably the largest factor limiting wildlife in urban environments. One of the greatest opportunities in landscaping for wildlife is the creation or preservation of a clean, dependable water source. Many wildlife species, including ducks, dragonflies,

When selecting food items for birds, think of the color red, which is particularly attractive to them. This robin is enjoying Washington hawthorn berries.

American toads have a voracious appetite for mosquitoes. They can be attracted by placing a large clay flower pot upside down in your yard.

and frogs, depend on water for their survival. Other animals also require water for digestion and metabolism, reducing body temperature, and removal of metabolic wastes. Wildlife can survive for weeks without food but only days without water.

If possible, preserve natural sources of water and wetland habitats. If natural water sources are not present, restore or create wetlands or ponds. Be aware that stagnant or still water is less attractive to wildlife than dripping or flowing water. Birdbaths provide little benefit to most wildlife species, and I don't recommend them as a general practice, although during winter, birdbaths can be important if they are kept ice-free.

Create a Diversity of Habitat Types

If your goal is to attract as many different types of wildlife as possible, you will need to develop different habitat types, such as an urban forest, a small prairie patch or meadow (wildflower garden), or a wetland (water garden). For instance, you might place a birdbath as a water source for some bird species. But by developing a water garden (or miniature wetland/aquatic habitat), you will not only attract a wider assortment of birds, you will also attract frogs, dragonflies, and other water lovers. This source of water would also attract insects and insect-eating birds and bats. It would also serve to attract such mammals as raccoons and opossums, none of which would visit the birdbath. A larger water garden might include flowering aquatic plants such as lilies and irises.

Use a Variety of Different Plant Groups

The greatest benefit can be derived from planting a variety of vegetative groups, including coniferous trees and shrubs, deciduous trees and shrubs, vines, grasses, legumes, wildflowers, and ferns. Within each group be sure to select plants of various sizes, to create a layering effect. A variety or diversity of vegetation equates to a variety or diversity of wildlife being attracted to the yard. An excellent cluster of plants that will provide year-round food for birds could be serviceberry (early spring flower, summer fruit), flowering dogwood (late spring flower, fall fruit) hawthorn (early summer flower, late winter fruit), and a cluster of azaleas (early spring through summer flowers that also serve to provide cover).

Use a Variety of Species within Each Plant Group

If one flowering dogwood is good, two is better, and three better yet. In the same line of thinking, if one flowering dogwood is good, one flowering dogwood and one silky dogwood is better, and one flowering dogwood, one silky dogwood, and one gray dogwood is even better. The message: plant a variety of species of one group of plants to provide year-round food for wildlife.

Select Plants for Year-round Flower and Fruit

Nature is amazing. Different plants are adapted to different growing conditions. Some plants flower in early spring, some in summer and some in the fall. Likewise, some plants produce seed in early summer, some in mid-summer, some in late summer, and some in the fall. During the planning stage, identify when various plant species flower and produce fruit. For example, serviceberry is one of the first species to flower, and its fruits mature in June. If you only planted serviceberry as a food plant, what would wildlife feed on in July through May? Similarly, American holly flowers in May and the fruits are not used by wildlife until late in the winter.

Diversify your plantings so you have something in flower (bloom) or fruiting every month of the year. In a typical backyard you might plant blue spruce, eastern hemlock, red cedar, and white pine for winter cover and nesting sites. Serviceberry, pin cherry, and elderberry would provide summer berries; flowering, silky, and gray dogwood would provide fall berries; and American holly and hawthorns would provide winter berries. This could be supplemented with a variety of wildflowers that produce seed during the fall and winter.

Select plants, such as this crab apple, that provide late winter food for birds like this cedar waxwing. Sumacs serve the same purpose.

Reduce the Amount of Lawn

It takes a considerable amount of time, probably at least 20 to 30 years, for an oak tree to reach the point of producing acorns. Planting large trees in urban environments is a long-term wildlife investment. Most people don't want to wait 30 years for large trees to mature. So consider where you can get the most immediate results from your habitat development. This would include reducing the amount of lawn and replacing it with various gardens—one for shade wildflowers, one for butterflies, one for hummingbirds, and one centered on water. Diane Heilenman, in her book *Gardening in the Lower Midwest,* suggests creating several gardens: night (good for moths and creatures that eat moths—bats), container, water, flower arranger's, cook's, cottage, grasses, "gone wild," herb, and collector's. Areas that are not planted to garden should be landscaped with small, medium, and large flowering and fruitbearing shrubs and small flowering and fruit-bearing trees. Finally, think about where other habitat attributes, including feeders, habitat structures, and water, can be developed.

Follow the Lead of Nature

Humans like everything ordered and symmetrical. Nature likes organized chaos where very few things grow in a straight line. Use nature as your model when planning urban landscapes—think curved, crooked, and clustered. Look for every opportunity to arrange your plantings in clusters or naturalistic clumps. Gentle curves in landscape planting give visual appeal to the property. And keep in mind the spatial needs of the wildlife you're trying to attract when arranging various habitat components. For instance, tree swallow nest boxes must be located at least 25 yards apart to avoid territorial disputes among the swallows.

Sometimes you may think you have provided a large quantity of potential food, water, and cover, but they appear to be unused. Why? One possible reason is because the components are too far apart to suit the

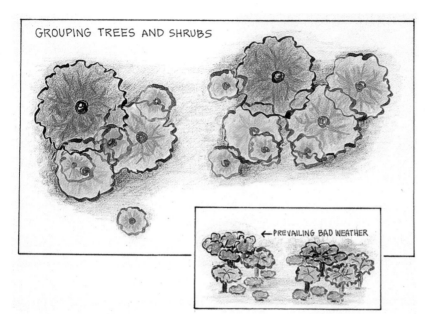

GROUPING TREES AND SHRUBS

←PREVAILING BAD WEATHER

Follow the lead of nature when planning. Plant in clusters or groups to achieve maximum wildlife use. Taller shrubs or trees should be placed on the windward side of the plantings.

needs of animals in the area. An animal can travel a long distance to find water if necessary, but it will do little good if the animal starves or is eaten by a predator along the way. Properly arranging the habitat's components is important to ensure that each component benefits wildlife. Providing food supplies does little good, and potentially more harm, if those food supplies are not protected. Imagine a severe winter when temperatures drop below freezing and there is a mighty north wind howling. Now add a small bird like a goldfinch that is trying to eke out a living while avoiding the cold and wind. Now picture that bird coming to a bird feeder or a wildflower garden full of seeds that is within ten feet of cover and is sheltered from the cold wind by a dense thicket of conifers.

Think of it as a puzzle. All the pieces of the puzzle

Food and cover should be planted in clusters to provide maximum benefit to wildlife, like these winterberry shrubs at Jefferson Memorial Forest.

Reptiles such as this five-lined skink need basking habitats—large rocks, an old wooden fence, or a decaying tree on the ground.

must be present and in the proper placement for the puzzle to be complete. The greater the mixing of habitat types in an area, the better for urban wildlife. This is important because wildlife have a tendency to be more abundant in areas with several habitats where food and water are close to cover. In the case of bird feeding, feeders should be placed within ten feet of significant cover to allow birds to view and escape potential predators. Keep in mind that the primary reason you are feeding birds is to view them at the feeder site. This means you must develop some cover near your feeder sites (close to the house).

The same holds true if you are planning a water garden. Don't place it in the far corner of the property where you won't be able to see the wildlife using it. This also means you must develop cover and food plantings near the water source.

Just as having food close to cover is important, so is having good vertical layering. Some wildlife species may use the ground layer (herbaceous) for food but also need the tallest layer (tree canopy) for shelter. The middle layer between the tree canopy and the herbaceous layer is comprised of shrubs. Every forest community has different vertical layering. Some may have a variety of layers comprised of grasses, broadleaf weeds, shrubs, small trees, and large trees, whereas others may have only one distinct layer of tall trees. Forests with little layering do not provide as many "niches" for wildlife when compared to the forest stand with a variety of layers. Generally speaking, urbanization reduces vertical stratification, and native midstory, understory, and herbaceous vegetation is replaced with shade-tolerant grass. You should attempt to re-create this vertical layering in your landscape efforts.

Finally, think about the proper arrangement of structural habitat components. Some species are highly territorial, including tree swallows that will only use nest boxes placed a minimum of 25 yards apart. Other species, such as purple martins, are social animals and like having others of the same species around them. This is important when considering where to

Every species of bird has a special place for nesting and feeding in the habitat it uses.

Habitat Niches Used for Nesting by Backyard Birds

Overstory Trees
(maximum height 50 feet and taller)

American beech	white pine
American elm	sycamore
black cherry	white oak
persimmon	tulip poplar
pin oak	sweet gum
red maple	eastern hemlock
shagbark hickory	

Birds Found in Overstory

scarlet tanager
American crow
great horned owl
blue jay
northern oriole
cedar waxwing
red-tailed hawk
common grackle

Understory Trees
(maximum height 20 to 50 feet)

American holly	hawthorn
box elder	plum
Ohio buckeye	sassafras
flowering dogwood	sourwood
redbud	hornbeam
serviceberry	

Birds Found in Understory

American goldfinch
blue-gray gnatcatcher
orchard oriole
red-eyed vireo
American robin
mourning dove

Shrubs
(maximum height less than 20 feet)

sumac
witch hazel
arrow-wood viburnum
wild hydrangea
spicebush
winterberry holly

Birds Found in Shrubs

brown thrasher
northern mockingbird
white-eyed vireo
yellow-billed cuckoo
ruby-throated hummingbird
gray catbird
chipping sparrow
song sparrow
northern cardinal

Birds found in Tree Cavities
(and Nest Boxes)

American kestrel	Carolina wren
great-crested flycatcher	house sparrow
screech owl	European starling
Carolina chickadee	wood duck
house wren	purple martin
tufted titmouse	woodpeckers
white-breasted nuthatch	

Birds Found on or Near the Ground

eastern meadowlark
field sparrow
rufous-sided towhee
Canada goose
killdeer
common nighthawk
mallard

Birds Found on Ledges or Vertical Structures

American robin
chimney swift
rock dove
barn owl
barn swallow

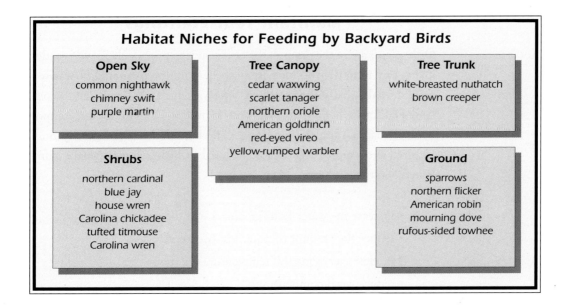

Habitat Niches for Feeding by Backyard Birds

Open Sky
common nighthawk
chimney swift
purple martin

Tree Canopy
cedar waxwing
scarlet tanager
northern oriole
American goldfinch
red-eyed vireo
yellow-rumped warbler

Tree Trunk
white-breasted nuthatch
brown creeper

Shrubs
northern cardinal
blue jay
house wren
Carolina chickadee
tufted titmouse
Carolina wren

Ground
sparrows
northern flicker
American robin
mourning dove
rufous-sided towhee

place the nest boxes. For example, purple martins and bats like open areas next to water. Wrens like houses in the open near shrubby vegetation.

Consider Potential Pest Problems

There will be times when animals are in the wrong place at the wrong time. Or from the animals' viewpoint, in the right place at the right time. Specific wildlife can become a nuisance or a pest. The best advice is to try to anticipate where potential problems can occur and prepare in advance to prevent them, or have a plan of attack if the problem arises. For instance, a garden can be fenced to prevent groundhogs and rabbits from devouring beans, peas, and tomatoes. If you develop water, raccoons and opossums will visit your yard. Develop a contingency plan for dealing with these potential unwanted species. More detailed information on handling wildlife problems is provided in chapter 8.

Raccoons will be attracted if you develop habitat for birds. To prevent damage, gardens should be fenced and chimneys should be capped.

Maintain Your Plantings

Once plants are in the ground, the next step is to provide them with tender loving care until they become established. Wildflowers should be watered often until they become established. Mulch around trees, shrubs, and woodland wildflowers helps to insure plant survival and is an important component of maintaining the landscape. The best mulches are usually fine-textured and nonmatting organic materials. Organic mulches have many benefits in the landscape. They

- increase the water-holding capacity of the soil;
- reduce the amount of water lost by runoff;
- moderate extreme soil temperature fluctuations;
- reduce weed competition;
- reduce the incidence of soil-related diseases;
- prevent soil erosion;
- reduce soil compaction, improve soil structure, and add nutrients and humus to the soil;
- create an aesthetically pleasing design feature;
- prevent mechanical damage to trees and shrubs caused by mowers and weedeaters; and
- prevent splash-back and staining of house foundation and siding.

Woody landscape plants need an application of three inches of a good mulch. This should be applied under the plant and at least out to the drip line, because the root system can extend two to three times the spread of the plant. Mulch should be pulled away from the trunk of the plant to keep the plant's bark dry. Trees have a very large spread, and mulching to the drip line will give good protection during a severe drought. When using mulch near the house, it is important to be sure that the mulch is at least six inches below untreated wood siding and at least eight inches below any untreated wood structural members such as sills, joists, and plates.

Enjoy, Enjoy, Enjoy

The final step in the process is to enjoy the beauty that surrounds you. This is what all the hard work, perspiration, planning, and expense are about.

Remember to be patient; habitat develops over time and it takes time for wildlife to find appropriate habitat. It is worth the wait.

The best way to attract wildlife to urban environments and create a sustainable urban ecosystem is to think ecologically. This means you should create a diversity of habitat types or ecosystems (forest, wetland, meadow or prairie), use a variety of plant types (evergreen trees and shrubs, deciduous trees and shrubs, vines, grasses, legumes, wildflowers, and ferns), use a diversity of plant species within each plant group (such as oaks, hickories, maples, walnut, American beech as overstory or canopy trees), and use structural habitat components if you wish to attract a wide variety of wildlife to the urban environment. It also means understanding how to create and arrange the three components of wildlife habitat: food, cover, and water.

References

Adams, G. 1994. *Birdscaping Your Garden: A Practical Guide to Backyard Birds and the Plants that Attract Them*. Emmaus, Penn: Rodale Press. 208 pp.

Aldrich, J.W., and R.W. Coffin. 1980. "Breeding Bird Populations from Forest to Suburbia after Thirty-Seven Years." *American Birds* 34: 3-7.

Board of Supervisors of Fairfax County. *Virginia v. Wills and Van Metre, Inc.* at Law No. 35094, Nineteenth Judicial Circuit of Virginia, 14 Sept. 1976.

Henderson, C.L. 1987. *Landscaping for Wildlife*. Minneapolis: Minnesota Department of Natural Resources. 144 pp.

Holpin, A.M. 1996. *For the Birds: A Handy Guide to Attracting Birds to Your Backyard*. New York: Henry Holt. 96 pp.

Kelley, John, Mary Haque, Debra Shuping, and Jeff Zahner. 1991. *Xeriscape: Landscape Water Conservation in the Southeast*. Clemson Univ. Cooperative Extension Service Pub. ED 672.

Pope, T., N. Odenwald, and C. Fryling, Jr. 1993. *Attracting Birds to Southern Gardens*. Dallas: Taylor Publishing. 164 pp.

Schneck, M. 1992. *Your Backyard Wildlife Garden: How to Attract and Identify Wildlife in Your Yard*. Emmaus, Penn.: Rodale Press. 160 pp.

Tufts, C., and P. Loewer. 1995. *Gardening for Wildlife*. Emmaus, Penn.: Rodale Press. 192 pp.

Design for Inhabiting the Urban Landscape

3

Man is that uniquely conscious creature who can perceive
and express. He must become the steward of the biosphere.
To do this, he must design with nature.

—Ian McHarg

"WE'RE LOOKING FOR SOMETHING different . . . please, no taxus or begonias!" This sums up the most common plea I've heard over the years as a professional landscape designer, and I've thought long and hard about what my clients and friends really mean by "something different." It is apparent that the typical urban landscape leaves much to be desired and leaves many needs unmet, although most people are quite unsure about what is missing.

For years I have closely observed the landscapes where people live, work, travel, and play in their daily lives. Whether large or small, public or private, inner city or urban fringe, our landscapes typically perform only the most limited function of covering bare ground. We pave with turf, caulk with shrubs, maybe put a tree here and some color there. Our outdoor places are literally an afterthought created from leftover spaces. Once established, someone must fulfill the endless role of outdoor janitor. I don't have the space here to trace the lineage of such landscapes or to sort out the blame for the lifeless mess of urban sprawl; the point is that we must realize how barren, how wasteful, how boring it has all become.

In a very real sense we are stupefied and enslaved by our surroundings. Far removed from the family homeplace, with grandma's garden a faint memory, we have lost our human heritage as garden makers. We no longer inhabit our daily landscape, and the landscape is lost without us. Yet living inside each of us, however vague or inarticulate, is an intimacy with fruit and fragrance, some memory of a rambling rose, a reverie of birdsong, sustenance, and sanctuary.

My hope and purpose in this writing is to help us remember what is missing, and then to set about the business of recreating it. Our home, our plot of ground is the foothold, no matter how small or seemingly misplaced. We cannot design our landscapes simply for wildlife or for nature's sake. A "sustainable approach to landscape design" is a trendy term for sensitive, skillful design that blends the needs of people, plants, and wildlife into a seamless whole. It is an approach to design that is dynamic and ongoing, that sees the life of a place unfolding out of a particular past into a desired future. Good design is an ongoing exercise in belonging to one's place.

In this chapter I outline the basic steps and thoughts involved in designing landscapes. Because guidelines for assessing habitat and attracting wildlife are covered in other chapters, here I focus more on how to make the landscape habitable for people. In this book I've geared the information toward those who are

- working with a relatively small-scale, residential setting (though much of the information will be applicable to other sites as well);
- are interested in hands-on design and gardening, even if professionals will be hired in the process;
- are interested in the long-term rewards of staying in one place, and,
- are longing for "something different."

What Is Design, Really?

Designing and creating landscapes is like living a good, sensible life. You need to be mindful of the past, fully aware of the present, and concerned for the future. You try to take care of the needs of all things entrusted to your care. You need patience and perseverance to see things through to a good end. You pay close attention to the details without losing sight of the overall objective. You stay open to, and expect, mystery and surprises. Above all, you keep learning.

Some of the most lively, generous, perceptive, and sensible people are gardeners. And the most pleasing gardens are not necessarily those found in fancy gardening magazines, but those that are lovingly designed and handcrafted over time and are unique to a particular place and personality. Gardeners work with the earth and the earth works on them in the most delightful ways. It is in those people and those places that landscape designers find inspiration for their work. I suppose you could say that an

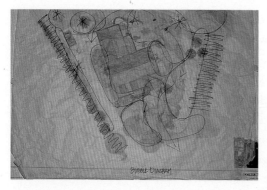

Using bubbles to determine uses for
the property.

These photographs show the planning process,
from start to finish, of a landscaping project
in Lexington. Native species were not used in
this design but could be substituted for many
of the more traditional horticultural plants
used. Notice the gently curving lines and the
reduction in lawn.

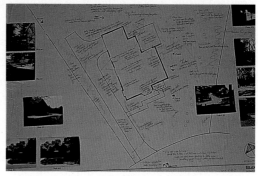

Conducting a site analysis and
drawing a technical plan.

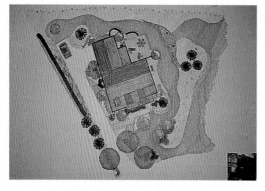

Selecting plants and drawing
a final plan.

The finished product.

ultimate goal is to create more gardeners, for as Henry Mitchell puts it, "Gardeners are the elect of the earth, cured in humility and grace and other good things." Design—teaching and sharing while doing it—is my principal tool.

I do not advocate any particular style of landscape design. The goal is more life, more comfort, and contact with nature at one's very doorstep—landscapes that are fully functioning and beautiful on many levels. If a certain style is desired or emerges, that is secondary to the process of fitting needs and desires appropriately to a place.

Most successful designs begin as a plan on paper, whether it be a sketch or a full-blown blueprint. The point of a landscape plan is to see the whole property at a glance, to verify the size and location of everything, and then to work out all the elements in relation to one another before planting and installation begin. A plan establishes the framework for the landscape, but often as things grow, one's understanding grows also. Ideas evolve and the landscape changes over time.

A Few Words about Hiring Help

Ideally, we would all have the skills, the interest, and the time to create our own special places. A truly rich and functional landscape may require, sooner or later, a broad range of knowledge and skill, involving soil science, grading, pruning, disease management, carpentry, masonry, and sheer artistry. If you are thinking about hiring someone to help with your project, you should begin with an experienced designer or landscape architect with broad knowledge and a thoughtful, sensitive approach to design.

You will want to show the designer or architect any pictures or gardens that inspire you, and you should definitely be pleased by examples of that person's previous work. But, above all, you want to sense the beginning of a great dialogue. The designer you choose should be highly observant, asking a lot of questions and listening intently to everything you say right from the start.

If you start out with a solid, creative plan, you will then know what parts you could accomplish on your own or what specialists may be needed to bring the landscape to life. One of the most important roles of a designer can be to identify those projects that may be tackled first while allowing other more complicated issues to be resolved. If I have clients who have just recently moved into a new place, I strongly encourage them to live through a cycle of seasons before making any major changes. Take your time, find someone willing to take the time with you, and proceed to learn more about the design process in the following steps.

The Design Process

Step 1. Landscape Functions: Knowing What You Need

First, take an inventory of what you and your family truly need. *What practical day-to-day functions should the landscape serve?* Think about how your needs may change with the seasons and with the passing of years. The following checklist may help you get started:

Driving/parking:
- driveway
- parking spaces
- room to back up or turn around
- garage or carport
- access for trucks for future construction or mulch delivery

Pathways:
- front entry walk
- to and from garage, toolshed
- garden pathways
- passage to neighbor's yard
- mail delivery route
- others (paved or mown)

Sports and games:
- volleyball
- badminton
- croquet
- Frisbee
- other

Play space:
- swings
- play equipment
- sandbox

Food production:
- vegetables or herbs
- greenhouse
- cold frame
- fruits, orchard

Social gathering:
- sitting area
- barbecue, picnic
- decks, patios

Private space:
- hammock
- reading
- meditation

Pet needs:
- dog house
- dog run
- fencing

Storage:
- firewood
- garbage cans, recycling bins
- compost
- tools, toys
- potting shed

Views:
- screening, buffering
- preserving vistas
- revealing desirable views

Focal points:
- pond, fountain, birdbath
- sculpture, sundial
- specimen plants

Any good design should bring structural forms and plants in harmony with one another.

Step 2. Landscape Character: Knowing What You Want

Next, take a careful look at your heart's desires, those intangible qualities or values that you may associate with being outdoors. *What qualities or characteristics are desired on the site?* Often we have landscape images that are rooted in childhood memories or special places we have visited. With my clients, I find it's important to search for these sometimes hidden or unarticulated ideas—they are often the keys, the spark, that brings clients to a deeper involvement in their own garden. Some of these might include

- Woodsy shade, dappled areas
- Filling the house with cut flowers
- A quiet oasis or retreat
- An apple orchard
- A cozy place for family picnics
- Frogs croaking at night
- Lying in a bed of leaves
- Unstructured, "wild," natural setting
- A safe, secure place for children
- An English cottage garden
- A formal herb garden
- A secret, hidden garden
- A nostalgic "grandmother's garden"
- A garden full of fragrance
- Eccentric or artsy found objects
- A grape-covered arbor

Step 3. Inventory and Analysis:
Knowing Your Site

Every site offers unique opportunities and challenges, and every good design grows out of a thorough understanding of the existing conditions. Every place consists of an intricate web of elements, relationships, and potential. Often the issues are complex and tangled, and it requires patient and thoughtful observation to sort out the many parts of the whole situation. Many mistakes are made in the process of rushing to solutions. Often the real problems and the potential are hidden. Consider the following items in your design.

The base map. A map of your site drawn to scale is the foundation of a landscape plan. The map should show all existing features of your property including the house, garage, driveway, pathways, and major trees. Be sure to include or approximate those features that you cannot see, such as underground utilities, the property lines, the north-south-east-west orientation of the site, and any areas along the street side that may be designated as public right-of-way.

It saves time if you can build the base map from a site survey or plot plan that usually comes with the deed to a property or may be found at the county courthouse. The scale of a plot plan is usually 1 inch = 20 or 30 feet, which is much too small a drawing to work with in any detail. You will need to have it enlarged to a more workable scale, such as 1/4 or 1/8 inch = 1 foot, depending on the size of your property. This becomes the "base" for noting site features and later for sketching design ideas. You can use tracing paper on top of the base plan to layer several ideas. If you can't locate a site survey and are not graphically inclined, you can hire a landscape designer, architect, or surveyor to provide one. A surveyor is able to locate the exact property corners on the ground, which is particularly helpful if you intend to build a fence. If you enjoy working with computers there are many programs available that will assist you in developing a landscape plan.

Soils and drainage. Soil is the most elemental building block, and often the most limiting factor, in the urban landscape. It is often the case around newer homes that the topsoil—the dark, loose, living layer of soil full of earthworms and organic matter—was stripped away prior to construction. The reason your spade may barely pierce the ground is that you are dealing

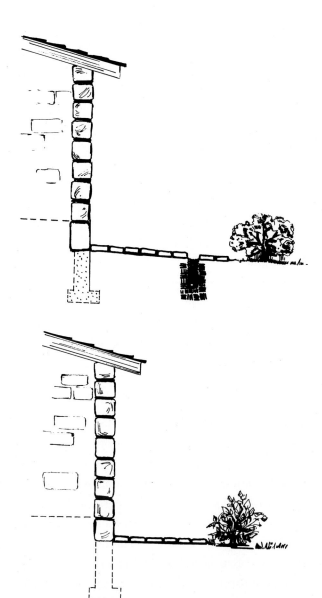

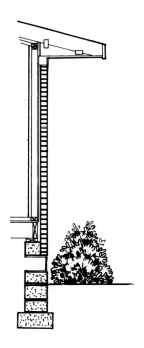

For homes with moisture or insect problems, you can install a subsurface drainage system to move water away from the foundation, or move plants away from the foundation to eliminate the need for watering under the eaves or roof overhangs.

with subsoil, tight clay material, to begin with. When compacted by heavy equipment, the subsoil becomes cement-like; water, air, and roots cannot easily penetrate it. You also may find areas where gravel or rubble was left behind, where water will pass through quickly and create droughty conditions. It is important to dig around to discover, and possibly map out, the mosaic of soil conditions.

In addition to the physical structure, you need to know the nutrient content and pH level (measure of acidity or alkalinity) of your soil. Your local County Extension Service can test a sample of your soil and provide information about corrections that may be needed. If you have discovered a patchwork of soil conditions in your yard, several samples and separate tests may be necessary. Where food gardens or play areas may be located, a test for lead in the soil is a very good idea, particularly around older buildings or adjacent to busy streets.

Next, you need to know how water moves through your site. Watch during and after a rainstorm: does water pool, collect, or stand for hours in low areas? Such areas could be ideal spots for moisture-loving plants instead of lawn. If water gathers near the foundation, you definitely want to regrade for positive drainage away from the house. Does water rush down slopes or drives, causing erosion and dumping sediment elsewhere?

We in urban areas are cursed by this compounded situation of hard ground, too much asphalt, and water that either stands where you don't want it or rushes away. Ideally, as in nature, you want the force of rain drops to be intercepted by multiple layers of leaves and then slowly absorbed into the earth. The goal is to slow the water down and retain it on site for your use.

Orientation and exposure. The location and intensity of sun, shade, and wind are also keys to understanding what plants and people will need to thrive in your setting. These factors change dramatically throughout the day and the seasons. Try to become intimately aware of the timing and the ways in which the sun reaches all the areas of your site, noting that the sun rises and falls lower in the sky in early spring and late fall, lighting up areas that may be in shade when the sun is high above the horizon in summer. Make notes and map out the extent of full-sun hot spots, areas of deep shade and in-between zones of dappled shade, morning sun only, and so on. Note also the orientation of the house and yard to the cardinal directions, keeping in mind that summer breezes are usually coming from the southwest and winter winds from the northwest.

In our climate of extremes, it is important to maximize the levels of comfort to be found outdoors throughout the year. People gravitate to a shady, breezy spot in the heat of summer and to a protected, sunny nook in spring, fall, and winter. There are many ways to modify the "micro-climates" in your yard, as well as the climate within the house, by careful placement of plant materials, arbors, trellises, and so on, yet this issue is too often overlooked in site planning.

Existing vegetation and habitat. Make sure that trees, shrubs, garden beds, and so on are accurately drawn to scale on the base map, including the extent of any tree canopies. You may need to get help from a nursery, garden center, or arborist in identifying your plants and assessing their health and likely longevity. Learn what you can about the plant's needs and what it has to offer throughout the season.

Do not be hasty in removing any plant material at this point! Preserve your options for working with what you have. You may decide later to move existing plants to more desirable locations, or to prune a large gangly shrub into a small tree. Certain shrubs may be rejuvenated by cutting them to the ground. If you do have rampant, invasive plants taking over the yard, such as Japanese honeysuckle vine, creeping euonymus, or mulberry seedlings, go ahead and take these out. At this stage, however, the focus is on learning and observation.

The built environment. The key concepts to keep in mind as you evaluate the built structures in your landscape (such as walkways, drives, fences, stairs, porches, and the house itself) are these:

1. Are elements functional and in good repair, and are they in the best place? These elements are often laid down without much foresight, particularly if your house was built as a "spec" house. Or your needs may be quite different from the previous owner's.

2. Can you get from one place to another with safety and ease? Are the stairs too steep, the path too narrow, the back porch or yard inaccessible from the kitchen?

3. Do the materials blend and complement one another? Or do you have a dizzying array of brick walks, stone walls, iron railings, and wood siding?

Rarely do we find, in this culture, a pleasing, fluid relationship of the house to the ground and surrounding landscape. What we generally do is isolate one from the other; "in" and "out" are entirely separate places—in physical terms, and therefore psychologically and culturally as well. Rigid foundation plantings merely emphasize the separation. When you are inside, are you drawn into the outside and vice-versa? Whatever happened to great porches, breezeways, and summer kitchens? In your design endeavors strive to think like the best architects; imagine ways to weave the house and garden together, allowing inside and outside to join in a complete living space.

The built features form the infrastructure (or the "bones" as the garden writers say) of the entire landscape. If the infrastructure is inappropriate or the bones are broken, your landscape efforts will be superficial and cosmetic. Invest in correcting the infrastructure first.

Use and recreation. This topic raises a central question: In what way does the site promote, prohibit, or limit the activities you hope to carry out? The primary considerations related to outdoor activity are:

- flatness or steepness of the ground;
- access to the space;
- size and configuration of space;
- visibility of the space; and
- comfort factors like sun, shade, and privacy.

Most of these factors can be modified, to some degree, but the key is to understand the inherent limitations of the site and to work as creatively as you can within those limits. In working out the spatial arrangement of activities, keep in mind those things that you may want close to the kitchen door—the vegetable, herb, or cutting garden—or areas that should be clearly visible from many vantage points, like the swing set.

Views in and out. Now take a visual inventory in and around your residence. Generally, such an inventory falls into four categories:

1. Clutter, storage areas, or utility units in your or your neighbor's yard that you may want to move or hide, such as garbage cans or compost areas.

2. Unobstructed views from the street or neighbor's yard into areas you wish could be more enclosed and private, such as bedrooms and patios. (On the other hand, if you live in an area where security is a concern, good visibility throughout the property is important.)

3. What a new visitor sees upon entering the property and approaching the house: Is it pleasant and welcoming? Is there confusion about where to park or which door to enter?

4. Pleasant views from your property that may be revealed or enhanced: Is an overgrown hedge blocking your view into the park beyond the back yard? Could you borrow and frame a view of the neighbor's lovely cutting garden from some special vantage point in your house or yard?

Good design should draw the viewer into the architecture of the home and not distract from it. As the evergreens in the above illustration grow up, they will give the entrance an univiting, inhibiting appearance. In contrast, by graduating the plant sizes away from the house, as in the lower illustration, the apparent size of a two-story home is increased. (Redrawn from J. Cervelli-Schach, Landscape Design with Plants: Creating Outdoor Rooms.*)*

Look out of all the windows of your house as if they were frames of a picture. Really look and note what you see on the base map, and remember that the scenes will change throughout the year. This exercise may require some objectivity and a fresh perspective from a friend or neighbor. For years I saw my little one-car garage as just that, even though I rarely parked my car there. One day someone commented on what a charming appeal the building had, and now I'm planning to take out a big chunk of asphalt and wrap the patio around my "garden shed."

Surrounding context.   No landscape or home is an island. The way our site affects and is affected by its surroundings is often much more complex than we realize. It is extremely important to step back and see the larger context that your home is a part of. It can be very helpful to literally step back to view your property from across the street. Is it possible that the empty lot next door could be built on? Could street trees be planted or sidewalks installed in the public right-of-way in front of the house? Are there cooperative ways to divert the flow of water from the neighbor's yard into yours? Could scattered clumps of woodland in several yards be connected to attract and keep more wildlife in the neighborhood?

Step 4: Moving from Analysis to Design

For those working with a designer, you will be a rare and distinctive client if you have given lots of thought to the previous steps prior to the designer's coming on the scene. If there are daunting challenges on your site having to do with poor drainage, steep slopes, or the need for extensive changes in elevation, you should enlist the aid of a landscape architect. Presenting your hired help with a well thought-out list of needs, desires, and site ob-

A typical landscape will have a foreground, middle ground, and background. Generally speaking, foundation or background plantings are the base for the design, particularly with flower gardens.

servations should not only delight your designer but result in time and money saved.

As you sift through your desires and discoveries throughout the analysis, your awareness grows of the unique combination of ingredients contained within your surroundings. Great insights may have begun to surface; the time has come for some conclusions. You begin to bridge the gap between what is really going on on your site and what is really possible there. After you have sorted out your assets (a big maple provides shade in the side yard all afternoon) and your constraints (the rear patio is scorching hot all day), you begin to tie them together (think about moving the patio to the side yard).

The transition from analysis to design is a bit difficult to describe. It is usually the most challenging, mysterious, and delightful part of the process. Whether you are proceeding in this design adventure or are guiding a designer, the following things are helpful to keep in mind:

1. Your attention should shift back and forth, with greater and greater ease, between focusing on the parts and stepping back to see the whole.

2. You should resist grabbing onto the first or most obvious solution.

3. On the other hand, you do not want to be shy about doing something really drastic (like moving the patio or the tree) to make the right connection or flow in a crucial place.

4. As is often the case in life matters, there is usually some central challenge or difficulty which, when resolved, holds the key to sorting out the other dilemmas. (If we move the patio, then the vegetable garden could be in the sun right outside the door.) The word "problem" is from a Greek word for "thing thrown forward."

5. You begin to hear yourself say "Aha!" more and more often, as certain solutions for people, plants, and other creatures begin to overlap and fall together in harmony. (It dawns on you that a low retaining wall to hold that slope would make a nice place to sit, creating a flat space for plants as well.) In truth, I am simplifying greatly here—it takes time and experience to do this well.

Step 5. Ideas for Shaping a Sense of Place

To this point, I have looked mostly at existing conditions and ways to make the site functional. Now, form will follow and blend with function. If the functions of the landscape provide the contents, the forms speak to the spirit of the place. As you move further into the design process, consider

A patio covered with trumpet-vine, passionflower, crossvine, pipevine, or native trumpet honeysuckle vine may be a special "place to go" in the landscape and will also be attractive to hummingbirds and butterflies. (Redrawn from Kelly, et al., Xeriscape: Landscape Water Conservation in the Southeast.)

ways that gardens take on a certain higher intelligence and special character when ideas about form are considered.

Throughout the many ages and cultural expressions of garden making, there are certain forms and ideas that have been repeated and re-created to fit the given setting. A garden can be seen as a living metaphor; we move through space and time, we rest, find comfort, and some meaning in our midst. Just as we reach out to touch more of nature, we reach back to some link with our culture, our past. Though we aim at working on all levels, the truth is that nature and serendipity supply most of what we are after.

The pleasing path. We want to be led comfortably through a series of discoveries. Experiences along the way should unfold, in sometimes unexpected ways, which means that everything should not be seen all at once. Shaping the way the garden is encountered from the

This wooden path serves as a gateway to the gardens beyond.

This water garden in downtown Louisville serves as a focal point for the landscape.

path is one of the most important, yet overlooked, perspectives in garden design.

Places to go. Along the pleasing path there should be special places of arrival or pausing along the way. The front door to the house, the back patio or herb garden are typical destinations, but the garden should provide a succession of other landings and goals if possible. In these places, think of the pathway widening out and collecting like a pool where the stream of movement is delayed.

Enclosure. Our expanses of lawn fail to provide what we find most comforting in an outdoor setting—a sense of being protected and wrapped around by the landscape. A garden as a whole, and sometimes spaces within the garden, must somehow be contained and separate from the world outside, so that the eye can rest and focus on what is within. A sense of enclosure can be accomplished on many levels and in many ways, employing hedges, fences, slopes, arbors, trellises, the side of the house or garage, or a combination of all these things.

Gateways. At points of entry, or whenever a path moves from one realm of the garden to another, the transition should be marked or highlighted by something special. Gateways can be anchored with sturdy plants, an arched trellis, or a vine-covered arbor. They can also be made distinctive by a change in path materials, elevation, or the contrast of moving from shade into sunlight.

The focal point in this landscape is the patio surrounded by plants.

Focal points. By this I mean something that stands out, draws attention to itself, and has a special purpose, significance, and location in the landscape. The focal point may be a tree or specimen plant of some distinction, a pool, fountain, sculpture, bench, or birdbath. There can be many multiple focal points throughout the garden, but they should be selected and placed carefully so they do not clutter or crowd their setting. (Some glorious gardens break this rule and pull it off with fanfare and flair.) Likely locations include the end point or crossroads of pathways, a spot that is viewed from a cozy chair indoors or the top of a rise or hill.

Clumps and masses. If you planted one of every kind of plant that you have room for in the garden, you would have incredible diversity but not enough order or structure. It would be difficult to appreciate each and every individual plant. That is why, visually, we plant several or many of the same species together, creating groves, clumps and drifts, which is often the way we find them growing in nature.

Contrast and texture. Often in nature, contrasts are seen on a large scale: open meadows and dense forests, hills and valleys, towering trees and delicate wildflowers. In the garden, contrast is created on a much smaller scale, and the shapes, textures, and colors of plants generally carry the day. Since flowers are fleeting, it is important to pay attention to leaves, stems, bark, and berries as well. Big leaves next to feathery grasses, dark bluegreens against light bright greens, gray winter stems fronting evergreens are all pleasing combinations. I have found that dark surfaces provide a very effective backdrop for planting, allowing the more subtle aspects of plant colors and textures to be highlighted in the foreground.

Use leading lines and specimen plants to bring out a focal point in the landscape. (Redrawn from J. Cervelli-Schach, Landscape Design with Plants: Creating Outdoor Rooms.)

Engaging the senses. Once the basic layout of the garden is attained and knowledge of plant and wildlife increases, the heady business of sensory fulfillment takes precedence in the gardener's criteria. Gardeners spend a lifetime immersed, like a bee enfolded in a flower, in the interplay of hue and texture, nectar and perfume, shadow and light, sweetness and tartness, cricket drone, and frog call. The more all the senses and all of life are invited to participate in the garden scene, the more endlessly rich and satisfying the garden will be.

Come Outside

Antoine de Saint-Exupery wrote in *The Little Prince:* "It is the time you have wasted for your rose that makes your rose so important. . . . Men have forgotten this truth. . . . But you must not forget it. You become responsible, forever, for what you have tamed. You are responsible for your rose."

The urge to grow things is a signal of our own growth: we should lavish attention on such longings. Don't settle for a lonely landscape or someone else's personal vision of what it should be. Be bold, be patient, and plumb the depths of place making. In finding your way to something different, you may find you have fully arrived, at home, just where you want to be.

References

Bell, S. 1993. *Elements of Visual Design in the Landscape.* New York: Chapman and Hall. 212 pp.

Cervelli-Schach, J. 1985. *Landscape Design with Plants: Creating Outdoor Rooms.* University of Kentucky Cooperative Extension Service Pub. HO-62.

Cox, J. 1991. *Landscaping with Nature: Using Nature's Design to Plan Your Yard.* New York: St. Martins Press. 344 pp.

Druse, K. 1989. *The Natural Garden.* New York: Glarkson N. Potter. 296 pp.

Eck, J. 1996. *Elements of Garden Design.* New York: Henry Holt. 164 pp.

Fairbrother, N. 1974. *The Nature of Landscape Design.* New York: Knopf. 252 pp.

Frey, S.R. 1992. *Outdoor Living Spaces.* Emmaus, Penn.: Rodale Press. 342 pp.

Kelley, John, Mary Haque, Debra Shuping, and Jeff Zahner. 1991. *Xeriscape: Landscape Water Conservation in the Southeast.* Clemson Univ. Cooperative Extension Service Pub. EC 672.

Martin, E.J., Jr., and P. Melby. 1994. *Home Landscapes: Planting Design and Management.* Portland, Ore.: Timber Press. 175 pp.

Messervy, J.M. 1995. *The Inward Garden: Creating a Place of Beauty and Meaning.* Boston: Little, Brown. 256 pp.

Robinson, N.H. 1992. *The Planting Design Handbook.* Brookfield, N.J.: Gower Publications. 271 pp.

Smyser, C.A. 1982. *Nature's Design: A Practical Guide to Natural Landscaping.* Emmaus, Penn.: Rodale Press. 390 pp.

Strong, R., 1986. *Creating Small Gardens.* London, England: Conran Octopus. 139 pp.

Taunton Press, 1994. *The Best of Fine Gardening: Garden Design Ideas.* Newtown, Conn.: Taunton Press. 95pp.

Landscaping with Native Wildflowers

To make a prairie it takes a clover and one bee,
One clover, and a bee,
and revery.
The revery alone will do,
If bees are few.

—Emily Dickinson

WHAT'S THE HOTTEST RAGE in gardening? Going wild with native plants! Landscaping with native wildflowers is catching on at homes, schools, and businesses all across America. This chapter defines terms used in landscaping with natives and describes the basic principles of gardening the native way (working *with* instead of *against* nature).

What is a native plant? A *native plant* is one that originated naturally (without human intervention) and persists naturally in the wild in a particular region. It is well adapted to the climate of its region, which makes it hardy and self-reliant. In some cases, desirable native plants, like prairie blazing star or purple coneflower, have been cultivated for various traits. These are still native species or *cultivars* of native species, but their genetic qualities have been altered. They may be used in landscaping, but true native species are preferred.

An *exotic* is an organism not native to a particular region. Many familiar plants, like chicory, Queen Anne's lace, ox-eye daisy, and Deptford pink, are exotics. Exotics in Kentucky include plants from other regions of the United States and other countries. Common lantana and California poppy are North American wildflowers, but they are not native to Kentucky, so they are exotics. A *naturalized plant* is an exotic that was introduced into a region by humans but persists there in the wild on its own. Many of Kentucky's naturalized plants, including common yarrow, multiflora rose, bush honeysuckle, nodding thistle, crown vetch, purple loosestrife, Johnsongrass, winged and climbing euonymus, wild teasle, kudzu, garlic mustard, and yellow or white sweet clover, are particularly invasive and have become major pest species in the state and region. Because of their weedy tendencies, naturalized plants establish themselves without seeding. Avoid planting such species.

As cities grow and develop, native vegetation is destroyed and replaced with concrete, asphalt, buildings, and roads. This leaves little room for plants. Where replanting does occur, native plant species are often replaced by exotic species. Several studies in Europe have found that 60 to 65 percent of original native plant species are present in small towns, but only 30 to 50 percent of native species can be found in large cities. Approximately 41 percent of the plants in what was West Berlin, Germany, are exotics, and 58 percent of its native species are considered endangered. Similar patterns occur in the United States.

Invasion of the Aliens

Alien or exotic species are those introduced by man into environments they would not have reached by natural means. These species have transformed entire ecosystems in the United States. The American chestnut, a dominant tree in the Eastern deciduous forest, has been reduced to root sprouts and a few adults because of the imported chestnut blight fungus that ravaged our forests. The Everglades are being overrun by dense monocultures of an imported Australian tree. More than 10 million acres of grassland in California have been invaded by yellow star thistle. In Kentucky and Tennessee, European garlic mustard is a threat to the native rockcress, which is being considered for inclusion on the federal endangered species list. In central Kentucky, garlic mustard has invaded most natural areas to the point where it dominates the herbaceous layer of the landscape and has outcompeted native plants like Virginia bluebells, trilliums, and other beautiful woodland wildflowers. The resources of 109 national parks are being threatened by invasive alien plants, and at least 18 federally threatened or endangered species are being harmed throughout the country.

At one time, Shady Lane Woods near the University of Kentucky arboretum had a beautiful spring wildflower display. A visitor to the area 25 years ago would have been greeted by trilliums, purple phacelia, bloodroot, and numerous other spring wildflowers. Today there is no spring wildflower display. Why? Two invasive exotic plants, bush honeysuckle and climbing euonymus, outcompeted all the native plants: the entire understory is nothing but those two plant species.

Approximately 25 percent of the plants in this country today are exotics. Approximately 10 percent of them are considered invasive. This conversion from native to exotic has been referred to as biological pollution of natural ecosystems because of the tremendous ecological damage and management problems created by invasive exotics. These exotics compete with native species, occupy their habitat, and ultimately force them out. This results in an altered plant species composition, an altered community structure, and a reduction in native biodiversity. Once these species become naturalized, it is almost impossible to eliminate them from the environment. For example, multiflora rose (which was introduced to create living fences and as wildlife food or cover) has become so invasive that it is now listed as a noxious weed in Illinois, Indiana, Iowa, Kansas, Maryland, Missouri, Ohio, Pennsylvania, and Virginia. When a species is listed as a noxious weed, it is illegal to plant it and you must attempt to control it on your property, which means using herbicides.

Animals are not immune to threat from exotics either. E. Raymond Hall, author of *Mammals of North America*, stated in 1963 that "introducing exotic species of vertebrates is unscientific, economically wasteful, politically shortsighted, and biologically wrong." If only we had heeded those wise words. The European starling and the house sparrow have become major pest species and compete for nest sites with native birds like the eastern bluebird and tree swallow. As with invasive exotic plants, it is almost impossible to control pest species once they are naturalized. Other animal examples include the recently introduced zebra mussel, which is threatening globally rare mussels in the Mississippi River drainage, and the rusty crayfish, which has displaced four species of native crayfish now listed as endangered in Illinois.

Why, in light of growing evidence regarding the problems with exotics, do we continue to promote and use them? For the most part, exotic plants are hardy and disease-free, have few if any insect pests, reproduce easily, and potentially provide food or cover for wildlife. They are readily available and provide a large measure of profit for nurseries because they reproduce so well. Unfortunately, these are the exact characteristics that make alien species serious competitors to native species.

A shift in philosophy is beginning to take hold in the scientific and management communities. The Illinois Department of Conservation no longer produces exotic plant material in its nurseries. After much encouragement, the Kentucky Division of Forestry no longer grows or sells exotic plants in its nursery. Native plant nurseries are springing to life all across

Exotics and the Problems They Cause

The following are invasive exotic plant species that
should not be grown in Kentucky.

beefsteak *(Perilla frutescens* var. f.)
bittersweet, Asian *(Celastrus orbiculatus)*
buckthorn *(Rhamnus frangula)*
burning bush *(Euonymus alatus)*
chickweed *(Stellaria media)*
chicory *(Cichorium intybus)*
clover, white sweet *(Melilotus alba)*
clover, yellow sweet *(Melilotus officinalis)*
dock *(Rumex acetosella)*
duchesnea *(Duchesnea indica)*
eulaly grass *(Eulalia* spp.)
euonymus, creeping *(Euonymus fontunei)*
fescue, Kentucky 31 tall *(Festuca arundinacea)*
honeysuckle *(Lonicera morrowii* and
  Lonicera standishii)
honeysuckle, Japanese *(Lonicera japonica)*
honeysuckle, shrubby *(Lonicera maackii* and
  Lonicera tatarica)
hydrilla *(Hydrilla verticillata)*
ivy, English *(Hedera helix)*
ivy, ground *(Flechoma hederacea)*
Johnsongrass *(Sorghum halepense)*
kudzu *(Pueraria lobata)*
lespedeza, bicolor *(Lespedeza bicolor)*
lespedeza, Korean *(Lespedeza striata)*
lespedeza, sericia *(Lespedeza cuneata)*

loosestrife, purple *(Lythrum salicaria)*
mulberry *(Morus alba)*
mulberry weed *(Fatuoa villosa)*
mustard, garlic *(Alliaria petiolata)*
olive, autumn *(Eleagnus umbellata)*
olive, Russian *(Eleagnus angustifolia)*
onion, wild *(Allium vineale* ssp. v.)
Osage orange *(Maclua pomifera)*
paulownia *(Paulownia tomentosa)*
pennywort *(Lysimachia numularia)*
privet *(Ligustrum sinense)*
Queen Anne's lace *(Daucus carota)*
rose, multiflora *(Rosa multiflora)*
skullcap, false *(Musla dianthera)*
spurge, leafy *(Euphorbia esula)*
star of Bethlehem *(Ornithogalum
  umbellatum)*
steeplebush, Japanese *(Spirea japonica)*
thistle, bull *(Circium vulgare)*
thistle, Canada *(Circium arvense)*
thistle, nodding *(Carduus nutans)*
tree of heaven *(Ailanthus altissima)*
vetch, crown *(Coronilla varia)*
vinca *(Vinca minor* and *Vinca major)*
water lettuce *(Pistia stratiotes)*
watercress *(Nasturtium officinale)*

Characteristics of Invasive Exotics

Rapid growth and maturity
Prolific reproductive capacities
Highly successful seed dispersal, germination, and colonization
Rampant spreading; outcompetes natives
Costly to remove and control

the country. We have one herbaceous nursery and two woody native plant nurseries in Kentucky. More are sprouting up all over.

Finally, the concept of using natives versus exotics is persuasive when you consider that native wildlife species comprise 99 percent of those for which state agencies manage habitat, and those animals became adapted over time to using native plant species. There is also little evidence that exotic plants are superior to native species for wildlife. We know many native plants can be grown in nurseries (in contrast to what traditional horticulturists or

Examples of Problems with Introduced Organisms

American Chestnut Blight

Caused by a fungus introduced with the Chinese chestnut, this pathogen eliminated one of the most important hardwood trees in Eastern North America. It completely altered the plant species composition of Eastern forests.

Dogwood Anthracnose

This disease, which is just beginning to affect Eastern North American forests, has been suspected of arriving with the Asian dogwood. In parts of the Eastern United States, mortality of dogwoods in the forest has been 100 percent.

Dutch Elm Disease

This disease destroyed nearly 100 percent of one of America's premier urban trees, the American elm.

Kudzu

Considered to be the scourge of the South, kudzu was introduced in 1935, when the federal government planted 73 million seedlings to control erosion along road cuts. Where the plants are established, no other species can grow. Kudzu has spread widely and can now be found as far north as Michigan.

Hydrilla

Hydrilla was introduced for aquacultural purposes. Since 1980 Florida has spent more than $112 million to control it.

Purple Loosestrife

This plant creates a monoculture and outcompetes native plants that provide food and cover for wildlife. It is estimated to cost $45 million annually in damage to agriculture and wildlife in the Northeast and Midwest.

Balsam Wooly Adelgid

Introduced with exotic nursery stock in the early 1900s, this insect has destroyed more than 95 percent of the Fraser firs in the Great Smoky Mountains.

nurserymen tell you), and future management problems caused by introducing additional exotics can be reduced if we promote and plant native species.

Making Use of the Natives

Before discussing gardening with wildflowers, a distinction should be made between gardening and restoration. Gardening with native wildflowers is not the same as restoring native habitats. If restoration of habitats is your

Black-eyed Susan in a small or out-of-the-way area

goal, you must get seeds and plants of *local* origin (the local county or adjoining counties) to ensure that the genetic integrity of local species remains intact. You must try to collect seeds from plants or salvage plants prior to the destruction of a natural site because nurseries are inadequate in supplying local plants. If you want to restore habitats, contact the Kentucky Nature Preserves Commission or the Kentucky Nature Conservancy for more information.

Gardening with native wildflowers uses plants native to a specific *region* (the physiographic region of Kentucky, for example). Although you should try to salvage local plants, it is not always possible, and you will need to rely on nurseries to find regional plants suitable for your needs. Although not optimal for the protection of genetic diversity, gardening with native wildflowers is a realistic compromise that is better than gardening with exotics.

As with any landscaping project, your native wildflower garden begins with a survey of how you use your property. What outdoor spaces do you use the most and for what types of activities? Turfgrass lawns are usually used for outdoor recreation and as tidy transitional edging between the home and the garden border. Chances are at least one area of your lawn is not part of your outdoor activity space. Maybe it's a postage stamp–sized front yard, too small for a traditional garden but a nuisance to mow. Such areas provide excellent opportunities to convert turfgrass to an alternative perennial ground cover, such as pachysandra, combined with colorful spring wildflowers and ferns. Or maybe you have a large backyard where only the 20 feet closest to the house are commonly used for recreational activities. Why not convert the borders and background space into a native habitat garden that never needs mowing?

Your Native Habitat Garden

The following steps will help even the novice gardener use native plants to create attractive, low-maintenance habitat gardens for wildlife.

Planning Your Garden

1. Determine the environmental conditions of your planting site. To reap all of the conservation benefits of using native plants in the landscape, rely on species adapted to the environmental conditions of the planting site rather than trying to adapt the site to a set of preselected plants. You reduce labor and costs of site preparation, have much greater success, and minimize post-planting maintenance. As Ken Druse states in *The Natural Habitat Garden,* "Don't fight the site."

Depending on past land use, soils may need to be restored to make them capable of supporting native plants. Soils are often compacted and lack topsoil following construction activities. If the soil is inadequate, loosen it to improve aeration and drainage properties and replace lost nutrients before planting. Sites currently supporting landscape plants of any kind are probably capable of supporting native plants with little additional preparation.

2. Choose an appropriate natural community as a landscape model. As discussed in chapter 2, a natural community is an assemblage of plants and animals that co-exist in nature because they have similar requirements for natural resources and are able to compete successfully with each other for those resources. A natural community is usually characterized by its plant and animal species. We can predict the type of natural community that will develop on a site based on climate, soils, topography, and other environmental conditions. Natural communities are excellent landscape models because they are self-sustaining and support a diversity of plant and animal species. Once you have defined the environmental conditions of your planting site, determine the natural community type that occurs under similar conditions in your region of Kentucky. Plants characteristic of that community will grow well in your habitat garden.

Although many types of natural communities exist in Kentucky, they can be classified generally as upland or lowland forests or prairies. Most of the Kentucky landscape originally was forested, and, in the absence of grazing and fire, most sites eventually regenerate to forest. Various management techniques such as mowing, grazing, or burning are needed to main-

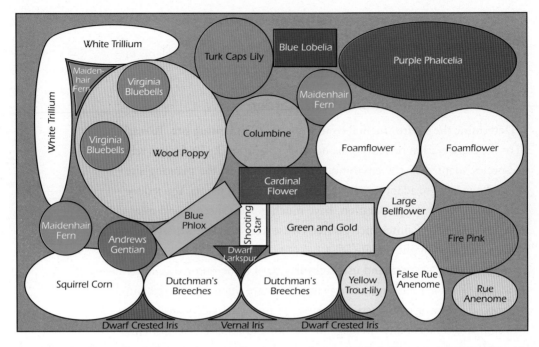

The labels within the figure read:
White Trillium, Turk Caps Lily, Blue Lobelia, Purple Phalcelia, Maidenhair Fern, Virginia Bluebells, Maidenhair Fern, White Trillium, Virginia Bluebells, Columbine, Foamflower, Foamflower, Wood Poppy, Cardinal Flower, Large Bellflower, Blue Phlox, Shooting Star, Green and Gold, Fire Pink, Maidenhair Fern, Andrews Gentian, Dwarf Larkspur, Squirrel Corn, Dutchman's Breeches, Dutchman's Breeches, Yellow Trout-lily, False Rue Anenome, Rue Anenome, Dwarf Crested Iris, Vernal Iris, Dwarf Crested Iris

An example of a woodland planting design. Fill in between plantings with wild ginger, spring beauty, and various wild violets.

tain open landscapes in most of Kentucky. For landscaping purposes, it is helpful to know the light and soil conditions common to forest and prairie communities.

In a natural forest, overstory trees create a canopy that filters the amount of sunlight reaching the forest floor. The leaf canopy creates conditions of dappled shade and sunlight. In some forests, little direct sunlight reaches the forest floor. Shrubs and herbaceous plants that grow in a forest are adapted to varying levels of shade. In a deciduous forest, the floor receives full sun throughout the spring until the leaf canopy develops. This sun promotes new spring growth of ferns and wildflowers. A backyard with mature shade trees creates conditions of shade similar to that of a natural forest. In contrast, the shade on the north side of a building is a dense shade not desirable for most plants, but many native forest shrubs and wildflowers do fine in dense shade if drainage and air circulation are adequate.

Forest soils generally have a high organic content. Leaves, bark, stems, and other plant debris litter the forest floor each year and begin the process of decomposition that builds the forest soils. This process can be replicated in the backyard by mulching with leaf litter and amending the soil with compost, peat, or other organic materials.

In contrast to the forest, a prairie is an open grassland characterized by a high diversity of grass and wildflower species and few tree or shrub species. It is a more extreme environment than a forest because it receives full exposure to the sun and elements. Most prairie plants tolerate a wide range of moisture conditions and are drought-tolerant. The bluestem prairie, which once covered millions of acres in Kentucky, ranged from wet to dry. In a wet prairie, plants are generally tolerant of saturated soil conditions (soil at maximum water-holding capacity), but most are also able to withstand dry periods of varying lengths. In dry prairies or glades, plants are tolerant of well drained to excessively well drained soil conditions. These plants are highly drought-tolerant and excellent choices for xeriscaping (landscaping to conserve water).

Prairie soils vary greatly from one community to the next. Most prairie plants are extremely efficient at utilizing available soil nutrients and do not require highly fertile soils. Some prairie plants grow in shallow, rocky soils, but getting them established in such soils can be difficult.

A restored prairie.

It is critical that you minimize competition from cultivated grasses and agricultural weeds. Most prairie plants thrive in a good garden soil if competition is minimized. Fertilizing with nitrogen only promotes the growth of annual invasive weeds. If there is a severe deficiency of phosphorus or potassium or if the soil needs liming (as determined by a soil test), apply these fertilizers following soil test recommendations. If a site supports a lawn or a healthy growth of weeds, it should be adequate for growing most prairie plants.

If your site contains overstory trees and is shady much of the day, model your garden after a forest community. If the site receives six or more hours of direct sun, particularly during the hottest time of the day (late morning to late afternoon), a prairie community is a better model. If the site stays wet much of the growing season or is prone to seasonal flooding, a lowland community is appropriate. The savanna community (or barrens on drier upland sites) might be a suitable model for large sites or sites with some shade and some sun. A savanna is an open meadow with scattered individual trees or groves of trees and is very park-like in appearance.

It is possible to plant trees to create shadier conditions or remove trees to create sunnier conditions. Creating wooded conditions is a worth-while, if long-term, process of great value to wildlife. Establishment of trees might be expensive, but maintenance is minimal. Any healthy, native tree should be considered a valuable landscape and wildlife asset. A single mature (30-foot-tall) hemlock tree purchased from a nursery can cost $12,000. A 60-year-old white oak is worth tens of thousands of dollars. Unless a tree is severely diseased or weedy and invasive (tree of heaven, for example), removal is not recommended. It is better to maintain existing trees whenever possible and convert already sunny sites to native prairie plants.

3. Create plant menus for each habitat garden. Create a menu of plant species for each landscape. Although not all-inclusive, the native wildflower matrix in Appendix A gives you a starting point for creating a menu of species adapted to your site. Native plant nursery catalogs provide avail-ability and cost information, and many contain detailed habitat and culti-vation information for the species they offer. Consult a field guide or bo-tanical book for more information and to see drawings or photographs of the species you intend to establish.

A plant menu can be a simple list of plant species but has more value if composed as a matrix containing functional and physical attributes for each species. Such information is crucial when you begin the landscape design process. Include plant type, sun tolerance, soil moisture tolerance, aesthetic characteristics (flowers and fruits, bark, form, autumn color), period of bloom, wildlife value, and potential uses (shade, evergreen screen, erosion control).

4. Use diverse plants. Most wildflowers and other native plants have dis-tinct flowering and fruiting periods that last a few weeks, rarely longer. For lots of color as well as nectar, fruit, and nut production, use a diversity of plant types (trees, shrubs, ground covers) and species. Diverse plant types provide assorted habitat elements that can be used by a variety of wildlife species. Select various species that bloom during spring, summer, and fall

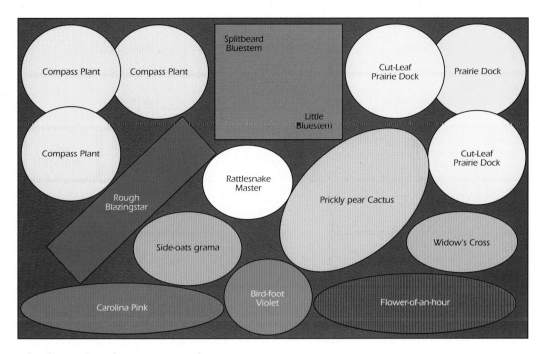

Plan for a rock garden using native plants.

Plan for a butterfly garden.

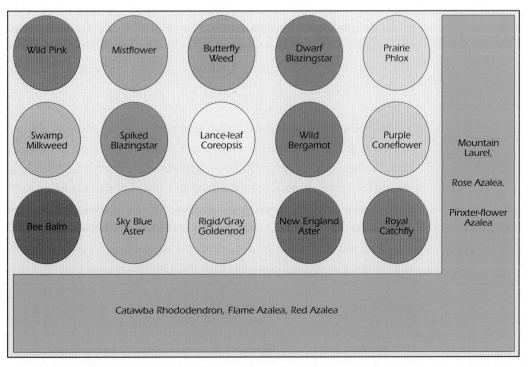

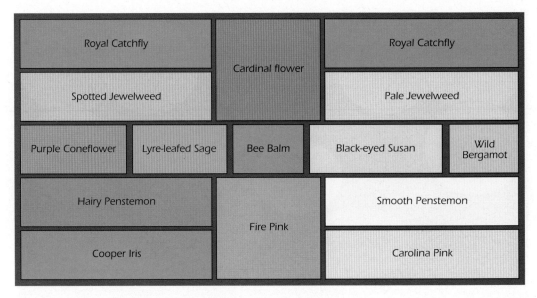

Plan for a hummingbird garden. On a trellis at the rear of the garden, the following vines would be placed: trumpet creeper, cross vine, passionflower, and Virginia clematis.

and plants that hold their fruits into winter. Native grasses provide good color in the garden in autumn and excellent wildlife cover in winter. In Kentucky, most forest wildflowers are spring-blooming, so add later-blooming species of woodland phlox, lobelia, aster, and goldenrod. Most prairie plants do not bloom until late spring. Some of the earliest bloomers include coreopsis, wood mint, sundrops, and downy phlox. Offering areas of both forest and prairie in your landscape provides year-round food and cover for wildlife.

5. Use clustering for enhanced beauty and wildlife value. Some wildflowers have large, showy flowers and can be used individually or in small groups with dramatic effect. Many wildflowers, however, are most attractive when planted in species clusters, or drifts. In nature, the most striking wildflower displays result from a tendency for species to grow in clumps. This tendency is influenced in large part by their methods of self-propagation and seed dispersal. Even in a garden, each species rearranges itself over time according to its own propagation patterns. One wild columbine is pretty for close-up viewing beneath a tree, but a drift of columbines in a wildflower border creates a solid block of color and texture visible from a distance. Planting species in clusters of several to dozens lends a natural quality and beauty to the landscape.

A summer wildflower garden.

A landscaped yard with spring wildflowers.

Clustering is also beneficial to wildlife. With the maximum amount of food in a single location, animals expend minimal energy to acquire it. Imagine the energy you would use if you had to go to one restaurant for an appetizer, another for the main course, and a third for coffee and dessert! Now think about a hummingbird—a bird with an extremely high metabolic rate-having to fly from one neighborhood to another just to find enough food for lunch. By planting large clusters of favorite foods (phlox, columbine, bee balm, cardinal flower) and hanging an artificial feeder or two you can feed many hummers with little effort on their part.

Establishing and Maintaining Your Garden

1. Eliminate all competing vegetation. In a natural community never degraded by logging, grazing, or other activities that alter the natural processes, vegetation is dominated by native species. In communities fragmented by roads, logging, or other human activities that create large openings in the forest canopy, it is common for exotic species to become established. In the United States, more than 4,000 species of harmful exotic plants have become established and are now part of the flora (U.S. Congress, 1994). Most people are familiar with the problems caused by kudzu and Japanese honeysuckle in our woodlands. The newer introduction of garlic mustard has, in just a few years, significantly affected the herbaceous flora in thousands of acres of Kentucky forest and woodland.

A significant obstacle to re-establishing native plants is competition

American columbine, a hummingbird favorite.

A grouping of bloodroot. Wildflowers need to be planted in groups or drifts to provide maximum viewing impact.

from exotic species. The first step in preparing a site for native plants is the elimination of all competing vegetation. Desodding, smothering, tilling, or applying herbicides (or a combination of these practices) will accomplish this goal. The method used depends on the type of site (past land use and existing vegetation), budget, time considerations, and equipment availability.

In a backyard that has a ground cover of turfgrass, desodding followed by light tilling works well. After tilling, water the area well to stimulate germination of weed seeds. Wait a few weeks, then hoe lightly to remove young weed sprouts. Plant or seed immediately with the native species you've selected. An alternative method is to till the site, rake away the sod, water, wait two weeks, hoe, and then plant. Be careful when tilling beneath trees not to damage surface roots. In fields, burning the field for two consecutive seasons prior to seeding produces good control of weeds such as fescue and Johnsongrass.

2. Decide whether to use plants or seeds. A habitat garden may be established using nursery stock, seeds, or a combination of the two. Advantages of using nursery stock are more control over design, quicker results, and better weed control. Usually, woody plants and woodland wildflowers and ferns are most successfully established using nursery stock (many are not available as seed). Nursery stock may be bare-root, in containers, or balled and burlapped (mostly trees and shrubs). You will be most successful if you transplant containerized wildflowers and ferns because they are not subject to the stress of being dug from a nursery bed prior to shipping. Many species of native trees and shrubs are available only as bare-root stock from mail-order nurseries. Bare-root stock is shipped and planted during dormancy (from November through early April, when leaves are off of the plant). Planting in spring when new growth has appeared in the forests and fields minimizes browsing impacts from deer and rodents. Balled and burlapped plants can be planted any time of year that the ground is workable.

Prairie plants are easily established using either stock or seed. It is often more economical to use seed on large, sunny sites. Many kinds of wildflower seeds and seed mixtures are now commercially available, but they vary tremendously in both quality and cost. The most successful mixes on the market today contain native grasses and perennials, with very few annuals or biennials.

Desirable native grasses include big and little bluestem, Indian grass, and prairie switch grass (grass seed is normally about 60 percent of the weight of the mix). The native grasses contribute wildlife food and cover, soil erosion control, autumn color, structure, and texture to the landscape.

Desirable native perennials include coreopsis, black-eyed Susan, yellow coneflower, purple coneflower, blazing star, aster, and goldenrod; native annuals include partridge pea and tickseed sunflower. Avoid mixes containing dames rocket, yarrow, ox-eye daisy, and Queen Anne's lace, which are nonnative and highly invasive.

Good seed contact with the soil is essential for a successful seeding. Hand and mechanical broadcasting are the preferred seeding methods on small sites. Because wildflower seed mixtures contain seed of many shapes, sizes, and textures, hand seeding affords better control of seed distribution. Seed may be mixed with inert materials to increase bulk and make handling easier. After seeding, a roller firmly presses the seed into contact with the soil without burying the seed too deeply. Light raking is another option.

Special drill seeders are often preferred on larger areas and erosion-prone sites because they eliminate the need for tilling. Use a broad-spectrum glyphosate herbicide, such as Roundup or Spectricide, to kill existing vegetation. The drill seeder places the seed in direct contact with the soil, and the dead plant material helps retain soil moisture and reduce weeds. The Kentucky Department of Fish and Wildlife Resources and chapters of Quail Unlimited have drill seeders adapted for seeding native plants.

In nature, it takes many years for a plant community to develop, and we cannot expect a habitat garden to spring up overnight. It requires several years for a native landscape to mature and begin producing an abundance of flowers, especially from seed. Some of the first species that begin blooming in the prairie garden are black-eyed Susan, partridge pea, and butterfly milkweed. By the second year, yellow coneflower, purple coneflower, ox-eye sunflower, and many of the grasses flower. Aster, blazing star, and goldenrod might not appear before the third year. As the planting develops, some species may become more abundant while others fade away, depending on site conditions and how the planting is managed.

3. Properly time establishment and maintenance. Native plants may be established from stock or seed almost any time of year that the soil is workable. Less maintenance is required during establishment if soil moisture levels are moderate to high and air temperatures are moderate. In Kentucky these conditions usually occur from spring through early summer and in the fall. Plants installed after mid-October should be mulched well after the ground freezes to prevent frost heaving.

During the establishment period, keep the root zone moist. Uniform soil moisture is necessary for good seed germination and seedling growth and development. Keep the full root zone of planted nursery stock moist until new leaves appear, then water as necessary to prevent wilting. Using a light mulch, such as leaves, clean straw, or shredded pine or hardwood bark, helps conserve moisture and reduce weed growth. In shaded areas established with forest wildflowers, apply an annual top dressing of leaf mulch in the fall.

Maintenance during the first couple of years after planting or seeding focuses on effective weed control. Hand pull weeds around established plants and in smaller seeded areas. Top annual weeds, such as foxtail, before they go to seed, and pull out perennial weeds by the root. In larger seeded areas, mow regularly to keep weeds less than 8 inches tall, thereby reducing weed competition and allowing sufficient sunlight to reach the seedling native grasses and forbs. In cases of severe competition by persistent perennial weeds like Johnsongrass or bull thistle, spot applications of a glyphosate herbicide or Plateau® may be warranted.

During the second year, you may mow to control weeds at the beginning of the growing season. Do not mow beyond mid-spring after the native plants have initiated rapid above-ground growth. It may be necessary to continue hand pulling or spot herbiciding particularly troublesome weeds, but in most cases this is not necessary.

Prescribed fire is the preferred method of maintaining prairie planting. Performed in early spring (late March for most of Kentucky), fire retards cool-season weeds and stimulates rapid growth of native plants. Do not use fire every year as it tends to promote grasses over forbs. Once your site is established, fire can be used every three to five years on average sites with good results. Prior to burning, mow fire lanes around trees and combustible structures. Your fire prescription should be prepared by someone knowledgeable about the use of fire as a management tool. Assistance is often available through stewardship programs such as the Kentucky Department of Fish and Wildlife Habitat Improvement Program and the Forest Stewardship Program.

Establishing a Prairie or Meadow from Seed on a Large Site

The first step is to select an appropriate site. Loamy soils are best for growing most prairie plants. Amend clay or sandy soils with a green cover crop (winter wheat) that is plowed under while the crop is actively growing. The site should receive at least six hours of full sunlight per day. Look for competition from trees, especially elms, basswood, or maples, because they have a high surface root density. Do not apply nitrogen fertilizer. If a soil test indicates fertility problems, add phosphorus and potassium accordingly.

The next step is to purchase high-quality native seed mix. The best mixes have a 60:40 ratio of grass to wildflowers. Do not use mixes that contain nonnative annual wildflowers or invasive exotics such as Queen Anne's lace, ox-eye daisy, common yarrow, or dames rocket. The mixture should contain big bluestem, little bluestem, Indian grass, side oats grama, and prairie switchgrass, with switchgrass being a *minor* component of the grass mixture.

It is important to select the appropriate seeding rate. Most prairie plantings are seeded at a rate of 6 to 8 pounds of pure live seed per acre if drilled with a native rangeland drill. If broadcast, double the seeding rate.

Select an optimum seeding date. The best seeding times are April 20 through June 20, but the range of planting dates can be from April 20 through July 1 and from September 1 until freeze.

Before seeding, prepare a firm, smooth, weed-free seedbed. The primary objective should be to clear the site of existing vegetation and eliminate all competing vegetation. The following methods work well:

• Burn existing fescue or grass in late March. When the grass is actively growing, apply Plateau herbicide following label directions. Two weeks later, seed directly into sod with a native rangeland drill.

• Mow, rake, and bale existing grass in late fall in the year preceding planting. After green-up in the spring, apply Plateau herbicide following label directions. After brown-down (two weeks), deep plow the site. Follow with a light disking or harrowing.

• Deep plow the site in the spring. Several weeks after plowing, disk lightly and rake to remove annual weeds. If you notice a large crop of annual weeds emerging, re-disk and rake several times.

Using the best seeding method is important. Because native plant seeds are light and fluffy, you cannot use normal plant seeders to create prairie. You will have the best success if the area is seeded with a native rangeland drill. Contact the Kentucky Department of Fish and Wildlife Resources or a Kentucky Quail Unlimited chapter to place your name on the list for use of and assistance with their native rangeland drills.

To get a head start, moisten the seed so it is just damp and place it in 1-inch-deep containers in a refrigerator for 30 days. Remove the seed and place it with paper mulch, proper fertilizer, and water in a hydroseeder. Hydroseed on a bare-ground (tilled), weed-free seedbed.

Hand broadcasting works better than commercial broadcast seeders for small areas. When hand broadcasting, seed slowly and cover each area in two directions. One pound of grass seed covers approximately 2,000 square feet. Flowers are seeded at a rate of 4 ounces per 1,000 square feet. Once the materials are sown, use a seed roller (available at most rental stores) to press the seeds firmly into the soil without burying them too deeply. On sloping sites, a light mulching of paper or clean straw keeps the seed from washing away.

After seeding, water once thoroughly, then as necessary to keep the seedbed moist. On larger sites, a nurse crop of annual rye or spring oats can be used to prevent erosion.

The final steps involve managing your planting. Prairie takes time to develop and requires patience and proper maintenance for several years. If you follow these steps and management guidelines, you will be rewarded with a spectacular landscape.

Year 1. Cut the planting two, three, or four times. At monthly intervals, use a scythe, mower, or line trimmer to cut the planting to a height of 8 inches. If using a mower, set it at the highest possible setting. Hand pulling can be used to remove individual invasive weeds

Costs Associated with Establishing Prairie

The major costs associated with establishing prairie are listed here. Many factors determine the costs; these are estimates.

Leasing equipment
(tractor with tillage equipment, mower, sprayer, seeder)

$25-$50 per hour (about five acres with a tractor)

Herbicide

(two or more applications may be necessary)

$80-$275 per gallon (will treat about four acres of fescue)

Plants:
One plant per square foot

$3 to $4 per plant

Seeds, warm-season grasses with wildflowers

$25-$250 per acre, depending on contents, and a seeding rate of 6 to 8 pounds per acre.

Total cost per acre: $250-$3,000

or woody plants. In severe cases, spot treatment with a herbicide may be required to control Johnsongrass.

Year 2. Mow once between mid-June and mid-August. Weed control and height regulation should help you decide if and when.

Year 3. Your patience has paid off, and your prairie planting has matured. You may mow your planting once a year (between mid-November and early May) if you desire as a clean-up procedure. A better alternative is to burn the prairie (January through March), but make sure to get the proper permits and follow all burning laws prior to conducting a burn. If you want to burn, you can get assistance from native plant nurseries or consultants.

To prepare a wildflower seedbed on a small site without the use of herbicide, follow these steps:

- Till the soil deeply to break up the sod and kill weeds.
- Rake the soil to remove weeds (and their roots) and prepare a seedbed.
- Water thoroughly; then allow several weeks for weed to sprout.
- Till lightly or use a hoe to remove the new weed crop. Disturb the soil as little as possible. Rake lightly.
- Sow seed immediately, roll, mulch lightly, and water.

Text continues on page 92

Some Favorite Woodland Flowers

See the native wildflower matrix in Appendix A for species native to Kentucky.

Dwarf crested iris

Wood (celandine) poppy

Bottle gentian can be used for fall color in the shade garden.

Foamflower

Some Favorite Early Spring Woodland Flowers

Wild geranium

Shooting star

Here is a nice combination of blue and white in a shade garden, with blue phlox, virginia bluebell, and shooting star.

Dutchman's breeches

Virginia bluebells

Some Favorite Rock Garden Plants

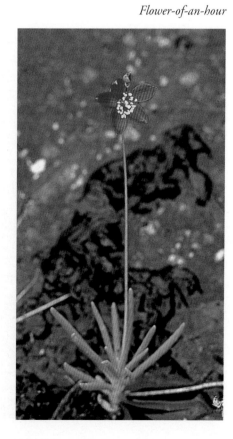

Bird-foot violet

*Compass
plant*

Flower-of-an-hour

White-false indigo

Flowers that Attract Hummingbirds

Wild petunia

Fire pink

Hairy penstemon

Spotted jewelweed

Prairie phlox

Hummingbird Wildflowers and Shrubs

Wildflowers

beardtongue (*Penstemon* spp.)
bergamot, or bee balm (*Monarda* spp.)
blazing star (*Liatris* spp.)
cardinal flower (*Lobelia cardinalis*)
columbine, wild (*Aquilegia canadensis*)
iris (*Iris* spp.)
jewelweed (*Impatiens* spp.)

mallow, rose (*Hibiscus* spp.)
petunia, wild (*Ruellia* spp.)
phlox (*Phlox* spp.)
pink (*Silene* spp.)
sage (*Salvia* spp.)
tea, New Jersey (*Ceanothus americanus*)
vervain (*Verbena* spp.)

Shrubs and vines

azalea (*Rhododendron* spp.)
creeper, trumpet (*Campsis radicans*)

cross vine (*Bigonia capreolata*)
honeysuckle, trumpet (*Lonicera sempervirens*)

Special Rock or Xeric Native Plants

Wildflowers

aloe, false (*Agave virginica*)
black-eyed Susan (*Rudbeckia hirta*)
blazing star, rough (*Liatris aspera*)
compass plant (*Silphium laciniatum*)
coneflower, pale purple (*Echinacea pallida*)
dock, cut-leaf prairie (*Silphium pinnatifidum*)
dock, prairie (*Silphium terebinthinaceum*)

flower-of-an-hour (*Talinum calcaricum*)
prickly pear cactus (*Opuntia humifusa*)
puccoon, hoary (*Lithospermum canescens*)
rattlesnake master (*Eryngium yuccifolium*)
stonecrop, pink (*Sedum pulchellum*)
violet, bird foot (*Viola pedata*)

Grasses

bluestem, broomsedge (*Andropogon virginica*)
bluestem, little (*Schizachyrium scoparium*)
broomsedge, Elliott's (*Andropogon gyrans*)

broomsedge, splitbeard (*Andropogon ternarius*)
grama, side oats (*Bouteloua curtipendula*)
Indian grass (*Sorghastrum nutans*)

Special Native Plants for Full Sun, Heavy Clay Soils

Wildflowers

aster, New England (*Aster novae-angliae*)
bergamot, wild (*Monarda fistulosa*)
black-eyed Susan (*Rudbeckia hirta*)
blazing star, button (*Liatris squarrosa*)
blazing star, prairie (*Liatris pyncostachya*)
compass plant (*Silphium laciniatum*)
coneflower, pale purple (*Echinacea pallida*)
coneflower, yellow (*Ratibida pinnata*)
cup plant (*Silphium perfoliatum*)

dock, cut-leaf prairie (*Silphium pinnatifidum*)
dock, prairie (*Silphium terebinthinaceum*)
indigo, cream wild (*Baptisia leucophaea*)
ironweed (*Vernonia gigantea*)
milkweed, butterfly (*Asclepius tuberosa*)
milkweed, common (*Asclepius syrica*)
rattlesnake master (*Eryngium yuccifolium*)
rosinweed (*Silphium trifoliatum*)
sunflower, ox-eye (*Heliopsis helianthoides*)

Grasses

bluestem, big (*Andropogon gerardii*)
Indian grass (*Sorgastrum nutans*)

switch grass (*Panicum virgatum*)

Why Many Nurseries Do Not Sell
Trilliums and Orchids

Native plant nursery personnel frequently hear the question, "Why don't you carry trilliums or orchids?" A good question, and the answer has to do with conservation ethics.

The primary reason many slow-growing woodland species are not available in nurseries has to do with their biology. Many are difficult to propagate in a nursery. For example, jack-in-the-pulpit, Virginia bluebell, and hepatica take three or more years to reach a salable size from seed in a nursery. Trilliums generally do not flower until the fifth through seventh year from seed. Ferns require special sterile conditions and several transplantings with tweezers before they are ready for small pots. Time is money, and woodland flowers propagated this way naturally would be expensive.

Orchid roots have a special relationship with specific fungi in the soil. The two are dependent upon one another, and both have specific soil requirements. Without this special condition, the plants are doomed to death. They will die when you bring them home and transplant them, even if you purchased them from a nursery. In addition, many orchid species in Kentucky are listed as state endangered or threatened species or are rare. There are severe penalties for even possessing these species. As more natural habitats are destroyed for development, more of these species will naturally perish. Why increase that rate!

References

Art, H.W. 1987. *The Wildflower Gardener's Guide: Northeast, Mid-Atlantic, Great Lakes, and Eastern Canada Edition.* Pownal, Vt.: Storey Communications. 180 pp.

Druse, K., and M. Roach. 1994. *The Natural Habitat Garden.* New York: Clarkson Potter. 248 pp.

Jones, S.B., Jr., and L.E. Foote. 1990. *Gardening with Native Wildflowers.* Portland, Ore.: Timber Press. 195 pp.

Phillips, H.R. 1985. *Growing and Propagating Wildflowers.* Chapel Hill: Univ. of North Carolina Press. 331 pp.

Stokes, D., and L. Stokes. 1992. *The Wildflower Book: East of the Rockies.* Boston: Little, Brown. 96 pp.

U.S. Congress, Office of Technology Assessment. 1994. Harmful Non-Indigenous Species in the United States. OTA-F-565. Washington, D.C.: GPO.

Wasowski, S., and A. Wasowski. 1994. *Gardening with Native Plants of the South.* Dallas: Taylor Publishing. 196 pp.

Wharton, M.E., and R.W. Barbour. 1979. *A Guide to the Wildflowers and Ferns of Kentucky.* Lexington: Univ. Press of Kentucky. 344 pp.

Wilson, J. 1992. *Landscaping with Wildflowers.* Boston: Houghton Mifflin. 244 pp.

Young, J.A., and C.G. Young. 1986. *Collecting, Processing, and Germinating Seeds of Welland Plants.* Portland, Ore.: Timber Press. 236 pp.

Gardening for Butterflies

5

There is no quiet place in the white man's cities.
No place to hear the unfurling leaves of the spring,
or the rustle of an insect's wings.

—Chief Seattle, 1854

INSECTS MAY BECOME your most welcome and diverse guests, but how often have you heard the saying "The only good bugs are dead bugs?" Is this true? I certainly hope not. Less than 1 percent of all insect species are pests and around 10 percent are beneficial to humans. From the standpoint of biodiversity and attracting wildlife to urban environments, there are a handful of mammals and birds that call Kentucky home, but most of the animals in this world and Kentucky are insects! Approximately 144 species of butterflies live in Kentucky and more than 2,200 species of moths can be found here. Untold other numbers of insects also inhabit the Commonwealth.

Insects are important members of the food chain, predators of many pests, recyclers of wastes, and responsible for silk production. Butterflies, honeybees, and other insects are crucial to the pollination of flowering plants. And some insects are beautiful. Although very few non-entomologists can appreciate a house fly, almost everyone can appreciate the grace and beauty of butterflies and, to a lesser extent, moths.

Butterfly Identification

Butterflies and moths belong to the group of insects named Lepidoptera (Greek *Lepis* = scale, *pteron* = wings). There are around 165,000 known species of butterflies and moths in the world, and about 750 species of butterflies in the United States. Butterfly watching has become a major leisure activity in the United States because of the wonderful colors and patterns of different species. The colors and patterns of butterfly wings

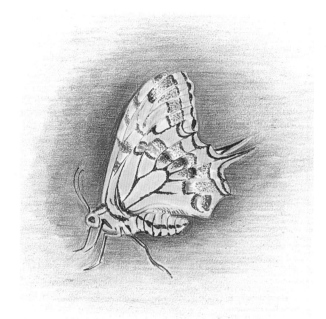

An adult butterfly at rest, showing the underside of the wings, the antennae, six legs, abdomen, thorax, and head.

come from modified hairs or scales that normally cover the upper and lower surface of all four wings. These scales come off easily when wings are touched. This trait helps butterflies escape spider webs, birds, and other predators, including people who attempt to grab them.

The order Lepidoptera can be further grouped into butterflies, moths, and skippers. How can you tell the difference between butterflies and moths? There are a couple of easy ways to make a quick determination, and a good field guide will help you better identify the insect. Butterflies are generally showy or exhibit more vibrant colors than moths. Butterflies are generally active during the day (diurnal), while moths are primarily active at night (nocturnal), although there are exceptions to this rule. Butterflies generally rest with their wings closed and held vertically over their back. Moths generally rest with their wings spread flat. Most moths form a silky cocoon in which to pupate, whereas butterflies generally form an unprotected chrysalis. Finally, butterflies generally have clubbed antennae and moths have feathery antennae. Skippers are a lesser-known group of lepidopterans whose characteristics are somewhat in between the butterflies and moths: they typically have hooked antennae, and at rest one pair of wings is out and the other pair is up.

Basic Butterfly Biology

Before you can begin to garden for butterflies, you must understand some basic butterfly biology and ecology. It is useful to know about each species' biology, ecology, behavior, and habitat requirements because every butterfly species is uniquely adapted and attracted to specific plants. To be suc-

The Seven Groups of Butterflies and Skippers Found in Kentucky

There are seven major groups of butterflies in Kentucky. They are grouped according to their anatomy, behavior, or ecological requirements. For instance, the skippers are unique in that they appear to be part moth and part butterfly, are small, and are usually not colorful. Individual butterflies and their larval or host plant requirements that occur in Kentucky are listed in appendix B.

Milkweed Butterflies (Danaids)
Identification: Medium to large (3-4" wingspan) butterflies. Wings are orange with black and white markings. Caterpillars feed on milkweed and butterfly weed.

Skippers (Hesperiids)
Identification: Small (1-2"), hooked antennae; at rest, the top pair of wings is up, while the bottom pair is down. The colors normally include brown, orange, and/or yellow. Host plants include many types of grasses. They are often found in meadows and other open areas.

Snout Butterflies (Libytheids)
Identification: Smaller butterflies (1-2" wingspan) with long pointed palpi (snout) jutting forward. The wings are pale orange with black and white patches, and the hind wings are gray underneath. Hackberry trees are host plants.

Gossamer Wings, Coppers, and Blues (Lycaenids)
Identification: Smaller butterflies (1 -1/2" wingspan), sometimes with tails, which prefer moist and open areas. Wing colors are orange and brown or blue and gray. Host plants include dock, sorrel, and buckwheat.

Brush-footed Butterflies (Nymphalids)
Identification: Medium to large butterflies (2-4" wingspan). This is the largest family of butterflies, and includes many species such as the admirals, anglewings, fritillaries, checkerspots, and our state butterfly, the viceroy. Most prefer open or moist areas, although the anglewings are more common in wooded areas. Larval food plants include aster, violet, thistle, nettles, willow trees, poplars, apple trees, hackberry, and milkweed.

Swallowtails (Papilionids)
Identification: Large butterflies (3-5" wingspan) usually with tails on their hind wings. Wings are black, yellow, or white with blue, orange, yellow and/or black markings. Swallowtails are found in both open areas and woodlands. Host plants include carrot or parsley (Black Swallowtail), sassafras, laurels, spicebush, and fruit trees (Tiger and Spicebush Swallowtails).

Sulphurs and Cabbage Whites (Pierids)
Identification: Medium-sized butterflies (2-3" wingspan), having yellow, white, or orange wings with black markings. These butterflies prefer open areas. Caterpillars are considered pests of cabbage, alfalfa, and soybeans, but the adults are pretty, and very common.

cessful in attracting butterflies, you will need to provide food and areas for all stages of a butterfly's life. Because of the importance of providing larval food plants (the host plants) to attract butterflies, a comprehensive listing of larval foods for Kentucky butterflies is provided in Appendix B.

A common wood nymph conserving heat with closed wings.

A butterfly's internal temperature must be 82 degrees Fahrenheit to fly. The ambient temperature must be at least 40 degrees Fahrenheit. Butterflies regulate their body temperature by basking (absorbing radiation from direct sunlight, with wings spread, which allows maximum body area exposure to radiation) or by shivering (without beating wings, which warms up flight muscles and generates heat). On cloudy days, butterflies conserve heat by keeping their wings closed. Because the underside of wings are often dull or drab, closed wings are less noticeable to predators. Butterflies overheat if air temperatures rise above 100 degrees Fahrenheit. They counteract the heat by heading for shady areas. So it is a good idea to leave open areas in a yard for butterflies to sun themselves and partly shady areas so they can hide when it's cloudy or cool off if it's very hot. As a general rule, butterflies can take flight when air temperatures are between 60 to 108 degrees Fahrenheit. For this reason, you'll want to situate your garden in a warm, sunny location protected from the wind.

A butterfly begins life as an egg, laid either singly or in clusters depending on the species. A tiny caterpillar emerges and, after consuming its egg shell, begins feeding on its host plant. Although some caterpillars, such as monarchs, are limited to only a few suitable host plants, others, such as tiger swallowtails, can feed on a variety of food plants. Caterpillars must molt, or shed their skin, to grow. Most caterpillars molt at least five times before changing into a pupa or chrysalis. Finally, an adult butterfly emerges from the chrysalis, often in the early morning hours. It must spread and dry its wings for several hours before it can fly away. This type of development is known as complete metamorphosis.

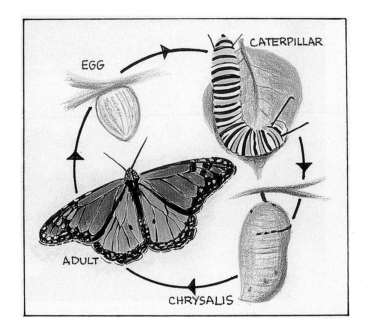

The life cycle, complete metamorphosis, of a monarch butterfly.

The larvae, or caterpillars, can be very interesting. A caterpillar's main objective is growing, sometimes gaining up to one thousand times its initial weight. Caterpillars have chewing mouthparts that are used to defoliate plants. Although they look much different from adults, they have the same basic insect anatomy: a head, a thorax with three pairs of true legs, and an abdomen with up to five pairs of abdominal legs or prolegs. The prolegs keep the abdomen from dragging and have hooked hairs called crochets at the tips, which allow caterpillars to cling to leaves, so they don't fall off on windy days.

Some caterpillars have a very interesting appearance to defend themselves from predators. For example, certain swallowtail caterpillars imitate snakes or bird droppings. Swallowtail larvae have a fleshy, forked appendage called an osmeterium, which when everted secretes a foul-smelling scent that discourages predators and parasites. Sulphur larvae are camouflaged, allowing them to blend into their surroundings. Many moth cocoons have

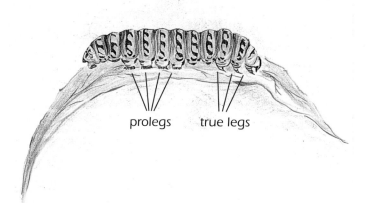

prolegs   true legs

A caterpillar, showing the head (on the right), the three sets of true legs on the thorax, and the abdomen with four sets of prolegs.

the appearance of a dead leaf, so you have to look closely to find them in trees. Painted lady larvae have protective spines. Last, but not least, monarch caterpillars are poisonous because of the milkweed they feed on.

The main method of attracting butterflies is to provide them with food, which comes in two forms: vegetative parts eaten by caterpillars, and nectar eaten by adult butterflies. To truly garden for butterflies, you need to provide specific plants for caterpillars, or larval food sources (host plants). Why? Most butterflies have very specific larval food sources. For example, the spicebush swallowtail caterpillars eat only the leaves of spicebush or sassafras. Black swallowtail caterpillars eat only the leaves of dill, parsley, carrot, and fennel. Monarch caterpillars feed exclusively on milkweeds. Red spotted purples like willows and black cherry, pearl crescents use asters, pipevine swallowtails like pipevines, and gulf fritillaries use passionvines. Knowing this tells what species of butterflies will come into the yard.

Before designing a garden, become familiar with the butterflies you are hoping to attract and their feeding and habitat preferences. It would be an exercise in futility to attempt to attract great purple hairstreaks if you are miles from trees harboring mistletoe, the only food for caterpillars of this species. Likewise, gardeners in Lexington are not likely to get pipevine swallowtails because they are found in the Eastern Kentucky mountainous region where the Dutchman's pipe (the sole caterpillar food for this species) is abundant. Diana fritillaries are not likely to be seen outside forested regions because their habitat consists of deciduous and pine forests close to a stream with a specific violet for their larval food.

How do you tell good caterpillars from bad caterpillars? Not an easy question to answer. The best advice: if the caterpillar is eating cabbage, cauliflower, broccoli, brussels sprouts, or other members of the mustard family, or if it forms a whitish bag in trees, it is probably a pest. Don't worry if caterpillars feed on dill, parsley, or other plants; remember, caterpillars grow into adult butterflies. Also keep in mind the old adage about planting an excess of corn, and plant an excess of larval food plants to supply both your needs and those of the caterpillars.

The type of food eaten by adult butterflies is nectar. Nectar is nothing more than sugar water with a sugar content between 8 and 76 percent. Most butterfly flowers have nectar with between 25 and 40 percent sugar, along with other compounds including amino acids, proteins, vitamins, enzymes, and flavonoids. The flavonoids are what give nectar its smell. To

Some host plants for larval butterflies include common milkweed, swamp milkweed, and aster.

An Edward's hairstreak on common milkweed.

A spicebush swallowtail on swamp or red milkweed.

A great-spangled fritillary on butterfly milkweed.

A meadow fritillary on aster.

provide nectar, you need to plant flowers. Although caterpillars have specific host plant requirements, adults are usually less particular about the type of plant they will get nectar from. The most important nectar plants in the Midwest, including Kentucky, are listed opposite, based on information in Carroll Henderson's *Landscaping for Wildlife*.

The amount and quality of nectar are important qualities in flowers because plants that produce high-quality nectar (low to medium sugar content and high amino acid content) are going to be more attractive than plants with less nectar, all other factors being equal. Environmental factors including temperature, humidity, wind, day length, sunlight, soil fertility, and plant health affect the quantity and quality of nectar produced by a

Plant	Approximate Number of Species Using the Plant	Plant	Approximate Number of Species Using the Plant
dogbanes	43	buttonbush	13
common milkweed	42	blackberry	12
swamp milkweed	20	Houstonia	11
asters	19	sunflowers	10
goldenrods	18	butterfly weed	9
winter cress	18	joe-pye-weed	9
vetches	14	ironweed	9
selfheal	14	vervain	9
New Jersey tea	13		

flower. It is important to plant several different species in the garden because nectar production will vary according to environmental factors. In the same vein, make sure you have wildflowers in bloom all season, from early spring until late fall, to provide nectar for butterflies. Finally, because nectar is the primary attractant for adult butterflies, do not water plants with overhead watering or a sprinkler during the day, as it dilutes nectar. Use a drip irrigation sprinkler or water in the early morning.

Maximum nectar is produced by flowers on a clear, hot day preceded by a cool night. Strong cold winds usually mean less nectar production. The amount of sunlight received by plants is one of the most important factors affecting nectar production. Why do butterflies seem to be most active in gathering nectar in open, sunny places? Because more sun means more energy available to the plant, which means more nectar can be produced. Butterflies may use plants growing in the shade, but they definitely prefer sun-loving plants; those plants that need at least 6 hours of full sun every day to flower. Common sense dictates that plants growing in fertile soils and healthy plants will produce more nectar.

All insects, including butterflies, have a head, thorax, abdomen, six legs, and one pair of antennae. Butterflies use the tips of their legs, called tarsi, to "taste" a food source before drinking. Butterfly mouthparts are modified to a long tube that is coiled at rest. Butterflies get all their nutrients through this tube, which limits them to nectar, standing water, and

Seasonal Color and Nectar for Butterflies

Trees

Plant	Blooming Period
redbud	April
bladdernut	April
wild plum	April

Shrubs

Plant	Blooming Period
pinxter flower azalea	mid-April
rose azalea	late April
flame azalea	early May
catawba rhododendron	early May
smooth azalea	mid-May to June
red azalea	June
longleaf rhododendron	July

Wildflowers

Plant	Blooming Period	Plant	Blooming Period
wild geranium	April to early May	prairie blazingstar	July to August
lanceleaf coreopsis	mid-May to late June	spiked blazingstar	July to August
eared coreopsis	early to mid-May	rattlesnake master	August
sundrops	May	joe-pye-weed	August to September
wild pink	May	mistflower	August
prairie phlox	May	tall coreopsis	August to September
wild bergamot	late May to June	New England aster	September to October
purple coneflower	June	silky aster	September to October
ox-eye sunflower	June to September	sky blue aster	September to October
dwarf blazing star	June to July	rigid goldenrod	September to October
common milkweed	July	gray goldenrod	September to October
swamp milkweed	July to September	rough blazingstar	September to October
butterfly weed	July to September		

other liquids. The length of the tube limits the types of flowers butterflies visit; for example, small butterflies cannot reach the nectar from daylilies. Thus flower shape affects which butterflies can use particular flowers, so to attract as many different species as possible, you'll need to plant a diversity of flowers. Certain flowers may be prolific in producing nectar but because they may have long tubes or stiff hairs surrounding the opening, only the largest butterflies or those with a long tube can feed on these flowers.

Flower size and cluster arrangement also affect which butterflies use a particular flower. Flowers with double petals make it difficult for butterflies to reach the nectar, and single, small flowers will probably not be visited by large butterflies. Do not, however, equate flower size with nectar production. Some plants that have small blossoms, such as wild cherry, may produce more nectar than a large showy flower like a wild petunia. In addition, individual flowers clustered together, like those found on milk-

Some common nectar plants.

A tiger swallowtail on lanceleaf coreopsis.

A giant swallowtail on button blazing star.

A silver-spotted skipper on wild bergamot.

A great-spangled fritillary on pale purple coneflower.

A tiger swallowtail on joe-pye-weed.

A monarch on dense blazingstar.

A monarch on goldenrod.

A fiery skipper with coiled tube extended for feeding.

weeds, provide a place for larger butterflies to land on. The insects can then travel easily to individual flowers to get nectar.

Butterflies have large, round compound eyes that allow them to see in almost every direction at once. Like most insects, butterflies are very nearsighted and are more attracted to large stands of a particular type of flower than those planted singly. They do not see red as well as we do, but they can see polarized light, which tells them the time of day by the angle of the sun, as well as ultraviolet light, which is reflected by many flowers and guides the butterflies to nectar sources.

This information suggests that flower color is important when designing a butterfly garden. Butterflies in general favor warm-colored flowers; reds, yellows, and oranges with purple, white, yellow, and pink being the most preferred. Most butterflies are not attracted to flowers in the greenish-blue to blue-green range. From a design standpoint, based on butterfly feeding preferences, plant groups of warm-colored flowers like purple coneflowers, and accent the planting with smaller groups of contrasting color. This will create a unified visual effect. Warm-colored flowers also give a stronger visual effect when observed against a green backdrop. Be sure to

provide foundation plantings of preferred host plants. In addition, because of a butterfly's near-sightedness you will want to design the garden with splashes of color or clusters of individual flowers of the same species that will flower at a particular time.

A clustering of lanceleaf coreopsis.

Clustering flowers and using certain colors will attract butterflies.

A swallowtail on rough blazing star.

A pearl crescent on black-eyed Susan.

A pipevine swallowtail on turk's cap lily.

A Diana fritillary on wild quinine.

A monarch on tall coreopsis.

A buckeye on rattlesnake master.

A red-spotted purple basking.

Butterflies also have a very well developed sense of smell with their clubbed antennae. Although sight is important in locating food plants, butterflies rely even more on the sense of smell. Some studies have found that scent marks on flowers are more common than visual marks. Have you ever noticed how you can smell a flower one day and the next day it has little or no smell and looks slightly different. This indicates that the flower has been pollinated and doesn't want to be bothered by more insects seeking to pollinate it. The flower is now busy making fruit. You can keep high-quality nectar available for the butterflies by getting into the habit of deadheading or pinching back flowers. Pinching back means clipping or pinching back the stems of flowers before the plant sets its flower buds. Deadheading is removal of fading flower blooms. These practices prolong blooming time and increase the number of blooms per plant. Finally, cutting back is the process of cutting stems after they have bloomed to keep them from looking unkempt. Make sure to leave plants and dead flower heads of those species (like native grasses and coneflowers) that provide food for wildlife or have a visual appeal during the winter.

Not all butterflies get their food and nutrition from nectar. Some species such as the goatweed butterflies, hackberry butterflies, buckeyes, ques-

Many wonderful moths can be attracted to the backyard.

tion marks, red-spotted purples, and satyrs go crazy over tree sap or over-ripe or rotting fruit (as do some moths). To attract these species try a technique called sugaring to bring them into view. Mix one of the following:

- Equal parts peach peels, brown sugar, and nonpasteurized beer
- Equal parts molasses, bananas, and grape juice
- Four parts sugar, one part nonpasteurized beer, one part cheap rum
- Equal parts old, rotten, fermented peaches and white granulated sugar
- Equal parts fermented bananas and dried apricots

Puddling Beds and Compost Piles for Butterflies

Constructing a Salt or Sand Puddling Bed

- Determine placement in the full sun near the flower garden (and close to a water source).
- Obtain landscape timbers, cut into 2' sections, nail together.
- Place heavy plastic as a liner to keep materials from entering the soil.
- Add to the frame a mixture of 1/2 to 3/4 cup of salt per gallon of sand.
- Add manure (preferably from a wild animal) at a rate of 1/2 to 3/4 cup per gallon of sand.
- Water liberally and keep moist at all times.

Constructing a Compost Pile

- Select a site near the back of the garden.
- Make a container of wood or wire no larger than 3' cubed. If using wood, leave 1" air spaces between boards.
- Place fresh vegetative material high in nitrogen on the bottom. This could also be straw or cow manure.
- Place a layer of high-carbon material like shredded leaves, newspaper, or sawdust on top.
- Alternate high-nitrogen and high-carbon layers.
- Add water occasionally to keep moist.
- Once a week, turn or mix the pile to aerate and keep decomposition occurring at a steady rate.
- Do not mix feces (even cat or dog), bones, meat scraps, fat material, vegetation with pesticides or herbicides, treated sawdust, or diseased plants into the pile.
- To reduce unwanted smells from fresh grass clippings, mix them with dry material like shredded leaves.
- Cut up melons and other foods into smaller pieces prior to placing in the pile.

A mourning cloak on common milkweed.

The concoction should be soupy (remember, it is the liquid the critters are after). Place the "soup" or bait in a large, shallow dish in the sun directly adjacent to your flower garden. To attract moths and uncommon urban butterflies like wood nymphs, spread the bait on a log or stump in light shade.

If you are using a butterfly feeder, mix 22 parts boiling water to 1 part granulated sugar and let it cool before placing it in the feeder outside. Butterflies may drink this nectar, but they probably will be more attracted to fruit placed around the sugar water. Place some overripe or damaged fruit like peaches, bananas, pears, plums, or persimmons in the feeder or in a bowl close to the flower garden.

Nectar may not supply all of the nutrients a butterfly needs. Often you may see large concentrations of butterflies at a mud or water puddle. You can get male butterflies to concentrate in this fashion by making an artificial puddling bed of sand, salt, and manure. Another method would be to create a compost pile.

What happens to adult butterflies as they age? Many species of butterflies overwinter or hibernate, with some species overwintering in various stages of the life cycle: swallowtails and hairstreaks overwinter as eggs; nymphalid butterflies, including the white admiral, red-spotted purple, and viceroy hibernate as caterpillars; and red admiral, mourning cloak, and goatweed butterflies overwinter as adults. Monarchs don't overwinter but migrate to the southwestern United States and Mexico for the winter. You can provide snags with deteriorating bark, trees with exfoliating bark, old fences or logs, and other structural sources for hibernating butterflies. I do not recommend hibernation boxes as they have a tendency to attract wasp colonies, and the numbers of butterfly species that would use the box are somewhat limited. And, by planting various late-season blooming flowers you will attract a greater diversity of butterflies that move or migrate prior to overwintering.

Control of Insect Pests

A vigorous butterfly garden will attract many visitors besides the desired butterflies and moths. Wasps, bees, beetles, and flies are attracted to pollen and nectar. In addition, there are numerous insect pests of flowers. A bit of tolerance is in order here, because chemicals that kill other insects may kill the butterflies or at least discourage them from entering the garden. All insects share the same general physiology. The best advice is to use native plants that can withstand some insect damage and to maintain healthy plants by leaving space between plants, making sure the plants are watered, fertilized, and taken care of.

One of the great benefits of using native plants is that they can withstand infestations of some insects. Every year aphids invade the butterfly garden at the Living Arts & Sciences Center in downtown Lexington. Following the outbreak of aphids there is an outbreak of ladybugs that devour the aphids. The plants recover and flower beautifully. In addition, these plants have been relatively free of Japanese beetles, an otherwise common pest.

There are two important points every gardener should understand. First, if you don't monitor your garden for pests regularly, small problems will become large problems. Second, you cannot begin to manage a problem correctly until you have identified what is causing it. Monitor your plants weekly. This involves no more than a walk through the garden. Many pests are likely to show up on the underside of leaves. Another sign to look for is dry, black, fecal pellets called frass. Finally, look for evidence of missing or damaged leaves.

Because you cannot use pesticides in the garden, there are a few pest control methods that are a fair compromise between no control and complete pest control. If the infestation is small, chemical-free control may eliminate most of the pests. Caterpillars and other pests have many natural enemies. Birds, frogs, skunks, praying mantids (a butterfly's biggest enemy), ladybugs, and spiders are only a few of the many predators that abound in nature. You may be able to order some species like ladybugs and lacewings from some nurseries and pest control companies.

Although this may sound ridiculous, hand removal of insects early in the season may pay off by mid-summer. Sedentary pests such as caterpillars can be hand-picked and thrown into a bucket of soapy water or drowned with a steady stream of water. Hand removal of the very first Japanese beetles will discourage others from ravaging your plants.

You can also spread some repellent plants throughout your planting to help with insect control. Insects avoid areas where these plants grow because of the plants' odor or because of the chemicals they release through their roots. Members of the onion family are the best repellent plants, although other plants like marigolds, nasturtiums, and nettles also are reported to have repellent properties.

Gardening for Butterflies

Butterfly gardens are a great source for your own enjoyment, for photo opportunities, or as an outlet for artistic talent. Flowers that attract butterflies are beautiful in themselves, but the added bonus of colorful wings and graceful, apparently carefree flight make the gardens come alive. Butterfly gardens can interest children in nature by providing a small window on local native inhabitants. The garden can become an outdoor laboratory—a place to observe caterpillars molting, increasing in size, and completing their life cycle, as well as identifying insect and butterfly diversity and habitats. Butterfly conservation is another important consideration in establishing a garden. Their habitat is constantly diminishing because of the increasing development of roads and housing, as well as modern methods of agriculture and forestry. There are normal fluctuations in butterfly populations, but when they are in decline, natural disasters like drought, hot or cold spells, and flood can decimate local butterfly populations.

Butterfly gardening can be as simple or complex as time and talent allow. The two most important factors in establishing a butterfly garden are enthusiasm and creativity. By definition, butterfly gardens contain plants and other structures attractive to butterflies. A butterfly garden can begin with only one container on a patio and develop into either formal or informal garden plans. Some wildlife need a habitat that resembles natural, undeveloped land, but butterflies don't care, so the garden can match the gardener's lifestyle. For better enjoyment, it may be advisable to place the most fragrant plants closer to high-use areas such as windows, a porch, patio, or the driveway.

Butterfly gardens have two basic constraints: plant requirements and available butterflies. Plants are the most healthy, and most resistant to diseases and other pests, when they are not stressed by inappropriate growing conditions. Plant cultivars should be suited to soil type, temperature zone, and shade requirements. It makes sense to plant only host plants for butterflies that are native to or common in the area already. Even though they are available in some catalogs, it is best not to import other butterflies to the area, as this may damage local populations. Consult the butterfly list from the Kentucky Lepidopterists' Society in Appendix B to determine which species are common in Kentucky. It may take some time for butterflies to build up to large numbers.

Remember the basic messages stressed in the beginning of this chapter when establishing the garden. Divide the garden into three main areas: background, intermediate area, and foreground. The background area serves as a wind screen and the foundation or backdrop for the flowers. This area usually consists of trees or shrubs. Consult the larval food plant list in Appendix B and the list of trees and shrubs in Appendix D for plants that could provide this "foundation." The intermediate area is the primary focal point in the garden. It should consist of clusters of colorful, medium tall to tall flowers. The foreground area defines the front boundary and requires low-growing plants. Remember to use plants with predominantly warm colors in the pinkish to purplish range with accents of blue flowers.

One final aspect that needs to be discussed is plant selection. Many food plants used by both larval and adult butterflies are classified as "weeds." But what is a weed? A weed is nothing more than an undesirable plant. Hence, one man's weed is another man's joy. For instance, if you are serious about butterflies, you are serious about milkweeds. Although it is true that some weeds beneficial to butterflies (and other wildlife) might try the patience of some gardeners with limited space, there are others that can be placed in the back, "out-of-the-way place" just for butterflies. These could include common milkweed for monarchs or nettles for red admirals. If you have a large area and these plants grow wild, don't mow them down or keep them along the fence or by some old building. They don't need any special care and will provide that little something extra in attracting butterflies. You can slow the spread of milkweed by pinching back and destroying the flower heads and mulching heavily around the plants to prevent them from suckering.

Try not to be a "neat freak"! Butterflies, their eggs, and larvae are relished food items of birds, lizards, spiders, parasitic wasps, and flies. Plant some protection, like native grasses, in the garden so these predators have to search for their food, rather than setting the table for them. Don't remove dead leaves, plant debris, or stubble that could harbor or shelter a future butterfly.

Attracting Moths to Your Garden

To attract moths, plant flowers that bloom at night. These include members of the genuses *Oenothera* and *Gaura*, such as *Oenothera biennis*, *O. fruitcosa* ssp. *fruitcosa*, *O. fruticosa* ssp. *tetragona*, *O. lacinata*, *O. linifolia*, *O. parviflora*, *O. perennis*, *O. pilosella*, *O. speciosa*, *O. triloba*, *Heliotropium tenellum*, *Gaura biennis*, *G. filipes*, *G. longiflora*, and *G. parviflora*. Moth host plants are listed below. Moths also use the same plants as butterflies during the day. One of the best activities you can do to benefit moths is to turn off your "bug zapper." These kill indiscriminately and destroy many more beneficial moths and insects than pests.

There are two methods of attracting moths for viewing. One is sugaring. The other is to place a white sheet between two trees or over a fence and place a bright light behind the sheet. A different group of moths will be attracted to the sheet if a black-light is placed behind the sheet. After dark on a moonless or cloudy night, turn the light on and check the sheet every few minutes to see which species have been attracted to it. If you are sugaring on tree trunks, check the trees occasionally after dark with a flashlight.

Common Showy Moths Known to Occur in Kentucky and Their Host Plants

Species	Caterpillar Food	Adult Food
Cecropia *(Hyalophora cecropia)*	ash, beech, birch, elm, maple, poplar, white oak, willow, wild cherries and plums	
Clearwings		
Hummingbird *(Hemaris thysbe)*	dogbane, hawthorn, wild cherry, viburnum	nectar
Snowberry *(H. diffinis)*	honeysuckle, snowberry	
Imperial *(Eacles imperialis)*	basswood, birch, cedar, elm, maple, oak, pine, walnut	
Io *(Automeris io)*	birch, elm, maple, oak, willow, others	
Luna *(Actias luna)*	beech, hazelnut, hickory, sweetgum, wild cherry, willow	
Polyphemus *(Antheraea polyphemus)*	ash, birch, grapes, hickory, maple, oak, pine, roses	
Promethea *(Callosamia promethea)*	ash, basswood, birch, maple, sassafras, spicebush, sweetgum, tulip, wild cherry	
Regal *(Citheronia relagis)*	ash, blackgum, hickory, persimmon, sumac, sycamore, walnut	
Rosy maple *(Dryocampa rubicunda)*	maple, oak	
Sphinx		
abbot *(Sphecondina abbottii)*	grapes	nectar, bait
azalea *(Darapsa pholus)*	azalea, blackgum, blueberry, viburnum	

Species	Caterpillar Food	Adult Food
Sphinx, continued		
big poplar *(Pachysphinx modesta)*	tulip poplar, willow	
blinded *(Paonias excaecatus)*	basswood, birch, elm, oak, poplar, wild cherry	
Canadian *(Sphinx canadensis)*	blueberry, white ash	
elm *(Ceratomia amyntor)*	basswood, birch, elm, wild cherry	
great ash *(Sphinx chersis)*	ash, plum, wild cherry	
hog *(Darapsa myron)*	grape, viburnum, Virginia creeper	
hydrangea *(Darapsa versicolor)*	buttonbush, water willow, wild hydrangea	
lettered *(Deidamia inscripta)*	grapes, Virginia creeper	
nessus *(Amphion floridensis)*	grapes	nectar, day & dusk
paw paw *(Dolba hyloeus)*	blueberry, holly, paw paw	
pink-spotted *(Agrius cingulatus)*	paw paw	
plebeian *(Paratraea plebeja)*	trumpet creeper	
small-eyed *(Paonis myops)*	birch, hawthorn, poplar, wild cherry, wild plum, willow	
twin-spotted *(Smerinthus jamaicensis)*	ash, birch, elm, wild plum, willow	
walnut *(Laothe juglandis)*	hickory, walnut, wild cherry	
waved *(Ceratomia undulosa)*	ash, fringetree, hawthorn, oak	
wild cherry *(Sphinx drupiferarum)*)	hackberry, wild cherry, wild plum	
white-lined *(Hyles lineata)*	apple	

In the planting plan, be sure to include plenty of flowers that bloom in August and September. Why? This is the best time to view butterflies in Kentucky because the last brood has been produced before winter and you can attract migrating species as well. The other reason this is an important period for attracting butterflies is that the flowers of late fall have less nectar than earlier blooming species, so the flowers need to bloom longer to attract pollinators, that is, butterflies. This means butterflies must move to more flowers to gain sufficient nutrients to complete their life cycle. A good combination to use during this period is asters (blues, whites, or purples) and goldenrods (yellow).

Butterfly Activities

Butterfly watching is the easiest and one of the best activities to enjoy in a garden. Butterfly watching can be as passive as simply relaxing in the garden during spare time. As interest grows, many butterfly enthusiasts use field guides and a notebook to identify and record butterfly visitors and their behaviors. Drawing, painting, photography, and butterfly collections are among the hobbies that go hand-in-hand with butterfly watching.

Butterfly conservationists plant several types of host plants in butterfly gardens to preserve or even build up numbers of butterflies. Caterpillars can be protected from predators with sheer fabric sleeves attached to the host plant, or by housing and rearing caterpillars in a separate location. Amateur entomologists might enjoy taking notes on the developing larvae.

Many butterfly enthusiasts enjoy making an insect collection. Materials needed include a butterfly net, a killing jar, insect pins, a spreading board, and a display case. Consult the nearest 4-H office for information on insect collection projects and techniques.

Several states have organized groups of professional and amateur lepidopterists that meet to exchange information, ideas, and the excitement of butterfly watching and collecting. For more information, contact the Xerces Society, 10 Southwest Ash Street, Portland, OR 97204, or the Kentucky Lepidopterists Society, c/o Charles V. Covell Jr., Biology Department, University of Louisville, Louisville, KY 40292.

References

Ajilvsgi, A. 1990. *Butterfly Gardening for the South.* Dallas: Taylor Publishing. 347 pp.

Covell, C.V., Jr. 1984. *A Field Guide to Moths of Eastern North America.* Boston: Houghton Mifflin. 496 pp.

Opler, P.A., and V. Malikul. 1992. *A Field Guide to Eastern Butterflies.* Boston: Houghton Mifflin. 396 pp.

Scott, J.A. 1986. *The Butterflies of North America: A Natural History and Field Guide.* Stanford, Cal.: Stanford Univ. Press, 583 pp.

Stokes, D., L. Stokes, and E. Williams. 1991. *The Butterfly Book: An Easy Guide to Butterfly Gardening, Identification, and Behavior.* Boston: Little, Brown. 96 pp.

Xerces Society. 1990. *Butterfly Gardening: Creating Summer Magic in Your Garden.* San Francisco: Sierra Club Books. 192 pp.

Woo Wildlife
with Water

At present, in this vicinity, the best part of the land is
not private property; the landscape is not owned, and the
walker enjoys comparative freedom. Hope and the future for me
are not in lawns and cultivated fields, . . . but in the
impervious and quaking swamps.

—Henry David Thoreau, *Walden*

W HO TO WOO? Most homeowners do not think about
providing water for wildlife in a state like Kentucky. Yet
the absence of water and food are probably the two largest
limiting factors in urban environments. Animals of all types are drawn to
wetlands, so many in fact that wetlands have been called "nature's cities."
Wildlife large and small, ranging from dragonflies and water striders to
Canada geese and great blue herons, will be attracted to any source of
good, clean water. One homeowner in Lexington placed a water garden (a
type of artificial wetland) in the backyard, and the young woman's father
warned her, "You'll get all kinds of critters and vermin back there!" Was he
ever right—raccoons, opossums, dragonflies, and birds, just to name a
few. At the Living Arts & Sciences Center the pump to the pond had just
been turned on when a variety of birds including mourning doves, blue
jays, and a rose-breasted grosbeak were observed drinking from the stream.

Why provide water in an urban environment? Although many wildlife species do not *require* freestanding water, most will not pass up the
chance to stop by for a drink. In addition, water is important for many
metabolic processes including digestion, respiration, and cooling of the
body. Insects, mammals, and birds use rainwater, puddles, and morning
dew to obtain much of the water they require. But wildlife of all kinds,
types, and colors are drawn to a water garden or wetland.

Many wildlife species, particularly birds, use water for bathing. Why?
Bathing is used to cleanse the feathers for proper insulation. Tiny inter-
locking feather webs, called barbules, must be free of oils produced by their
bodies. Bathing helps clean the barbules, which help to keep the birds

Keep ice-free water available during the winter. Birds such as this house finch prefer to use water sources on or near the ground.

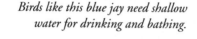

Birds like this blue jay need shallow water for drinking and bathing.

warm, so water is also important in the winter. Bathing also cleans the feathers of external parasites (as does dusting) and offsets the discomfort of new feather growth. And birds bathe to keep cool.

Another reason to provide water deals with habitat requirements of certain wildlife species. Mammals like the raccoon are associated with water habitats; dragonflies with their aerial acrobatics need water; bats and purple martins prefer to feed on insects above water sources. The list goes on and on.

Finally, some species are absolutely dependent on water during some period of the year. Amphibians need water for their eggs and tadpoles, adult frogs need water, wading birds need water for feeding, and waterfowl require water for feeding, loafing, and brood rearing.

What kinds of water birds can you expect to use larger ponds in an urban environment? Herons, kingfishers, geese, ducks, shorebirds, and many others will visit permanent water sources. I used to watch a green-backed heron sit in a willow tree adjacent to the pond at the Ashland Oil Head-

Blue-spotted salamanders and other amphibians must have water to reproduce.

Mallards and other waterfowl can be attracted to ponds by feeding with shelled corn.

Many herons, including black or yellow crowned, great blue, and green, can be observed feeding in larger ponds.

quarters in Lexington every summer. I would watch it walk through the shallow water looking for fish or tadpoles. I would also find great blue herons in the deeper parts of the reservoir. Yellow-crowned night herons, a state endangered species, and killdeer used to nest in or adjacent to Shady Lane Woods next to a storm water basin pond that was located on the University of Kentucky campus. Black-crowned night herons nest in wetland areas in the Louisville Zoo. These water birds have unique leg and bill adaptations that allow them to capture different types of aquatic food in different depths of water.

Other bird life can also abound near water in an urban environment. Chimney swifts and purple martins dart across the sky in search of flying aquatic insects. Kingfishers plummet into the water after fish. Wood ducks, mallards, and American coots loaf on ponds of various sizes. Warblers and other songbirds can be seen around ponds seeking an insect meal of a

Birds love the sound of dripping water. One simple method of creating this situation is to punch a hole in the bottom of a bucket and fill it with water. (Adapted and redrawn from G.H. Harrison, The Backyard Bird Watcher.)

Every species of bird has a unique method of obtaining water. Most prefer misting, dripping, or flowing water.

dragonfly. Even screech owls, Cooper's hawks, and red-tailed hawks are attracted to a water source in search of the birds and mammals that live there.

What mammals would come to drink or eat? Squirrels and chipmunks will all find their way to water. Bats will come out when the sunset gives way to night as they feed on mosquitoes and other aquatic insects. Opossums and raccoons will be attracted in search of an easy meal of fish or frog.

Finally, those wonderful creepy crawlies of the amphibian world will arrive in spectacular style, beginning with the mass of eggs, followed by tadpoles, and ultimately adults. Spring will be heralded with the delightful chorus of spring peepers and tree frogs. This will give way to the deep "croak" of the bullfrog in the summer. Slimy critters like the eastern newts (along with the colorful land form called a red eft) will find their way to a pond.

When planning to provide water in urban environments there are several general principles.

Be imaginative in your ways of providing water for birds. Shallow water, no more than 2 inches deep, is best.

You must decide if you want fish or amphibians in your pond. You can't have both. Never stock aquatic turtles in a pond because they will eat either fish or amphibians.

First, dripping or flowing water is more attractive than standing water. You can provide this in a number of ways ranging from a hanging bucket of water with a hole in the bottom, to a sophisticated piece of equipment from a bird-feeding store, to a stream associated with a wetland or water garden. Hummingbirds are attracted to a fine mist of water.

Second, shallow water is preferred over deeper water for many activities. If you are providing a bird bath, it should be no more than 2 inches deep, and the bottom should be of a rough texture. This is not to say you should not provide deeper water. Many species like waterfowl and wading birds need deeper water. If you are planning a water garden it will need to be more than 3 feet deep if you want to overwinter amphibians. And take care not to create death traps for wildlife. Water gardens constructed with a preformed liner are potential death traps for many wildlife species because they do not have any shallow access into or out of the pond. To make these usable for wildlife, place a log, rock, or some other structure that will

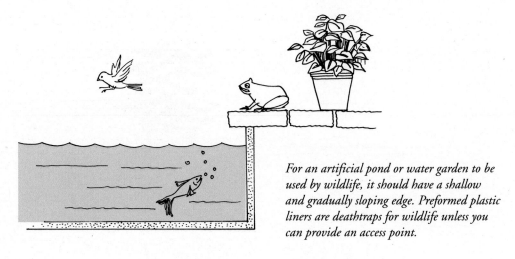

For an artificial pond or water garden to be used by wildlife, it should have a shallow and gradually sloping edge. Preformed plastic liners are deathtraps for wildlife unless you can provide an access point.

allow wildlife the opportunity to get out of the water and not drown. Many water gardens are only 18 to 24 inches deep. Most of these shallow ponds will require heaters in winter to provide water for birds and keep fish and plant life healthy. Most permanent outdoor ponds should have a portion at least 3 or 4 feet deep. This allows the fish an area deep enough to resist most winter freezes and a cool retreat during hot weather. A depth of 18 inches is sufficient in Kentucky, as long as only a few fish are stocked and plenty of floating aquatic plants are provided for shade.

Third, keep the water (or a portion of it) open during the winter. This will allow fish and aquatic plants to overwinter. It will also provide a source of water for winter birds. Remember, birds need to bathe in the winter too!

Fourth, provide cover around a portion of the pond for wildlife that need plants, and keep part of the pond edge open to allow for roosting of species like mallards.

Fifth, planning is the most important aspect of developing any dependable water supply for wildlife.

Landscape around one side of the pond and leave the other side clear. This provides an unobstructed view for wary birds.

Sixth, try to achieve a balance of 50:50 between vegetation and open water to provide maximum interspersion and use by wildlife.

Providing water in the backyard can be as simple or complex as you want. As with all other aspects of landscaping for wildlife, the more habitat you provide, the more wildlife you will attract. Let's begin by discussing the simplest method: the birdbath. Most birds will not use a birdbath during the summer; they serve best as a winter water source. Some species, like the American robin, will use the time-honored birdbath on a pedestal. You can increase bird use of a birdbath by cutting off the pedestal and placing the bath at ground level. In this case, the birdbath must be placed in a location where there is no tall vegetation surrounding or near it. Why? Predators will find easy pickings on unsuspecting birds. One good method of providing standing and dripping water is to place one birdbath on a pedestal with a water hose (conveniently concealed) that slowly adds water to the bath. Place another birdbath under and to the side of the pedestal birdbath so it can catch the overflow water.

Other simple forms of water supply could be anything from old whiskey barrels cut in half, to large plastic buckets, or even a submerged bathtub. When creating these small watering structures you will want to fill the bottom of the container with a good loamy soil. Once water has been trickled into the container, plant a water lily or other aquatic plant.

Except for creating a wetland, the final method of creating a dependable water supply is to construct a water garden. This has become an increasingly popular option for many gardeners and homeowners.

Ornamental Garden Ponds or Water Gardening

Ornamental ponds, long common in the Orient, are becoming very popular in the United States. The soothing, visual beauty of a pond is enhanced by aquatic plants, the ever-changing view of fish swimming among these plants, and the play of light and shadows reflected in the water. Ponds can be found in private backyards, public parks, hotel lobbies, mall courtyards, restaurants, apartment balconies, and even basements in colder climates. In Japan, where ornamental ponds have been popular for centuries, pond and garden designs are highly artistic. Some Japanese extend the pond into their living rooms, where fish watching becomes a restful evening activity.

Ponds can be relatively expensive to build and maintain, although many beginners start with little expense by using an old wash tub or a child's wading pool. Construction costs for most ponds can range from several hundred to several thousand dollars depending on size, depth, materials used, and labor. Labor costs can be reduced by doing the work yourself or acting as back-up labor for the professionals you hire. A word of advice: Most pond owners regret not building their ponds larger.

Before beginning any water gardening project, check local ordinances. Why? Some cities (Lexington, for instance) state that any water source greater than 2 feet deep is considered a swimming pool and must have a fence surrounding it. This may be fine for small water sources like bird baths, but one section of a water garden must be at least 3 feet deep if you wish to overwinter some amphibian species and plants. Local ordinances will also dictate what types of electrical system will be required, and so on. Planning is probably more important for water gardening than anything else discussed in this book. Construction plans should be reviewed by local governmental departments (for example, Building and Zoning) to ensure that the proposed system complies with all building codes. Many commercial firms selling pond equipment offer consulting services on design, construction, and maintenance of water gardens. Use available expertise and your own creativity to design a pond that reflects your own imagination and taste.

Pond Location, Size, and Type

The first step in building a pond is actually thinking about what type of pond to have. Do you want a water garden with or without fish? If you want a pond for amphibians, you can't have fish in the pond. The fish will readily eat the eggs and adults of frogs, toads, and salamanders. Generally speaking, fishless ponds are easier to maintain because you do not have to worry much about water quality, oxygen content, and filtration. If you want fish in the pond, use native species like mosquito fish or some of the small darters that eat small microscopic plants or animals. Do not place predatory fish like bluegills or bass in a water garden because you have no prey base to sustain the animals and most water gardens are not large enough to support more than a few of these fish. Be sure not to collect fish from native populations, as they can bring in diseases and probably will not survive because of the increased stress from collection and transportation. Finally, do not stock turtles in any pond because many turtles are carnivores and will readily eat fish or amphibians.

Once you have determined which type of pond to build, the next step is to consider where to put the pond. Pond location can be critical, not only in regard to your enjoyment but in regard to the maintenance and biological performance of the pond. The following guidelines should be followed when planning and selecting a site for the water garden.

• The site must receive a minimum of 6 hours of sunlight each day. Sunlight is needed for photosynthesis by pond plants including algae, which provide oxygen to the pond. Abundant oxygen means a healthy environment for fish and other organisms. One exception is a small container garden with less than 100 gallons of water. It will do best with 1 to 2 hours of shade during the hottest part of the day.

• Avoid any area that receives runoff that could contaminate the pond with fertilizers, herbicides, or insecticides. These will quickly kill plants and animals. The site should be level.

• Do not place the pond under trees or under large overhanging branches. Ponds should not be located directly under trees, as their roots hamper excavation and eventually cause structural damage to the pond. Also, leaves can foul the water and overhanging branches may exude toxic substances into the pond.

• Do not locate a pond above utility services. If you plan to excavate, check with utility companies on the location of underground gas, water, sewer, and electrical lines before moving one shovel of soil.

There are several advantages to locating the pond within view of the house:

• to enhance enjoyment by making it easy to view the wildlife and plants in the garden;

• to more easily supervise children playing around the pond (being sure to take precautions, such as controlling access, to ensure the safety of children);

• to help you spot and ward off predators of fish, such as birds, raccoons, or snakes; and

• to reduce the expense of pipes, electrical hookups, and pumping, which are usually lower for ponds built close to the house.

Once the decision has been made on location, you must decide what type of pond or garden you want. Ponds are built out of several types of material. Some of the more common construction materials are earthen, flexible plastic liners, fiberglass, and concrete. They have the following advantages and disadvantages:

• Earthen materials are inexpensive, especially for larger ponds, but seepage can be a problem and wild plants may become established. Soil must be at least 20 percent clay.

• Flexible plastic liners make construction easy, but punctures are possible and the pond must be pumped or siphoned to drain. The type of liner will determine the lifetime, usually 10 to 20 years.

• Fiberglass or plastic is durable and good for plant-only ponds. They are usually shallow and are not a good year-round habitat for fish. They can crack if water freezes. Very small ponds, however, can be moved inside during the winter.

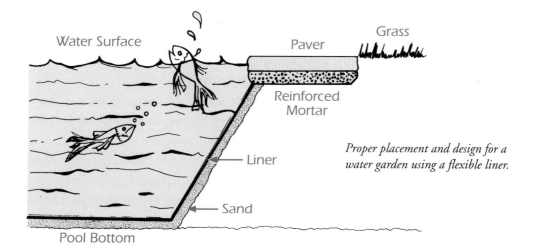

Water Surface

Paver

Grass

Reinforced
Mortar

Liner

*Proper placement and design for a
water garden using a flexible liner.*

Sand

Pool Bottom

• Concrete ponds have very long life but are expensive and must be cured. Decorative tiles can be added. They may need coating with epoxy or pool paint to stop the leaching of minerals.

Before you start to dig, plan how pipes, filters, fountains, or water heaters will be concealed. Decide where electrical and water lines should be placed for night lighting, pumps, fountains, or waterfalls. This is also the time to set foundations for such structures as stepping stones, a walking bridge, or the base of a fountain. Equipment and materials that you may need for your pond include:

• pipes, drain structures, nets, buckets

• spare tanks for acclimating and isolating fish; feed, chemical brushes, and test kits to measure oxygen, pH, and so on

• electrical hookups, lights, pumps

• filters: biological or mechanical, filter media such as zeolite or charcoal

• sand or stone overlays or borders

• fountain, waterfall, aerator

• plants, plant enclosures

Ponds without drains are common, particularly those with liners, but a drain allows for easier management. Draining facilitates cleaning and fish removal in cases of maintenance or disease problems. Of course, ponds can be drained by pumping or, in some cases, siphoning. Before building the pond, plan how it will be drained. Draining into city sewer lines or a storm drain is probably legal, but draining onto a neighbor's property is not. When in doubt, consult local government agencies.

An important consideration when constructing a pond is to make sure the bottom slopes at least 1 percent (1 foot decline per 100-foot distance) so the water will drain. A catch basin, usually 6 to 12 inches deep, in the deepest part of the pond will help concentrate fish during draw-down (when draining the pond for cleaning or other purposes). Remember, the drain, pump, or siphon intake should be covered with mesh so no fish will escape during draw-down.

Ponds that are least two-thirds below ground level retain heat in cold weather and keep the pond cooler in hot weather. Ponds that are built totally above-ground may have to be drained during the winter, requiring that fish and plants be moved indoors.

Excavated ponds can have problems from water run-off. First, care should be taken during construction so that run-off water does not flow into the pond. If the surrounding terrain is higher than the pond, a berm may be required to control run-off. Run-off water can introduce chemical contaminants or cause muddiness or oxygen problems. Second, rainwater saturation of the soil under the pond may cause the pond to overflow or float out of the ground. To prevent this problem, you will need a special under-pond drainage or water-pressure relief system. Consult the USDA Natural Resources Conservation Service on soil characteristics in your area.

Liners are very popular because of their versatility. Liners allow for relatively quick and less expensive construction and allow future changes in the size or shape of the pond.

Vertical pond sides can erode rapidly and let dirt, leaves, and other debris build up along the edge of the pond bottom. Tiered or sloping sides encourage movement of detritus toward the deepest part of the pond where the material can be drained or siphoned out. The pond sides should be cut in two or three tiers, each about 12 inches wide. Tiers help to hold liners in place and provide ledges for plants and other decorative items. To protect a liner from puncture by roots and rocks, the dirt along the pond sides and bottom should be covered with sand before installing the liner. Firmly pack the pond sides and bottom, especially if liners are used. Smooth the pond corners so they will not become detritus traps.

Borders that overhang the water by 1 to 2 inches are visually pleasing and help conceal liner edges and hide openings to equipment. The pond's exterior borders may be decorated with washed sand or rocks. Aquatic plants such as lilies, lotus, reeds, and submerged plants add to the aesthetic beauty of the pond and function as biological filters and shade for fish in the pond.

In building the pond, remember that water will be level but your construction may not be. Unless leveling is accurate during construction, you may end up with an exposed area at one end of the pond and water about to overflow the other end. *Make sure the shoreline of your pond is level!*

For advice on construction, consult a professional pond builder or plumbing contractor. For advice on liners, consult an ornamental fish dealer, pond builder, plant nursery, or Extension fisheries specialist.

Water Source

Whether your ornamental pond is a plastic tub or a backyard wonder with waterfalls and hidden lights, good water quality must be maintained. If not, the pond declines in beauty and the fish become stressed and susceptible to diseases. Once the basics of water quality are understood and practiced, maintenance will become second nature and require only a few hours per month.

The most common water sources are city water and well water. Surface water from a creek or pond is not recommended as it may contain contaminants, diseases, or wild fish, any of which may harm the pond's ecosystem. If city water is used, it must be dechlorinated. One week of sunlight (or less, if continuously aerated) will dechlorinate city water if the chlorine source is liquid or gaseous chlorine. If the chlorine source is chloramine, it is best removed by chemical dechlorination. Commercial dechlorinators made from sodium thiosulfate are available in liquid or pelleted forms from most aquarium and pond suppliers. If you do not dechlorinate the water, any animals placed in the pond will die rather quickly.

Water Volume and Weight

The water volume of the pond must be determined before you select a filter or pump or perform a chemical treatment. Knowing the pond's water weight is very important before a free-standing pond is placed on a patio, roof, or living room floor. Be careful to check your structural support, because water is very heavy. For information on calculating area and volume, request Southern Regional Aquaculture Center Publication No. 103, by M.P. Masser and J.W. Jensen, from your county Extension agent.

Water Quality

Water quality is always a concern in any type of aquatic management. Water quality factors of common concern are dissolved oxygen, ammonia, nitrite, pH, alkalinity, hardness, carbon dioxide, and contaminants or pollutants (such as pesticides). Not all of these factors deserve equal consideration. The following is a brief discussion of their importance as applied to ornamental ponds.

The amount of oxygen that will dissolve in water (D.O.) is very small and is measured in parts per million (ppm). The amount of oxygen in a pond can range from 0 ppm to more than 20 ppm. Oxygen dissolves directly into the pond from the air if the water is agitated (by winds, waterfalls, and so on) or from underwater plants, which excrete oxygen as a byproduct of photosynthesis. The amount of oxygen in the pond will vary, depending on the amount of agitation, numbers of fish and plants, time of day, and water temperature. More oxygen can dissolve in cool water than in warm. As temperature increases in the summer, fish increase their metabolism and less oxygen will be dissolved in the pond, particularly at night when underwater plants are also using oxygen in respiration. Fish will become severely stressed at less than 3 ppm D.O. and will die if oxygen concentrations fall near 1 ppm.

Pond nutrients come from fish feed, wastes, decomposing leaves and other debris, and from fertilizers applied to pond plants. In a well-balanced pond, ornamental plants will remove nutrients rapidly and suppress algal growth. Excessive nutrients stimulate rapid algal growth or blooms. The clinging, filamentous kind of algae are not as much of a problem as the free-floating blooms. Algal blooms quickly become a nuisance, causing the water to become a cloudy green and restricting the view of fish. Dense algal blooms may cause oxygen depletions at night or during extended cloudy weather. Mechanical aeration, such as waterfalls or fountains, can maintain minimum dissolved oxygen concentrations and remove excess carbon dioxide.

Excessive algal blooms should be controlled. The best method is to avoid overstocking and overfeeding fish or overfertilizing pond plants. Another good method is to ensure a healthy emergent plant population that can shade some areas of the pond. Biofilters (which can be purchased or made) can be used to remove excess nutrients on which algae flourish. Finally, you may need to replace or flush water through the pond to dilute nutrients and disperse algae.

Ammonia is the major nitrogen waste excreted by fish. Certain types of bacteria decompose or nitrify ammonia to nitrite. Ammonia and nitrite are both toxic to fish but are seldom problems in ornamental ponds. These compounds are normally removed from the water by pond plants and used as nutrients for growth. Ammonia and nitrite can become problems if the pond is overfed or overfertilized, or from rapid decomposition of organic matter (leaves, dead plants, fish, and so on). You can remove excess ammonia and nitrite by biofiltration, by flushing, or by adding bacterial water conditioners.

Water pH (acidity) is measured on a scale from 0 to 14, with 7 being neutral (less than 7 being acidic, more than 7 being basic). Pond pH changes cyclically each day because of photosynthesis and respiration of plants and other organisms. Under normal conditions, pond pH can fluctuate from 6.5 to 9 without harming fish. A pH much above or below this range will stress or even kill fish. If the pH is fluctuating above or below this range, the pond needs buffers.

Alkalinity is a measure of bases in water and is therefore related to pH. Alkalinity is measured in ppm (or milligrams per liter: mg/l) and can range from 0 to more than 300 ppm. Sufficient alkalinity buffers or resists pH changes. Alkalinity can be increased in the pond by adding carbonates (agricultural limestone, oyster shell, or bicarbonate of soda). In general, an alkalinity of greater than 20 ppm is considered adequate, but 50 ppm or greater is better.

If you suspect any chemical contamination of the water, you can perform a simple bioassay using a few fish. Place three or four small fish in a minnow bucket and float it in the pond for 24 hours in an area that gets some circulation but not direct sunlight. If no deaths occur, the water is probably not contaminated. Use fish that look healthy to minimize the risk of introducing diseases into the pond. Do not set these fish free into the pond unless they are specific individuals you want stocked in the pond. Once you release fish into the pond, it will be very difficult to remove them without draining the pond.

Filtration

Not all ponds need filtration. Ponds with abundant plants and a modest number of fish should not need it. The key is to maintain water quality and relatively clear water. Again, ornamental plants are active biological filters, and if a balance is maintained between the number of plants and the amount of nutrients the pond receives, no other filtration may be necessary.

Keeping the proper balance is as much an art as a science. For this reason, many pond owners become frustrated with trying to maintain balance and opt for additional filtration. The two types of filters are mechanical and biological.

Mechanical filters remove or trap particles of dirt and organic matter. Typical mechanical filters include leaf skimmers, sand beds, foam or cartridge filters, and settling basins. Leaf skimmers, foam filters, or some type of settling basin are the most commonly used mechanical filters. Sand filters and cartridge filters, like those used in swimming pools or hot tubs, are not generally used in ornamental ponds because they clog or channel quickly and require fairly large volumes of water for backwashing.

Biological filters remove excess nitrogen and decomposition of organic matter. Natural biological filtration comes from nutrient removal by plants, algae, and bacteria. Decorative plants remove nutrients and slow water currents that cause suspended particles to fall out of the water column.

Bacteria also remove nutrients, but only if provided with the proper substrate and environment. Bacterial biofilters are becoming common in ornamental ponds, particularly those in which fish are the major attraction. Biofilters require little maintenance if properly designed and installed. These biofilters rely on bacterial growth to clean the water of wastes. Biofilters contain layers of gravel or coarse sand, corrugated plastic sheets, plastic rings, mesh, foam, or some other material as a substrate or medium on which bacteria grow. Like plants, the bacteria remove wastes as nutrients for growth. Biofilters operate best at a pH of 7 to 7.5 and an alkalinity of around 50 ppm. Adjustments in pH and alkalinity can be done using agricultural limestone, oyster shell, and bicarbonate of soda.

Undergravel filters, common in aquariums, are one of the simplest types of biofilters. In these filters, the gravel acts as a mechanical filter and is colonized by bacteria. Large gravel filters can be built into the pond bottom or into the bed of a stream or brook that flows into the pond. The problem with gravel filters is that they become clogged with solids and require laborious cleaning.

The Formula for Creating a Balanced Pond

1. Fill the pond with water.

2. Dechlorinate the water.

3. Plant and place your aquatic plants in the pond, including submergents. Cover at least 50 percent of the water surface with floating leaf plants.

4. Place one bunch of submergent plants per square foot of pond surface area up to 100 square feet. Place two bunches of submergent plants per square foot for ponds with more than 100 square feet.

5. Wait two weeks for the pond to "cure." The water may turn green but don't drain the pond. If the green color bothers you, use an appropriate algicide to kill unwanted algae.

6. Stock fish at a rate of no more than one 12-inch fish per 4.5 square feet of pond surface area. Add snails and bullfrog tadpoles as scavengers at a rate of one per square foot of pond volume.

7. Ensure that the total volume of water in the pond recirculates every two to six hours.

A common type of in-pond filter uses plastic media and foam surrounding or connected to a submersible pump to accomplish both mechanical and biological filtration. The pump draws water through the filter media, trapping sediment and providing an area for bacteria to grow. This type of filter requires that you remove sediment periodically and clean the foam every one or two days. Sediment should not be allowed to build up in the bottom of the filter.

An upflow biofilter is another popular design. As the name indicates, water enters the filter from the bottom and exits through the top. Stainless steel or plastic mesh is used to hold the biofilter medium off the bottom, thus creating a sediment basin. Plastic beads and other coarse media are colonized by bacteria. Plants can be added to the surface of the filter for added nutrient removal. Upflow filters are usually self-contained and separate from the pond. There are other biofilter designs available; you should consult a professional for more information concerning these filters.

Aquatic Plants

Aquatic plants not only add beauty to an ornamental pond, but they are also effective filters and nutrient absorbers. They are the first items that should be placed in any pond. Because many aquatic plants are invasive, all plants used in a water garden should be placed in containers to prevent them from taking over the entire garden. Three different groups of plants should be placed in any balanced garden; emergents that are rooted in the bottom and extend above the water surface (iris, rushes, and so on); submergents *Myriofillum or Ceratophyllum* that stay beneath the surface of the water (and are very important for oxygenating ponds); and floating leaf plants like water lilies. When placing submergent plants you should probably put them in a wire or plastic container to prevent them from taking over the pond. Try to achieve a 1:1 ratio of open water to vegetation to provide maximum habitat for wildlife. These decorative plants, just like other garden plants, will need periodic pruning, dividing, repotting, and fertilizing.

Plants may need to be protected from the fish by surrounding them with wire or plastic mesh. Choose plants that will not drop debris into the pond, because organic matter can clog filters and deplete oxygen as it decays. Hardy aquatic plants such as water lilies and water iris are winterized by cutting off the growth and placing the pots in the pond below the freeze line. Check with the ornamental plant dealer as to the best care for the plants.

Several pieces of equipment should be assembled before you add plants to your water garden. You will need 3-1/2-quart or larger containers for iris, water lily, and moist soil plants. For lotus and spatterdock you will need a 12-inch container (minimum). You'll also need sufficient heavy garden topsoil (with clay content of about 20 percent). Don't use a commercial potting soil or any soil that has been tainted with pesticides or herbicides. Aquatic plants are very sensitive to these chemicals. Obtain sufficient clean (rinsed with water) pea gravel (1/2 to 3/4 inch in diameter) to cover the plants in each container to a depth of 1/2 inch. Do not use limestone gravel. Fertilizer will also be needed. You can use commercially formulated tablets or a 10-10-10 mixture of soluble fertilizer.

When you've assembled these items, follow these steps to complete the planting.

- Rinse off your plants and keep them wet while planting.
- Fill the container about halfway with soil.
- Position the plant properly. For water lilies, plant the rhizome at a 45° angle. For lotus, keep the growing tip of the plant 1/2 inch above the soil. For iris, plant so the root and white area above it are covered.
- Tamp the soil firmly.
- Cover the soil with 1/2 inch of the pea gravel.
- Lower the container into the pond to saturate the soil.
- Finally, lower the container to the appropriate depth.

Native Perennials for Water Gardens

Showy Moist Soil (Bog) or Shallow-Water Plants

arrowhead (*Sagittaria latifolia*)
iris, copper (*Iris fulva*)
iris, southern blue flag (*Iris virginica* or
  versicolor)
Joe-Pye weed, spotted (*Eupatorium maculatum*)
lizard's-tail (*Saururus cernuus*)
mallow, rose (*Hibiscus militaris* and *Hibiscus
  moscheutos*)

marsh marigold (*Caltha palustris*)
meadowbeauty, Virginia (*Rhexia virginica*)
pickerel rush (*Pontederia cordata*)
spiderlily (*Hymenocallis occidentalis*)
sweet flag (*Acorus calamus*)
violet, marsh blue (*Viola cucullata*)

Showy Floating Leaf Plants

lotus, American (*Nelumbo lutea*)
primrose, water (*Jussiaea repens*)
spatterdock (*Nuphar advena*)
water lily, wild white (*Nymphaea odorata*)

Submergent Plants

Stock in the pond at a rate of 1 cluster or
  bunch per sq. foot of pond

coontail (*Ceratophyllum* spp.)
milfoil, water (*Myriophyllum* spp.)

Emergent Plants for Interesting Greenery

bulrush, dark green (*Scirpus atrovirens*)
bulrush, softstem (*Scirpus validus*)
burreed (*Sparganium americanum*)
cattail, common (*Typha latifolia*)
fern, cinnamon (*Osmunda cinnamomea*)

plantain, water (*Alisma subcordatum*)
rush, scouring (*Equisetum hyemale*)
rush, soft (*Juncus effusus*)
sedge, fox (*Carex vulpinoidea*)
sedge, Frank's (*Carex frankii*)

*Copper iris. Irises are
excellent for attracting
hummingbirds.*

*Southern blue
flag iris*

Native Perennials for Water Gardens, continued

Spatterdock

American lotus

Pickerel rush

White water lily

Arrowhead

*Cardinal flower.
Hummingbirds
love this plant.*

Native Perennials for Water Gardens, continued

Spiderlily

Great blue lobelia

Water primrose

Rose mallow

After planting you'll need to fertilize water lilies and lotuses twice monthly and bog plants monthly. Before winter, stop fertilizing, prune dead leaves and stems. After the first killing frost, lower the plants to the deepest part of the pond. The plants will survive better if ice is not allowed to form around them.

Fish

The last step in creating an ornamental pond for fish is to stock the fish. Do not stock the fish until after the pond has become balanced for water quality. The first common mistake made by novice ornamental pond owners is to place fish in the pond before getting the vegetation established. The second most common mistake is to stock too many fish. Many people do not consider the number of fish the pond can safely support. A pond is suitable for fish as long as it can supply adequate oxygen and decompose the wastes. Most of the fish commonly placed in ornamental ponds grow rapidly and may keep on growing unless they are kept on a limited diet.

Pond carrying capacity—the number of fish the pond can support—depends on the size of the pond, temperature, amount of sunlight the pond receives (which influences oxygen levels), whether aeration is provided, and how well the filtration system removes wastes. The stocking rate, or number of fish to put in the pond, should not exceed the pond's estimated carrying capacity. The following examples give stocking rates recommended by fish hobbyist magazines.

First, determine the pond's surface area in square feet. Stock an *unaerated pond* with one 12-inch fish (not including the tail) per 4.5 square feet of surface area. Stock an *aerated pond* with one fish per 2 to 3 square feet. Conservative hobbyists suggest stocking only 1 to 6 inches of fish per 5 square feet of surface or 8 to 12 inches of fish per 16.5 square feet of surface area. For example, if a pond measures 9 by 15 feet, the surface area is 135 square feet. Dividing 135 square feet by 4.5 square feet = 30, the units of 12-inch fish bodies per unit, or 360 inches total.

Problems in Ponds

Water Quality Problems with Fish

The two most common water quality problems in a pond with fish are oxygen depletion and the build-up of toxic nitrogenous wastes. Oxygen depletion occurs because the total amount of plant and animal life has exceeded the carrying capacity of the pond or because of an excessive rate of decomposition. Fish gasping at the surface are almost a sure sign of oxygen depletion. Aeration, the best management for oxygen depletion, should begin immediately; then the cause of the depletion should be determined.

The other common water quality problem is the accumulation of toxic wastes such as ammonia and nitrites. This occurs because of overfeeding, rapid decomposition, or biofiltration failure. When high ammonia or nitrite concentrations are discovered, reduce or stop feeding, flush with good quality water, and check the mechanical or biological filters.

Algae Control

If the algal bloom starts to cut down on visibility, the natural tendency is to treat with herbicides. This is not recommended as it can easily kill fish if the herbicide is not applied properly, or if the decaying algae deplete oxygen. Herbicides may also kill the decorative aquatic plants in the pond. A heavy algal bloom is usually a sign that the pond contains too many nutrients derived from fish wastes, uneaten feed, or overfertilization. To treat the problem, you may need to flush the pond with fresh water, reduce feeding or fertilization, add more aquatic plants or nitrifying bacteria, or reduce the number of fish in the pond.

References

Harrison, G.H. 1979. *The Backyard Bird Watcher.* New York: Simon and Schuster.

Masser, M.P., and J.W. Jensen. *Calculating Area and Volume of Ponds and Tanks.* Auburn, Ala.: Southern Regional Aquaculture Publication 103.

Muhlberg, H. 1982. *The Complete Guide to Water Plants.* London: E.P. Publishing Ltd. 392 pp.

Robinson, P. 1987. *Pool and Waterside Gardening.* Middlesex, England: Collinridge Books. 124 pp.

Stadelmann, P. 1992. *Water Gardens.* Hauppauge, N.Y.: Barron's Educational Series. 145 pp.

Swindells, P., and D. Mason. 1990. *The Complete Book of the Water Garden.* Woodstock, N.Y.: Overlook Press. 208 pp.

Bird Feeding
for Success

7

The chickadee. These spritely little birds, with their cheerful
cries and black caps, are the charmers of the winter woods.
Perhaps you know what I mean. After all, have you ever
met a chickadee you didn't like?

—Roger Tory Peterson, 1996

THESE ELOQUENT WORDS from one of the best known ornithologists in the world express the views of many who feed birds. It would be pretty difficult to argue against the popularity of bird feeding because this activity is the only interaction some people have with wildlife. Birds are diverse, colorful, and entertaining, and they add life to a sometimes monotonous winter landscape. Feeders bring birds close, where they can be observed, identified, photographed, or simply enjoyed. Watching birds at a feeder is excellent therapy for people confined indoors by illness, accident, or winter weather. And bird feeding is inexpensive relative to many forms of recreation. Many people also see bird feeding as a way to help birds survive hard times.

It's understandable, then, why bird feeding is one of the most popular ways to enjoy wildlife in our country. In 1990, scientists estimated that 65.4 million Americans (age 16 or older) fed wildlife around their homes, mostly birds (96 percent). Survey respondents indicated they feed birds an average of seven months each year. Collectively, they spend just over $2 billion on bird food, of which 75 percent is commercially prepared and packaged.

The idea that feeding helps birds is sometimes contentious. Most amateur and professional ornithologists believe feeding is beneficial to birds and people but recognize that it may not always be entirely in the birds' best interest. Feeding can reduce natural competition among birds and subject them to diseases and predation. Also, certain species such as the northern cardinal and northern mockingbird have extended their ranges in recent years, probably in response to food availability at feeders. Depending on one's outlook, such range extension can be viewed as good or bad. It seems logical that feeding could be harmful if it is not continued through the winter, but little scientific study has been devoted to "feeder dependence." One such study conducted at the University of Wisconsin concluded that the survival of chickadees was not compromised when bird feeders were withdrawn from their range. The severity of the weather and availability of natural foods and other feeding stations in nearby woodlands, meadows, and along streams actually determine the potential for harm. Because feeder birds are opportunistic foragers (taking what is available), don't feel guilty if you abandon or discontinue feeding for a period of time. It shouldn't harm the birds.

This chapter is a basic guide for the beginner embarking on the hobby of feeding birds, but it should also help veterans improve their feeding stations. It contains tips to help you maximize your feathered guests' benefit and safety, deal with pests, and select equipment and food. If you heed the cautions, both you and the birds should benefit from and enjoy the experience.

Bird feeding does not have to be complicated or expensive. It can simply mean throwing out sunflower seeds on a picnic table for northern cardinals or tossing a few handfuls of sunflower seed and white millet under a bush for sparrows, dark-eyed juncos, and northern cardinals. At the other extreme, you can purchase specialty feeders and feed for different finches. One of the hottest trends in feeding is putting out insects, such as mealworms or crickets, for species like eastern bluebirds. One homeowner near downtown Lexington told me she actually had a male bluebird come into her insect feeder—a most unusual situation because bluebirds don't particularly like cities. Another trend is feeding fruit for northern orioles. A visit to a bird feeding "specialty" store can be bewildering for the rookie feeder. When you go into the store, do not be afraid to ask for advice or ask friends what works for them.

Birds at Feeders

The following table lists birds observed at feeders throughout the United States during the winter of 1993-94 as part of the Cornell Laboratory of Ornithology's Project Feeder Watch. Only Kentucky species are listed.

Ranking	Bird
1	dark-eyed junco
2	American goldfinch
3	blue jay
4	mourning dove
5	downy woodpecker
6	northern cardinal
7	house sparrow
8	European starling
9	white-breasted nuthatch
10	common grackle
11	red-bellied woodpecker
12	hairy woodpecker
13	red-winged blackbird
14	song sparrow
15	white-throated sparrow
16	purple finch

Purple finch populations are declining at feeders because of competition from the house finch. Purple finches (female at left, male at right) can be distinguished from house finches by the light stripe above the eye and the notched tail.

Male and female house finches on a tube feeder. The house finch is the most common urban feeder bird in Kentucky. It has a straight tail and does not have the white eyebrow of the purple finch.

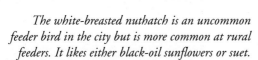

The white-breasted nuthatch is an uncommon feeder bird in the city but is more common at rural feeders. It likes either black-oil sunflowers or suet.

The red-breasted nuthatch is most commonly seen feeding on suet during migration at Kentucky feeders because the species prefers pine habitats. The red-breasted has a rufous belly and white eye stripe when compared with the white-breasted.

The northern cardinal is Kentucky's state bird and a common feeder bird. It prefers sunflowers and safflower seeds and will feed at a feeder or on the ground. The female is seen at left, the male at right.

There are probably 20 different books available telling you how to feed birds. Most of them show you dozens and dozens of different species of birds that will come to feeders. For the most part, that is unrealistic unless you live in a rural area. In the city, house finches will be the most common species at a feeder. Other common species will include northern cardinals, blue jays, dark-eyed juncos, mourning doves, house sparrows, European starlings, common grackles, white-throated sparrows, downy woodpeckers, Carolina chickadees, tufted titmice, Carolina wrens, and American goldfinches. Other birds that might come will depend on a number of factors including the distance to large wooded areas or parks and the number of other people who feed birds in the neighborhood. These species can include hairy and redbellied woodpeckers, purple finches, white-breasted nuthatches, song, chipping, and fox sparrows, and rufous-sided towhees. You might also get some species during migration including white-crowned sparrows, red-breasted nuthatches, indigo buntings, and rose-breasted grosbeaks. Some people who have fed birds for a long time remember when evening grosbeaks, common redpolls, and pine siskins were common at feeders. Because we don't have a great deal of natural pine habitat, these species are very uncommon at feeders in Kentucky.

When beginning any bird-feeding program, the first guideline to remember is that what you feed is far more important than what type of feeder you place the feed in. Because this is the most important point, that is where we will begin.

Marie Sutton had an ingenious idea to keep European starlings from suet. She encloses the suet log in chicken wire, which allows smaller birds, like this Carolina wren, to feed while it discourages European starlings.

The downy woodpecker is the commonest suet feeder in Kentucky. It is smaller than the hairy woodpecker, has a shorter bill, and lacks outer white tail feathers. The hairy is not so common at feeders.

The red-bellied woodpecker is more common at rural feeders than in cities. It will eat suet or black-oil sunflower seeds.

What to Feed

There are many different seeds and other food items you can purchase for bird feeding. Many people purchase their seed at the supermarket or discount department store. You can purchase seed by individual variety or in mixed form. What and how you buy depends on a number of factors, including bird-feeding goals, cost, and availability. Many seeds commonly found in inexpensive supermarket or discount department store mixes, such as wheat, peanut hearts, hulled oats, and rice, are relatively unattractive to most birds. Such commercial mixes might be cheaper, but you will not

Text continues on page 146

A white-throated sparrow.

Sparrows are common ground feeders that like millet,
The white-throated is the commonest feeder sparrow.
It has either black and white or tan head stripes,
yellow lores, and a distinctive white throat. The
white-crowned sparrow lacks the yellow lores and
distinctive throat patch. It is uncommon at urban
feeders and is most likely to be seen during migration.

Song sparrows and chipping sparrows are common
ground feeders that prefer millet. Song sparrows
have a distinctive streaked breast and dark spot
that chipping sparrows lack.

*The indigo bunting (blue), which is most likely to be seen during migration at rural feeders, is sharing this
platform feeder with a chipping sparrow.*

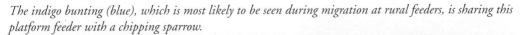

House sparrows are introduced species that are common at urban feeders. They like agricultural grains. Their populations at feeders appear to be declining as a result of competition from house finches. House sparrows are not true sparrows but a weaver-finch (note the big thick bill). The male is at left, the female at right.

The Cornell University Lab of Ornithology lists the dark-eyed junco as the commonest feeder bird in North America. It is a ground feeder that likes millet.

Three common ground-feeding birds are the common grackle (left), the brown-headed cowbird (lower left), and the European starling (lower right). All like agricultural grains and are aggressive, chasing other birds from feeding stations. If you do not want these species at your staion, do not feed their preferred seeds.

Bluejays prefer unsalted peanuts in the shell. They will also eat gray-striped sunflower seeds.

Mourning doves are common ground-feeding birds that like millet and black-oil sunflower seeds.

The rufous-sided towhee is a common rural ground-feeding species that is less common at feeders in the city because of the lack of dense shrubby habitat.

The thistle sock is an inexpensive method of feeding niger seeds to American goldfinches.

A summer feeding program should focus on feeding only black-oil sunflower seeds for species like the male American goldfinch.

attract as many birds compared with purchasing individual seeds and making your own mix with preferred seeds. Unattractive seeds probably will be eaten, but preferred seeds will be eaten first and tend to attract birds that might not otherwise visit a feeder. For example, niger seed attracts finches, safflower seed attracts northern cardinals, and peanuts in the shell attract blue jays.

The black-oil sunflower provides the best seed for the bird-feeding dollar. Small black-oil–type sunflower seeds have virtually replaced traditional large gray or black-striped seeds. Although traditional sunflower seeds are excellent food for blue jays and cardinals, most birds, when given a

The Carolina chickadee is one of my favorite feeder birds that likes safflower and black-oil sunflower seeds. It is shy and often feeds early in the morning and late in the afternoon when other, more aggressive birds are not at the feeder.

The tufted titmouse is a common feeder bird, although it can be shy. It likes safflower and black-oil sunflower seeds. It is seen here on a counter-treadle type house feeder designed to discourage squirrels.

The ruby-throated hummingbird is a summer resident that can be attracted with specialized feeders. Males have the iridescent red throat patch. Use a solution of 1 part granulated sugar to 4 parts water for a feeding solution.

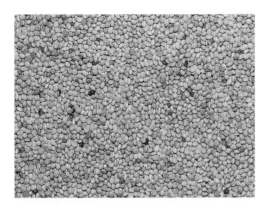

White proso millet

Safflower seed

Black-oil sunflower seed provides the most value for your bird feeding dollar.

Gray-striped sunflower seed

choice, take the small black seeds. About 70 percent of an oil-type seed's weight is in its kernel, while only 57 percent of the weight of a traditional sunflower seed is in the kernel. Oil-type seeds are inexpensive and readily available. Among mixes, those with high proportions of these seeds are your best bet. Also, if you plan to have only one feeder or are just getting started, use black sunflower seed. A second choice would be white millet. Because this seed is very attractive to brown-headed cowbirds, grackles, and house sparrows, don't place a large amount of seed in a feeder. The best advice is to throw a handful under a bush or tree with branches that hang close to the ground. This will attract dark-eyed juncos, white-throated, song, and chipping sparrows, and mourning doves.

You can choose from many other seeds and food items. In the 1970s, the U.S. Fish and Wildlife Service determined the following food preferences of common bird species:

American goldfinch	niger seeds, hulled sunflower seeds, oil-type sunflower seeds
blue jay	whole peanut kernels, large striped sunflower seeds
northern cardinal	oil-type sunflower seeds, large striped sunflower seeds, safflower seeds
chickadee	oil-type sunflower seeds, large striped sunflower seeds, hulled sunflower seeds
mourning dove	oil-type sunflower seeds, white and red proso millets
purple finch	oil-type sunflower seeds, large sun flower seeds, millets
common grackle	hulled sunflower seeds, cracked corn
dark-eyed junco	red and white proso millets, canary seeds, fine cracked corn
song sparrow	white and red proso millets
white-crowned sparrow	oil-type sunflower seeds, white proso millet
white-throated sparrow	same as white-crowned sparrow
tufted titmouse	peanut kernels, all types of sunflower seeds

Undesirable species at a feeder:

brown-headed cowbird	white proso millet, other millets, canary seeds
house sparrow	white proso millet, most small seeds
European starling	peanut hearts, hulled oats, table scraps

Recently, more than 5,000 volunteers contributed data on bird-food preferences as part of the Seed Preference Test administered by the Cornell University Laboratory of Ornithology. Each volunteer used the same cardboard feeders, placed on the ground and filled with equal presentations of millet, milo, and sunflower. The data indicated that all three seed types are eaten by various species. However, 15 common arboreal (off the ground) species, such as chickadees, nuthatches, jays, and finches, strongly favored sunflower seeds. Common ground-feeding species, such as sparrows, towhees, and doves, favored millet. Milo was not preferred among typical eastern bird species. At my feeders, northern cardinals, Carolina chickadees, and tufted titmice prefer safflower seeds. Dark-eyed juncos, white-throated sparrows, and mourning doves prefer white millet. Downy woodpeckers and Carolina wrens prefer blueberry-flavored suet.

Suet appeals to many species, especially woodpeckers, chickadees, titmice, and wrens. Most people use beef suet, but hunters find suet from a deer is also attractive. Beef suet used to be free for the asking at the local butcher shop or grocery store. Now that its popularity as a bird food has created a market for it, you probably will have to pay for it. Suet can be fed as is or melted and mixed with dry foods to attract a variety of species. The most efficient mixes (those that are entirely edible) combine suet with oatmeal, hulled sunflower kernels, peanut hearts, or cracked corn. Whole seeds can be provided more efficiently in other feeders. Bacon fat can be used but tends to be soft and messy. Peanut butter can be used in the same way and is attractive but quite expensive. Mix peanut butter with dry foods, suet, or both because birds can have trouble swallowing straight peanut butter. Commercial suet cakes are available in all shapes and sizes with ingenious devices to present them to the birds. I have found that the fruit-flavored commercial versions are the most popular with birds.

You can supplement seed supplies with stale bakery products, table scraps, and fruit, but these foods have disadvantages. Table scraps and bread often attract less desirable species, such as house sparrows, starlings, grackles, and pigeons. Fruit is attractive to American robins, European starlings, northern mockingbirds, gray catbirds, and northern orioles, and so it is better as summer food than winter food. Simple feeders are available for providing orange halves to northern orioles during summer, and diced apples and raisins can be fed to help American robins through late spring storms. A cut apple can attract northern mockingbirds when snow covers the ground. Northern mockingbirds are somewhat sedentary and will not find the fruits on hollies, hawthorns, and other plants as American robins do. Some commercial mixes contain diced dried fruit.

Don't be afraid to experiment with your own feeder designs, seed mixes, or food items. Once you know a little about your area's common birds and their needs, you might have some creative ideas. Some people are experimenting with providing insect larvae, such as mealworms, for eastern bluebirds and other primarily insectivorous species. Be observant and use your imagination to follow up on ideas. For an exhaustive discussion of bird feeding, I recommend *Wild About Birds: The DNR Bird Feeding Guide* by Carroll Henderson.

The Results of Starting a Bird-Feeding Program in Urban Lexington

A simple bird-feeding station was established, consisting of a plastic hanging feeder; a thistle sock; 25-pound bags of white proso millet, black-oil sunflower seed, and safflower seed; and 10 pounds of whole peanuts and niger seed. Costs were $10 for the feeder, $6 for the thistle sock, and $50 for seed. The feeder was placed in a bush at a height of approximately 5 feet, and a ground-feeding station was set up below it on bare ground. The thistle sock was placed in the same tree. Once a bird was seen at the feeding station, it was seen on all successive days. The feeding station was established in November and maintained through the summer.

Results of a Feeding Program in Lexington

New species	Time of first sighting	Feeder station and feed eaten
Blue jay	day 2	ground: peanuts
Mourning dove	day 2	ground: millet
Common grackle	day 2	ground: millet
Dark-eyed junco	day 3	ground: millet
Northern cardinal	day 3	ground and feeder: safflower and sunflower
House finch	day 3	sunflower
House sparrow	day 3	ground: millet
Brown-headed cowbird	day 3	ground: millet
European starling	day 3	ground: millet
Carolina chickadee	day 7	feeder: safflower and sunflower
Northern mockingbird	day 7	peanut butter and sesame seed pine cone
Tufted titmouse	day 8	feeder: safflower and sunflower
Carolina wren	day 13	ground: millet
Song sparrow	day 18	ground: millet
American goldfinch	week 3	feeder: niger
American crow	week 3	ground: millet
White-throated sparrow	week 4	ground: millet
Purple finch	week 4	feeder: safflower and sunflower
Downy woodpecker	week 4	suet
Catbird*	May	ground: sunflower
Rose-breasted grosbeak*	May	feeder: safflower
White-crowned sparrow*	May	ground: safflower
Indigo bunting*	May	feeder: millet
Pine siskin*	May	feeder: niger

*Stopped at feeder for up to three weeks during spring migration.

Tips on Buying Birdseed

Buying seeds in bulk quantity is substantially cheaper than purchasing smaller amounts. Buying in 50-pound bags saves money and allows you to get the seeds you want and make your own mixes. Do not underestimate the quantity of seed you will use. Fifty pounds of seeds might last all season at an urban feeder, but an active rural feeding station can require 500 pounds or more in a single winter. The Buckley Hills Audubon Society has a special program that enables you to buy seeds in bulk at special prices during October and January in Lexington.

Plan for the cost of feeding the birds all season so you do not have to close down your feeder in mid-January for financial reasons. Thistle seed at $2 a pound adds up quickly if you are fortunate enough to have a flock of hungry goldfinches in the neighborhood. It is probably better to put out less expensive (and less preferred) mixes for the entire feeding season than to stop feeding mid-season.

Store seed in a dry place. Plastic or metal trash cans with tight-fitting lids make excellent storage containers. For smaller quantities, five-gallon plastic buckets work well. If you do not plan to feed year-round, use all the seed before summer because insects will destroy seed left through the summer.

Types of Feeders

There are probably more different kinds of feeders on the market today than you could ever imagine using in a lifetime. Many feeders have been designed to solve a common problem of bird feeders, such as making them squirrel proof or allowing preferred birds to feed while discouraging unwanted birds. Some of the ideas have merit. For instance, the suet feeders that only allow birds to feed hanging upside discourage European starlings from feeding because they can't hang upside down. Metal feeders with counter treadle devices discourage squirrels because the weight of the squirrel closes the feeder opening. Unfortunately there is no feeder designed to prevent house finches from feeding. House finches don't like to hang upside down on the special goldfinch feeders or thistle socks, but they will if they have to.

When selecting a feeder, avoid cute feeders designed to attract buyers more than birds. Look for durable materials, large seed capacity, sensible

design, and a feeder that is easy to fill and clean. A feeding station may be one simple feeder or a dozen or more assorted feeders scattered around the yard. Let your interest and financial resources determine your level of involvement. All feeders can be grouped into one of four designs: shelf, house, tubular, and suet.

The *shelf feeder* is a simple platform that can be mounted on a post or attached to a window sill. It suits many species, can be built easily and inexpensively at home, and is easy to fill with seed. On the negative side, a simple shelf is exposed to snow and rain (unless you put a roof on it) and provides easy access for squirrels. In addition, large quantities of seeds can be scratched from the feeder onto the ground, making the feeder less attractive to birds that prefer to feed above the ground.

The *traditional wooden* or *house feeder* is basically a shelf with a roof and modifications for dispensing food items. Typically, it has a glass or plastic hopper that holds seeds and dispenses them to the feeding area by gravity. Some models have rack-like structures on the ends to hold suet cakes, or wooden pegs on which to impale bakery products and scraps to prevent them from being carried away whole. This type of feeder is usually mounted on a post or railing and is suitable for most birds. If you are considering only one feeder, this is probably the best type to select.

More sophisticated versions of the traditional feeder are made of metal or plastic and can include modifications to fend off squirrels, increase seed holding and dispensing capacity, or feed only certain species. Feeders can be made selective for certain species by using a weight-activated treadle device as a feeding perch. Other methods of selecting for certain species, such as specialized feeders and special food items, can be as effective as counter treadle devices. Whether you want to select for certain species is a matter of personal preference. A bird one person considers a pest might be another's favorite.

Woodpeckers, nuthatches, chickadees, and titmice are attracted to *suet feeders* or *log feeders*. A suet feeder can be simple (an onion bag filled with suet and hung from a limb) or more sophisticated (a basket constructed from scrap wood and quarter-inch-mesh or larger hardware cloth or chicken wire). You can mix melted suet with dry food and pack it into any kind of mold or container. A variation of the suet feeder is the log feeder. This feeder has a common rustic design and consists of a 1- or 2-foot section of a log or limb, usually 2 to 3 inches in diameter. Suet or peanut butter mix is packed into holes bored into the log. Usually a small peg is added below each hole to serve as a perch.

The popular, modern-style *tube feeder* consists of a tube of clear plastic or glass with evenly spaced feeding perches and access holes. A modern version of the log feeder that dispenses seeds instead of suet, it is efficient and durable and comes in a variety of sizes. Different versions are designed to dispense different seeds. On high-quality feeders, the holes through which the birds get seed are armored with metal. Inexpensive plastic feeders can be destroyed quickly by squirrels.

A *thistle sock* is a variation of the tube feeder designed specifically for American goldfinches. It is a fine-mesh tubular bag designed to dispense niger seed. Small birds cling to the sock and remove the small seeds. It is an inexpensive feeder that quickly pays for itself by conserving expensive thistle seeds.

Another specialized feeder is the *hummingbird feeder*. The most common version is a plastic bottle fitted with one or more tubular funnels that hold and dispense sugar water. You use it in summer, when hummingbirds are present. Feeding hummingbirds is discussed in detail later in the chapter.

If you live in a rural area, you can construct large feeders to attract quail, turkeys, and other ground-dwelling species. A tepee or lean-to made of tree limbs or lumber provides shelter and a place to spread grain, particularly cracked corn, for these species.

If you or someone in your family is handy with tools, you can probably make your own feeders. Many are easy to build. Contact the Kentucky Department of Fish and Wildlife Resources or your local county Extension offices for plans. Some excellent feeders can be fabricated in minutes from recycled materials such as two-liter pop bottles, milk cartons, and glass jugs.

Feeder Placement

You should consider several things when deciding where to place feeders. First, you want them to be visible from a favorite window. After all, seeing and enjoying birds is a main reason for feeding them. Second, feeders should be sheltered from prevailing winds that make filling difficult or unpleasant. Third, feeders mounted on poles or suspended from limbs or wires should be 5 to 6 feet from the ground. Fourth, and perhaps most important from the birds' standpoint, feeders should be no more than 10 feet from cover (shrubs, trees, or both) to provide a place of retreat from cats or other threats, a gradual approach route for "shy" birds, and a convenient perch for opening a sunflower seed. This distance also allows an open area so that birds can see cats or other predators. Finally, feeders should be placed to accommodate birds that feed in different niches. This includes feeders placed on tree trunks, feeders situated on low, stable platforms, and free-swinging suspended feeders.

A good feeding station should have four major feeding niches: ground, table-top, post-high or hanging, and tree trunk. (Adapted and redrawn from G.H. Harrison, The Backyard Bird Watcher.*)*

*Providing ice-free water will en-
hance your bird-feeding efforts.
(Redrawn from S.R. Craven and
R.L. Ruff,* Bird Feeding: Tips for
Beginners.*)*

Windows can be excellent spots for feeders. All sorts of lightweight
plastic seed trays come with suction disks to attach them directly to glass.
This brings the birds close, but it poses a hazard if they perceive the glass as
a clear flight path. Do *not* put a window feeder on a window with a sight
line through the house to another window.

The ground also is both a feeder site and a feeder. Mourning doves,
dark-eyed juncos, most sparrows, and most other birds prefer to feed on
the ground. Blue jays, for example, prefer to get unsalted sunflowers in the
shell from the ground, retreat to a nearby tree to break them open and feed,
and return for another peanut. Normal spillage might accommodate
ground-feeding birds; if it doesn't, sprinkle some seed directly on the ground
or mount a low shelf or platform at ground level.

Hummingbirds

When the heat of mid-summer rolls around, bird feeding is a distant
memory for most people. But for those who enjoy our tiniest yet perhaps
most spectacular bird, summer presents a wonderful opportunity—a time
to attract and feed hummingbirds.

Hummingbirds are best known for their small size, iridescent beauty,
and amazing flight. Their name comes from the distinctive humming sound
created in their flight. Upon first observing a hummingbird, most people
exclaim, "I can't believe it's a bird." Identification should be no problem in
our region, because we have only one species, the ruby-throated hummingbird. About the only creature it could be mistaken for is a hawk moth,
which is similar in appearance and behavior around flowers.

Ruby-throated hummingbirds breed throughout the eastern half of
North America. They are here from April or early May through September
or October, when frost eliminates their food supply. Your feeder should be

placed and filled with sugar water no later than April 10 in Kentucky. Hummingbirds migrate and leave by November at the latest. By keeping that feeder out during the late fall, you may get the opportunity to see an unusual species such as the rufous hummingbird, which is usually found in the western United States. Migratory North American hummingbirds winter primarily in Mexico and Central America. It is hard to imagine a bird that weighs three grams making a round trip to Mexico, but they do. In fact, ruby-throats fly across the Gulf of Mexico, a 600-mile flight that requires the fuel contained in about 2.1 grams of fat.

Ruby-throats are general in their selection of habitats throughout their broad range. They use deciduous and mixed woodlands, clearings, edges, parks, orchards, and suburban areas with adequate plantings and gardens. Because of the broad range of suitable nesting habitat, reasonable diversity in your yard is all you need to attract them. Efforts at attracting hummingbirds are best focused on providing a food source, either natural or artificial.

There are several styles of hummingbird feeders on the market. All consist of a glass or plastic storage bottle with one or more tubular nectar dispensers, often terminating in a perch or plastic flower. The feeders should be filled with a boiled solution of four parts water to one part white sugar. Commercial nectar mixes are also available; they are convenient but cost more. Do not use formulations containing honey because of potential mold or fungal disease problems.

Hummingbirds key in on red flowers, so most commercial feeders incorporate red perches, "flowers," or other parts. This is enough red; it's not necessary to dye the sugar solution. A homemade feeder without red parts might benefit from a red solution. As with all bird feeders, hummingbird feeders should be kept clean. An active feeder will be emptied rapidly. Each week, if the sugar solution has not been used by the birds, the feeder should be emptied and cleaned using a brush and mild detergent.

An active feeder is a great source of pleasure. Birds may arrive as early as 30 minutes after sunrise and stay as late as an hour after sunset. Don't be discouraged if birds don't respond immediately to a newly placed feeder. It might take a while or require some attractive flowers nearby. Do not be concerned about yellow jackets (hornets) sharing the sugar solution. They are more of a problem for you than for the birds. If you wish to deter them, try rubbing Avon Skin-So-Soft™ or Off Skintastik™ on the plastic red flowers to repel them.

A few final tips:

• The best method of attracting hummingbirds is to provide a natural food supply. Red tubular flowers are considered best, but several orange and yellow species also work. Some good plants are listed in chapter 4 and Appendix D.

• Many people worry about preventing the birds from migrating by keeping feeders filled late into the fall. This concern is unfounded. By providing that little extra food, you actually might attract some late migrating hummers or even a wayward rufous hummingbird (not unheard of in Kentucky).

• Do not hang your feeder in front of a large window because this represents a safety hazard.

All of this might seem like a great deal of trouble, but the hummingbirds are well worth your effort.

Dealing with Uninvited Guests

Do you get angry when your neighbor's cat stands guard under your bird feeder? Do you reach for the shotgun when you observe a gray squirrel poised to leap onto your feeder? Do you run screaming from the house when your favorite cardinal becomes breakfast for a passing Cooper's hawk? If your answer is yes to any of these questions, you have uninvited guests at your bird-feeding station. Fortunately you can solve most of these problems, or at least modify your own response, so that you can relax and enjoy your feeder without periodic bouts of stress.

Cats

Coping with cat problems around a feeder is more often an exercise in diplomacy than wildlife management. In the rare event that you know beyond reasonable doubt that the offending cat is a stray, the animal can easily be captured in a live trap (such as a Hav-a-hart® or Tomahawk®). Bait the trap with sardines, cat food, fried chicken, or a similar food, and turn the captured cat over to the local Humane Society. Do *not* relocate the cat to a farm or distant neighborhood in the mistaken belief that the cat will be better off.

If you know the cat's owner, it's time to negotiate. Few cat owners are willing to come to grips with the predatory capabilities of their "harmless pets." Enlighten them in a diplomatic way. Ask the owner to keep the cat indoors, attach a bell to the cat, or make an effort to keep the cat out of your yard. For your part, remove concealing ground vegetation and frighten the cat every time you see it. You might try using a super-soaker type squirt gun to deter the cat. If you have a dog, it can be a tremendous aid in frightening the cat.

Squirrels

Squirrels cause frequent, persistent problems at all types of feeders. They monopolize seed supplies, frighten birds, and damage feeders by enlarging seed ports or destroying feeder covers to gain access. Gray squirrels, chipmunks, and even flying squirrels are all potential pests.

The gray squirrel is arguably "Feeder Pest No. 1." Gray squirrels have enormous appetites and can clean out your feeder quickly and repeatedly. On the other hand, squirrels can be fascinating and funny as they leap, dangle, climb, swing, and drop to get to a feeder. If you can protect your feeders from damage, you can feed the squirrels right along with the birds. Several specialized feeders, corn cob holders, and other devices are available to make squirrel feeding practical and entertaining. If you are not now (or are not likely to become) a convert to the merits of squirrels, the following suggestions can help in the ongoing struggle between you and them.

- Use feeders with metal armor to protect seed ports, covers, and so on. They are more expensive but worth it in the long run.
- Try one of several so-called squirrel-proof feeders. They operate with counterbalanced treadles that close the feeder when an animal heavier than a bird tries to feed.
- Suspend your feeders from thin cables or wires. Further protect the feeders by running the cables through short lengths of old garden hose (which will spin around) or old LP records or similar discs.
- Position your feeders away from tree trunks, limbs, roofs, and other points from which a squirrel can jump.
- Protect pole-mounted feeders with a squirrel baffle, inverted cone, sheet-metal guard, or sliding weighted sleeve. These devices can be purchased at specialty bird-feeding stores.

• Provide an alternative food source (corn, nuts, seeds) away from your bird-feeding station. (This will either help solve the problem or attract more squirrels!)

• Remove squirrels by live-trapping as described for cats. Use only sunflower seeds and peanut butter as bait.

• Grin and bear it, or consult *Outwitting Squirrels—101 Strategies to Reduce Dramatically the Egregious Misappropriation of Seed from Your Bird Feeder* by Bill Adler Jr. It is very entertaining.

Chipmunks

Chipmunks are a major problem from April through November. Particularly in late summer and fall, chipmunks carry off large amounts of sunflower seeds or whole-grain corn from feeders. They fill their cheek pouches with the seed and take it beneath the ground for winter storage. During the primary birdfeeding season, chipmunks are resting comfortably below ground with a nice supply of your seeds safely cached. If you have children, chipmunk control is not recommended. Learn to live with them, and let the kids enjoy watching them. Control can be implemented if you do not have children, you can't bear the thought of a mammal near your feeder, or the chipmunks are doing other damage, such as extensive excavation of a rock wall or garden.

Other Mammals

A few other mammals might be problems. Raccoons can be destructive pests. They tear apart feeders to get to corn or sunflower seeds. In some urban areas or farm settings, rats might use bird feeders. They are capable climbers but usually forage on the ground below the feeder. Telltale half-dollar-sized holes in the snow can indicate the presence of rats. Get rid of rats with a rat trap placed under a box with holes on the sides or under a tepee arrangement of boards so birds will not be caught accidentally. Smaller holes in the snow can indicate the presence of voles or shrews—mouse-sized dark gray animals that also visit winter feeders. Don't worry about them; they are not a problem and are fun to watch.

Birds

Some birds also qualify as uninvited guests, even at a bird feeder. People have varying degrees of tolerance for rock doves (pigeons), house sparrows, and European starlings. In some urban settings, these species may be the only feeder visitors and are certainly preferable to no birds at all. If pigeons, sparrows, or European starlings are detracting from more desirable species, however, they can be discouraged by several practices.

- Avoid feeding table scraps, stale bread and pastry, and low-cost seed mixes.
- Stick with the most attractive seeds (sunflower) and specialty seeds (niger, safflower).
- Try using an unstable hanging feeder. Some people claim these are less attractive to house sparrows.
- Trap and remove house sparrows, pigeons, and starlings. These three nonnative species are unprotected, but check state and local regulations or clear your trapping operation with your local conservation officer. Be absolutely sure no "nontarget" birds (those you are not trying to capture) are captured or injured.
- Develop a feeding station using cracked corn or millet on the ground far away from your other feeding station.

The hawk-cardinal scenario described at the start of this section could occur at your feeder and involve any of several raptor and prey species. Such predation is a perfectly natural event. It should not be viewed as a disaster or be held against the offending raptor. Instead, it provides an opportunity to observe another link in the food chain. If your birds have shrubby escape cover reasonably near the feeder, you have done all you should to protect them from natural predators.

Remember, pests are a matter of perspective. Squirrels, rats, sparrows, and other "pests" are doing nothing more or less than cardinals, finches, and woodpeckers—trying to find a square meal.

Feeder Maintenance and Sanitation

Feeders subjected to the rigors of winter weather and the abuse of squirrels and pets might need routine maintenance. Tighten loose screws or fittings and replace damaged parts. Replacement feed ports, spill trays, and other components are available for most quality feeders. Feeders made from recycled materials may simply be replaced when they no longer function properly.

The most important aspect of feeder maintenance is sanitation. It is important for the health of your feathered guests to keep your feeders clean.

Sick birds are easy to spot. They usually appear lethargic; they don't feed or fly much; and their feathers are often messy, ragged, or fluffed up. If you find sick or dead birds around a feeder, poor sanitation is probably a contributing factor. A high concentration of birds at a feeder facilitates the spread of disease, and feeders themselves can become contaminated. A bacterial infection called salmonellosis is spread through fecal droppings. As droppings accumulate, the problem gets worse. Finches and sparrows are especially susceptible to this disease.

It is a good idea to clean your feeder at least once a month, more frequently if it gets heavy use. Remove moldy seed and fecal droppings. Painted, varnished, or metal feeders are easy to clean. To disinfect feeders, dunk them in a weak bleach solution (one part liquid chlorine household bleach in nine parts water) and let them dry before refilling with fresh seed. Remove accumulations of spilled seeds and seed coats from the ground because this material can be a source of fungal diseases such as aspergillosis.

Disease problems are especially likely to occur if you continue to feed into the summer. Warm weather promotes the survival and growth of many disease organisms. Especially if mourning doves are frequent visitors to your feeders, clean the feeders and do not begin feeding again until fall. Mourning doves are susceptible to a parasitic disease called trichomoniasis, which is easily spread at feeders when contaminated food drops from the mouth of an infected bird and is then eaten by another bird.

Diseases

Birds do get sick. Disease is one of many natural processes affecting wild species. The following four diseases commonly affect bird species that typically use feeders. (Other diseases occur in the bird world, but not all bird species visit feeders.)

Salmonellosis (sal-muh-nel-LOW-sis)

Salmonellosis is a general term for any disease in animals and people caused by a group of bacteria known by the Latin name *Salmonella*. Birds can die quickly if the *Salmonella* bacteria spreads throughout the body. Abscesses often form in the lining of the esophagus and crop as part of the infection process. Infected birds pass bacteria in their fecal droppings. Other birds get sick when they eat food contaminated by the droppings. Salmonellosis is the most common bird-feeder disease.

Trichomoniasis (trick-oh-mo-NYE-uh-sis)

The trichomonads are a group of protozoan (one-celled microscopic) parasites that affect a broad variety of animals, including humans. One trichomonad species afflicts only pigeons and doves. The popular and widespread mourning dove is particularly susceptible. Birds afflicted with trichomoniasis typically develop sores in their mouths and throats. Unable to swallow, they drop food or water contaminated with trichomonads that other birds then consume, thus spreading the disease.

Aspergillosis (as-per-jill-OH-sis)

The *Aspergillus* fungus (mold) grows on damp feed and in the debris beneath feeders. Birds inhale the fungal spores and the fungus spreads through their lungs and air sacs, causing bronchitis and pneumonia.

Avian Pox

More noticeable than the other diseases, avian pox causes wart-like growths on featherless surfaces of a bird's face, wings, legs, and feet. The virus that causes pox is spread by direct contact with infected birds, by healthy birds picking up shed viruses on food or feeders, or by insects mechanically carrying the virus on their bodies. However, not all warty growths on birds are caused by the avian pox virus.

All four diseases can lead to death. Salmonellosis can kill the birds outright, and pneumonia from aspergillosis is nearly always fatal. Trichomoniasis can obstruct a bird's throat. Avian pox growths on the face can become large enough to impair vision or eating ability, and growths on feet and toes can affect a bird's ability to stand or perch. Sick birds are more vulnerable to starvation, dehydration, predation, and severe weather.

People who feed birds cannot ignore the disease issue. Eight relatively easy steps can be taken to prevent or minimize disease problems at feeders.

1. Give the birds space. Avoid crowding by providing ample feeder space. Lots of birds using a single feeder looks wonderful, but crowding is a key factor in spreading disease. If birds have to jostle each other to reach the food, they are crowded. This crowding also creates stress, which can make birds more vulnerable to disease.

2. Clean up wastes. Keep the feeder area clean of waste food and droppings. A broom and shovel can accomplish a lot of good, but a vacuum such as you might use in your garage or workshop helps even more.

3. Make feeders safe. Provide safe feeders without sharp points or edges. Even small scratches and cuts allow bacteria and viruses to enter otherwise healthy birds.

4. Keep feeders clean. Clean and disinfect feeders regularly. Use one part liquid chlorine household bleach in nine parts of tepid water to disinfect. Make enough solution to immerse an empty cleaned feeder completely for two to three minutes. Allow to air dry. Once or twice a month should do, but do this weekly if you notice sick birds at your feeders.

5. Use good food. Discard food that smells musty, is wet, looks moldy, or has fungus growing on it. Disinfect any storage container holding spoiled food and the scoop used to fill feeders from it.

6. Prevent contamination. Keep rodents out of stored food. Mice can carry and spread some bird diseases without being affected themselves.

7. Act early. Don't wait until you see sick or dead birds. With good prevention, you'll seldom find sick or dead birds at your feeders.

8. Spread the word. Encourage your neighbors who feed birds to follow the same precautions. Birds normally move among feeders and can spread diseases as they go. The safest bird feeders will be those in communities where neighbors cooperate with equal concern for the birds.

Bird feeding is not problem-free, but disease does not happen often. The risk of disease simply means you have an ethical obligation not to jeopardize wild birds. What is called for is intelligent bird feeding. Follow the precautions listed above, and you will minimize risk and continue to enjoy feeding healthy wild birds.

Other General Tips and Pointers

• A discarded Christmas tree provides shelter and cover near a feeder if natural cover is in short supply.

• A clasp from a dog leash makes a handy attachment for a hanging feeder—it makes the feeder easy to remove for filling or repair.

• A good field guide or several hours with a "pro" make bird identification simple and fun.

• You can mark the passing of the seasons by keeping track of the comings and goings of different species.

• A tray or pan mounted beneath the feeder reduces waste by catching a lot of spilled seed. Always provide some seeds on the ground, however, for doves, juncos, towhees, sparrows, blackbirds, and other ground-feeding species.

• A poor winter at the feeder—low numbers, few species—is usually a sign of a mild winter or abundant natural food rather than some sort of catastrophe.

• Cardinals, blue jays, and house sparrows are often the first visitors to a new feeder. When titmice, woodpeckers, and nuthatches come, you know you have established an effective feeding station.

• Don't be discouraged if it takes time for birds to respond to a new feeder. The amount of time it takes for birds to find your feeder depends on such factors as whether you live in a new subdivision barren of trees or a heavily wooded area on the edge of town and whether or not your neighbors also have feeders.

• Suet-seed mixes can be purchased in cakes, blocks, chunks, and other forms. They are more expensive, but more convenient, than homemade.

• If you attract a rare bird to your feeder, be discreet about publicizing it. You can easily be overrun with eager bird watchers.

• Most people concentrate their feeding activity from October to April. You can feed all year if you wish to see different species and parent birds with their young or to extend your enjoyment. You might need to adjust your foods and be alert for disease problems. The addition of nesting material (string, yarn, feathers) on or near the feeder in the spring will make it more attractive to the birds.

• If you happen to see a banded or color-marked bird, try to read the band number and report it to a known bander, a Department of Fish and Wildlife Resources employee, or the Bird Banding Laboratory, Washington, DC 20811. Banders work hard to recover information important to our knowledge of bird ecology. Banded birds are likely to return to a particular feeder year after year, so you can renew old friendships.

• If you wish to try your hand at homemade feeders or birdhouses, consult your local Extension office. These items make excellent gifts, fundraisers, and community service projects.

• Project Feeder Watch is a popular program run by the Cornell Laboratory of Ornithology. It is similar to the Seed Preference Test discussed in the foods section. Thousands of volunteers across the country monitor bird abundance and population trends at their feeders. The data are useful to biologists concerned about bird populations and ecology. If these kinds of experiments intrigue you, sign up for either project by contacting the Cornell Laboratory of Ornithology at P.O. Box 11, Ithaca, NY 14851-0011. There is a nominal charge, but you can have a great deal of fun while making an important contribution to ornithology. In addition, you receive some helpful information.

Feeding Deer and Other Mammals

Birds are the traditional target of most backyard feeding enthusiasts, but it is possible to attract deer and other mammals if you would like to. Is it desirable to do so? Be careful what you wish for when feeding to attract these critters. In most cases they can become overpopulated with an over-abundant food supply and may seriously damage ornamental and garden plantings in your yard. You have to draw your own conclusions and be aware of the consequences if you choose to attract deer, raccoons, opossums, and other mammals.

As noted earlier, some mammals visit feeders intended for birds; given the chance, even deer and black bears consume sunflower seeds. If you enjoy seeing such animals, consider a feeder just for them.

People frequently feed deer to bring them close for viewing and photography. This practice is especially common in northern states with harsh winters where deep snow impedes deer movement and their access to food. As with squirrels, corn is a popular choice for feeding deer. It is usually spread on the ground or low platforms, under lean-to structures, or in wire hopper-style feeders that dispense a regular supply. Hay, apples, sugar beets, carrots, and other agricultural commodities are also used, depending on local availability. The frequency of roadside advertising for "deer apples" or "deer corn" in rural areas speaks to the popularity of deer feeding. Salt and mineral licks are popular and easy to use. These often contain nutritional supplements designed to produce large deer or improved antlers, usually for hunting purposes. Such products are heavily advertised in sporting magazines, sporting goods stores, and feed mills.

Raccoons and opossums quickly respond to handouts of table scraps, pet food, or deer bait. Special feeders are not necessary; any shallow pan or tray will do.

If feeding mammals sounds easy, it is—if you have suitable habitat for these animals around your home. In fact, it is so easy that feeding animals like these can lead to too much of a good thing. One raccoon may be cute (and manageable), but what about two dozen of them? If these animals are not satisfied with your handouts, they might turn to gardens, trash, and other available sources for food. Some species might find the living so good they move in with you. Raccoons and squirrels, in particular, can be terrible problems in attics and walls. As the animals become bold and numerous, they might be a health and safety risk to you, your children, and your pets. Bites, diseases, and parasites are all possibilities. Consider these consequences before you add a few ears of corn for the squirrels or a salt block for deer to your backyard feeding station.

References

Adler, Bill, Jr. 1988. *Outwitting Squirrels—101 Strategies to Reduce Dramatically the Egregious Misappropriation of Seed from Your Bird Feeder.* Chicago: Chicago Review Press. 176 pp.

Craven, S.R., and R.H. Ruff. 1983. *Bird Feeding Tips for Beginners and Veterans.* Madison: Univ. of Wisconsin Cooperative Extension Publication.

Harrison, G.H. 1979. *The Backyard Bird Watcher.* New York: Simon & Schuster. 285 pp.

Henderson, C.L., 1995. *Wild about Birds: The DNR Bird Feeding Guide.* St. Paul: Minnesota Bookstore. 279 pp.

Jenner, J.V. 1995. *Backyard Birds: An Enthusiast's Guide to Feeding, Housing, and Fostering Wild Birds.* New York: Michael Friedman Publishing. 128 pp.

Mahnken, J. 1996. *The Backyard Bird-Lover's Guide.* Pownal, Vt.: Storey Communications. 310 pp.

Peterson, Roger Tory. 1996. *International Wildlife Magazine,* March/April, pp. 36-43.

Warton, S., ed. 1990. *An Illustrated Guide to Attracting Birds.* Menlo Park, Calif.: Sunset Publishing. 112 pp.

Managing Wildlife that Become Pests

These sprays, dusts, and aerosols are now applied almost universally to farms, gardens, forests, and homes . . . and have the power to kill every insect, the "good" and "bad," to still the song of birds and leaping of fish in the streams . . . . Can anyone believe it is possible to lay down such a barrage of poison . . . without making it unfit for all life?

—Rachel Carson, *Silent Spring*

A S THE STATE EXTENSION wildlife specialist, I receive hundreds of calls each year concerning wildlife damage. Problems range from chipmunks stealing birdseed to coyotes killing sheep. They also range from comical to critical. One humorous call was from an elderly woman who had a garter snake in the heating vent of her car. Every time the woman started her car and turned on the heater, the snake appeared and terrified her. Wildlife damage calls also vary with the season: slithering snakes, burrowing chipmunks, and tunneling moles in the spring; bats in the attic, groundhogs on the lawn, raccoons in the garden, and birds roosting under the eaves all summer; snakes again in the fall; squirrels in the attic, moles in the yard, skunks under the patio, and more roosting birds during late winter.

In your endeavors to create habitat for wildlife, you, too, might be aggravated by animals that are in the wrong place at the wrong time. Bats in the belfry, a chipmunk under the deck, woodpeckers on siding, robins in the grape arbor, rabbits in the vegetable garden, gray squirrels in the attic, raccoons in the chimney . . . the list goes on and on. Some species are just nuisances; others can cause significant damage to gardens, landscapes, or structures. Each problem has its own unique solution, and it would be impossible to provide answers here to every wildlife problem that can occur on your property. Rather, this chapter stresses proper planning to resolve problems *before* they begin and suggests general solutions to some common problems. For specific information on managing individual species

White-tailed deer are becoming a major nuisance in urban areas.

and the damage they cause, contact your local Cooperative Extension Office and ask for the appropriate species brochure listed in the table below.

Not every wildlife-human conflict necessarily requires control. Long-term damage that reaches an economic or personal threshold is what dictates corrective action. For example, you might tolerate squirrels raiding the bird feeder—until they take up residence in your attic. You might even tolerate squirrels in your attic—until they begin to breed and keep you awake at night.

When considering options for solving a problem, be sensitive to values other than your own. Although you may abhor swifts in your chimney,

Wildlife Damage Publications Published by the Kentucky Cooperative Extension Service	
Publication Number	**Publication Title**
FOR 37	*Managing Coyote Problems in Kentucky*
FOR 38	*Controlling Woodpecker Damage*
FOR 41	*Managing Chipmunk Problems in Kentucky*
FOR 42	*Managing Mole Problems in Kentucky*
FOR 43	*Managing Rabbit and Vole Problems in Kentucky Orchards*
FOR 44	*Managing Woodchuck Problems in Kentucky*
FOR 45	*Managing Tree Squirrel Problems in Kentucky*
FOR 46	*Snakes: Information For Kentucky Homeowners*
FOR 48	*Bats: Information For Kentucky Homeowners*
FOR 49	*Managing Skunk Problems in Kentucky*
FOR 50	*Managing Beaver Problems in Kentucky*
FOR 51	*Managing Muskrat Problems in Kentucky*
FOR 57	*Managing White-tailed Deer Problems in Kentucky*
FOR 62	*Managing Urban Pest Bird Problems in Kentucky*
ID 115	*Managing Commensal Rodent Problems in Kentucky*

your neighbors might sit on their patio and delight in watching the birds eat insects every evening. On the other hand, your neighbors might dread the tapping of woodpeckers creating holes and causing damage to their home, while you place suet bags around your deck to feed these interesting birds. Individuals have differing opinions on controlling wildlife pests. Be considerate of others' opinions and keep the lines of communication open between you and your neighbors. Strive to use nonlethal solutions first. Because of available technology for controlling pests, neighborhood relations, values other than your own, and laws related to the protection of wildlife, lethal solutions should be used only as a last resort.

Before you decide on a solution to a particular problem, learn about the wildlife species in question. You might want to rethink your original plan. Take the chimney swifts, for example. Once you learn of the chimney swifts' voracious appetites for destructive insects, you might decide your "problem" is not so bad in exchange for the benefit the swifts provide. You'll also learn that chimney swifts migrate in early fall, at which time you could have the chimney cleaned and capped before the return of the birds.

Always keep in mind that the primary objective in dealing with a pest wildlife problem is to alleviate the problem, not to destroy wildlife. The ultimate goal is peaceful coexistence between humans and wildlife.

General Principles of Managing Problem Wildlife

Base solutions to wildlife problems on the following principles:

1. **You cannot control the entire population.** In most cases, high reproductive rates and animal mobility make control of the entire population nearly impossible. After a control program, remaining individuals in the population produce more young, the young have higher survival rates because of the lowered population, and the population quickly returns to precontrol levels. Also, many species are highly mobile and have ranges that extend beyond the property under your control. It is not necessary to control the entire population anyway because damage usually is caused by just a few individuals. (An exception is when roosting or feeding of birds conflicts with human interests. In these special cases, hundreds of birds may be involved and special control measures are necessary.)

2. Remove the attractant. Once the animals causing the problem are removed, the damage will cease only if the habitat or attractant is removed. Excellent nesting or roosting habitat for squirrels, raccoons, bats, birds, and snakes is often created when houses and other structures are built. These and other animals exploit opportunities to enter the warm, cozy environment provided by a chimney, attic, or other space. Some animals can enter buildings through holes as small as 1/8 inch. To combat wildlife damage, you must make your home as animal-proof as possible. Replace or repair broken windows or boards, mend broken screens, tightly fasten floor drains, cap chimneys, cover vents, and repair holes and cracks in concrete or masonry. If you don't take these actions, features that attracted the original animal remain and might prompt another animal to move in and cause more damage. To borrow an old adage, an ounce of prevention is worth a pound of cure.

3. You are in the best position to solve the problem. Those experiencing the problem are in the best position to locate the individual animal and reduce damage or prevent economic losses. Armed with accurate information, a little creative thinking, proper equipment, and perseverance, you can solve most wildlife damage problems yourself. You can even cope with sticky situations, such as a skunk digging under the porch. In some cases, especially those involving bird roosts, resolution of the problem might exceed your capabilities and require professional assistance. (If you decide to solve bird-roosting problems yourself, you'll probably need help from your neighbors. At a minimum, let them know you will be using scare tactics-playing a distress tape, using loud noises and bright lights—to move the roosting birds.) Remember, the goal in solving wildlife-human conflicts is to reduce losses or aggravation to a level you can tolerate and maintain a peaceful coexistence with the wildlife around you.

4. Be proactive, not reactive. The time to solve a wildlife problem is *before* it exists. During the planning process of landscaping for wildlife, anticipate where problems might occur and take steps to prevent them. If you have a prized grape arbor and robins are common in your area, erect bird netting *before* fruit ripens. If rabbits or groundhogs are common, erect a quality fence *before* damage occurs.

5. Understand your adversary. Success in solving wildlife-human conflicts is enhanced by understanding the species causing the problem. If you know what the animal eats, you can remove enticing food sources from the environment or accurately select bait for traps. A good woodchuck bait, for example, can be made from the juices of persimmon and garden vegetables mixed with vegetable oil. Commercial trapping baits are based on animals' food preferences. This knowledge also curtails the capture of non-target wildlife (animals you are not trying to capture). Knowing where an animal lives gives you clues on trap placement, garden design, and how the environment can be made inhospitable by removing one or more of the animal's essential cover requirements. Knowing how prolific the animal is or how mobile it is also can help you understand the problem and devise possible solutions.

6. Investigate wildlife law. Before harassing, trapping, relocating, or killing a wild animal, find out what you can and cannot legally do. Some species (rats, house mice, pigeons, starlings, and several others) are not protected by state or federal laws. Wildlife is a public-owned resource, however, and most species are protected by either state or federal laws. Before beginning a wildlife damage control program, determine the legal status of the animal because laws influence which wildlife damage control techniques can be used. The U.S. Fish and Wildlife Service and the Kentucky Department of Fish and Wildlife Resources (KDFWR) are responsible for laws related to wildlife protection and management and animal damage control.

7. Integrated wildlife damage management is vital. Managing wild animal problems is different from controlling weeds or insects. Few chemicals are available for animal control, which is good because chemicals that kill wildlife can harm other animals and humans. There are no "cookbook" approaches (apply X to Y, then apply Y to Z, sprinkle, and the problem disappears) to dealing with wildlife damage problems. Each situation must be examined for a variety of factors, including:

- species of animal causing damage
- severity of damage
- season, duration, and location of damage
- legal status of animal
- biological and ecological factors
- management options available (lethal and nonlethal)
- economic considerations
- values of homeowner and neighbors

Laws and Regulations Regarding Wildlife

Federal Agency Regulations

The U.S. Fish and Wildlife Service is responsible for enforcing the Endangered Species Act of 1973 (as amended), the Fish and Wildlife Act of 1956 (as amended), and the Migratory Bird Treaty Act of 1918 (as amended). Because of these laws, it is illegal to kill, destroy, or harm any endangered or threatened wildlife species or any migratory bird except the feral pigeon, European starling, and English sparrow.

A federal permit must be obtained before a federally protected migratory species may be taken, possessed, or transported. This includes whole birds, any bird part, eggs, or nest. This permit is *not* required only when the following conditions are present under the provisions of the Migratory Bird Treaty Act:

Yellow-headed, bi-colored and tri-colored, red-winged, rusty and Brewer's blackbirds, cowbirds, all grackles, crows and magpies when committing or about to commit depredation upon ornamental or shade trees, agricultural crops, livestock or wildlife, or when concentrated in such numbers and manner as to constitute a health hazard or other nuisance.

Federal permit application form requests (including a $25 processing fee) should be made to:

U.S. Fish and Wildlife Service
Law Enforcement Permit Office
P.O. Box 4839
Atlanta, GA 30302
Telephone (404) 331-3555

State Regulations

The following state statutes apply to wildlife in Kentucky. The statutes are administered by the Kentucky Department of Fish and Wildlife Resources.

150.105. Destruction or Control of Animals Causing Damage

Notwithstanding any other provisions of this chapter, the commissioner may, with the approval of the commission, authorize conservation officers or any other persons to destroy or bring under control in such manner as he deems necessary any wild animals, fish or wild birds, protected and unprotected, which are causing damage to persons, property or other animals, fish or birds, or spreading diseases, and which in his judgment should be eliminated or controlled to prevent further damage.

150.170(8). Killing of Animals Causing Damage

Resident landowners, their spouses or dependent children who kill or trap on their lands any wildlife causing damage to such lands or personal property situated thereon, shall not be required to have a hunting or trapping license. Tenants or their dependent children residing upon said lands shall also have the same privilege. Upon destruction of any wildlife by the above-specified individuals, such act must be reported to the department or the resident conservation officer for the proper disposition of the carcass.

150.320. Birds Not Protected—Nests and Eggs

(1) No person shall take any wild bird except game birds or live raptors for which there is an open season, either under the laws of Kentucky and the regulations of the department or the laws of the United States, except those birds mentioned in subsection (2) of this section.
(2) This chapter does not protect or in any way limit the taking of the crow, the starling, or the English sparrow, but any persons taking any of them must have a hunting license.
(3) No person shall take, disturb or destroy the nest or eggs of any wild birds except for raptors as prescribed by regulation.

When control is appropriate, specific management techniques should be applied at the time and place the animal is most vulnerable. An integrated wildlife damage management approach, using several of these techniques, is essential to effectively solve most wildlife-human conflicts. The following options are used in wildlife damage management: exclusion (animal-proofing), repellents (visual, auditory, chemical), habitat modification, removal by toxicants (poisons), and increased tolerance.

Integrated Wildlife Damage Management

Exclusion (animal-proofing)

The Humane Society of the United States defines animal-proofing as "a common sense approach to animal-damage control . . . achieved by physically excluding wildlife, conditioning them to avoid the area, or inhibiting their breeding." Exclusion is the most important component of an integrated wildlife damage management program because physical barriers represent the only way to secure semipermanent or permanent relief from most problems.

Although exclusion, or "building out" wildlife, is viewed as a nonlethal way to solve a problem, this is not always true. When an animal's shelter is removed, the animal is forced to find alternative cover. The animal might have to go a tremendous distance to find suitable habitat not already occupied by other members of its species. In searching for a new home, an animal can die from starvation, predation, a collision with a vehicle, or a fight with members of its own kind if it invades their territory.

Excluding animals from buildings. Shelter is important to wildlife because it provides a place to relax, keep warm and avoid the weather, escape from predators, and raise young. Houses and other outbuildings can provide excellent shelter for animals. Animals that seek shelter in these structures can be a nuisance. Chipmunks burrowing around a foundation or a squirrel eating insulation off of electrical wires can cause significant damage; a roosting bird transmitting histoplasmosis—a respiratory disease caused by a fungus in bat and bird droppings—can create a health hazard.

Raccoons and gray squirrels are probably the most common wildlife species that cause nuisances or damage homes. They are not, however, the only species that invades structures. Big brown and little brown bats are common attic dwellers throughout Kentucky. Pigeons, starlings, and house sparrows often enter buildings via unboxed eaves or unscreened vents, louvers, or exhaust fans. Snakes find their way into cool, damp basements through basement or foundation cracks or crawl spaces. Five-lined skinks and blue-tailed lizards enter homes through cracks or crevices around foundations. Skunks, opossums, woodchucks, and chipmunks (ground squirrels) burrow around or near foundations.

After removing the problem animal(s), periodically check buildings for evidence of animal usage. Look for droppings, feathers, tracks, and dull or discolored paint or dull or worn-looking spots on boards. Common entry points include uncapped or unscreened chimneys, the juncture of the roof and sides of the house, unscreened vents and louvers, and foundation cracks. When wildlife invades homes or other buildings, begin animal-proofing with repairs. Replace broken boards, siding, and windows. Mend screens, patch holes, screen vents, and seal any opening larger than 1/8 inch. Board, caulk, or weatherstrip cracks and crevices. To avoid ani-

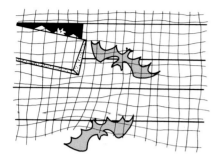

The only permanent, safe way to exclude bats is to build them out. All possible entrances should be located and sealed except one. Plastic bird netting or a one-way door should be erected on that entrance to allow bats to exit but not return.

mal reentry by gnawing or prying, use hardware cloth or heavy (26-gauge) galvanized sheet metal.

Never exclude animals from a dwelling when young animals are present. If you animal-proof at this time, you separate the parents from the young. The young will die if they are not mobile and ready to live without assistance from adult animals. If the young die, you have a smelly mess to clean up. Also, the adults might cause even more damage in a frantic attempt to reach their young. All in all, this is an unacceptable, inhumane way to manage the problem.

A unique exclusion device created a number of years ago is the one-way check valve, or door. It is especially useful in building out bats. The device is relatively inexpensive to construct because it can be made from plastic bird netting or hardware cloth and PVC pipe. The check valve allows bats to leave in the evening on their daily travels and prevents them from reentering the structure. Stephen Franz reported at the twelfth Vertebrate Pest Conference that

> birdnetting check valves were designed and effectively applied to exclude commensal bats from buildings or other structures. Bats were able to make their normal exodus at dusk without becoming entangled or trapped in the check valve netting. Upon returning to the roost site at dawn, bats were unable to circumnavigate the check valves, apparently because major cues for re-entry were not impaired. Birdnetting is relatively inexpensive . . . and fabrication can be completed during the daytime . . . . Installation can generally be completed by one or two people within a few days. The designs are

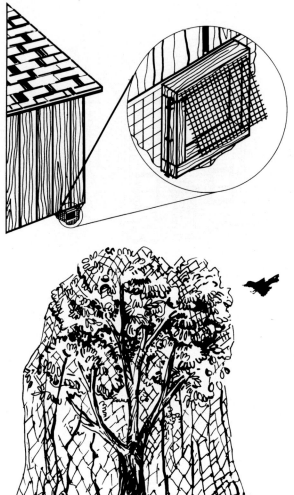

adaptable to a wide variety of points of egress: small or large, discrete or diffuse, on a pitch or horizontal, edge or ridge cap or roof, under soffits, around corners, etc., and do not interfere with house ventilation or aesthetic characteristics.

The details necessary to use these techniques successfully are contained in the species-specific bulletins listed in the table on page 168.

The best way to keep pigeons, starlings, and house sparrows from roosting or nesting on ledges and rafters or under eaves and other overhangs is to prevent them from landing in these sensitive locations. Bird

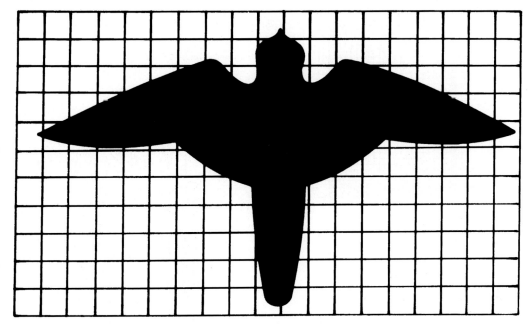

Enlarge the illustration above to approximately 6" high x 10" wide.

One method of keeping birds from crashing into windows is to cut a diving falcon silhouette from black construction paper and place it in a window. (Use template above)

netting is one of the best products available to exclude birds from structures, prevent birds from roosting in trees, and protect fruit trees or garden vegetables. Research has shown that netting can reduce damage to fruit crops by as much as 90 to 99 percent. Modifying the design or shape of the structure also keeps birds from landing or walking on it. When the roosting structure is a ledge, for example, place a metal covering or board on the ledge at a 45- to 60 degree angle. You can also use "porcupine wires" to deter birds. These short, heavy wire or plastic prongs stick out at various angles making it difficult for birds to land or walk about on a ledge. The plastic wires are cheaper and easier to use in many situations than metal ones.

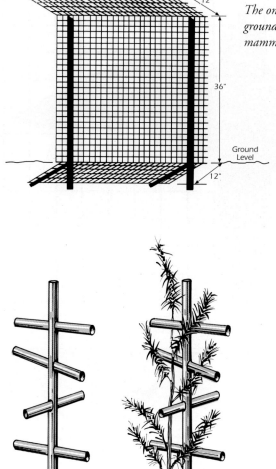

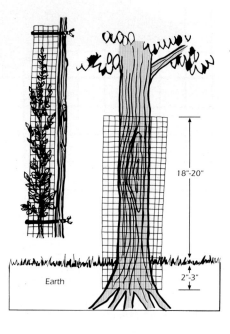

The only way to protect gardens from raccoons, groundhogs, and other burrowing or climbing mammals is to erect an exclusion fence.

One method of keeping deer, rabbits, and other chewing mammals from important trees is to install hardware-cloth protectors around the trees (above) or to place rebar structures to prevent deer from rubbing their antlers on the trees (left).

Using fences to exclude animals. How do you keep that persistent rabbit or woodchuck out of your garden? Short-term solutions are available, but the best long-term solution is to erect a good, stable fence that critters can neither burrow under nor crawl over. I don't mean a cheap chicken-wire fence, but a fence designed specifically to keep wildlife out of places you don't want them. Most fences useful in keeping out wildlife are constructed of hardware cloth (very expensive) or other types of welded wire. Be sure to match the mesh size to the pest you are trying to exclude. To exclude animals that are excellent climbers or diggers, the fence should be 30 to 36 inches tall, with the bottom 6 to 8 inches turned outward and buried un-

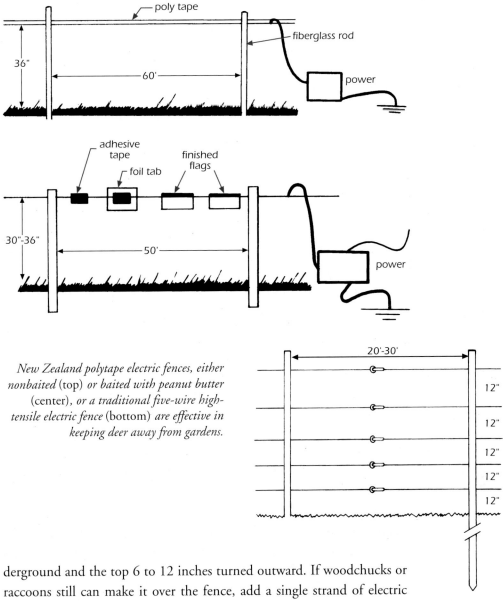

New Zealand polytape electric fences, either nonbaited (top) *or baited with peanut butter* (center), *or a traditional five-wire high-tensile electric fence* (bottom) *are effective in keeping deer away from gardens.*

derground and the top 6 to 12 inches turned outward. If woodchucks or raccoons still can make it over the fence, add a single strand of electric fence to the top.

During the winter, rabbits might chew on the bark of trees or shrubs. Small individualized fences, which you can buy or make yourself using hardware cloth, can be placed around individual landscape trees to protect them from browsing. Make sure the fences extend above the normal snowfall line.

Fencing out deer in urban areas can be problematic because the fences are expensive to build and maintain and they can appear unsightly. If deer are a problem and you decide to use fencing as the solution, contact your county Extension office or the Department of Fish and Wildlife Resources for information on fencing out deer.

Repellents

Repellents deter animals from doing damage or gaining entry by the use of visual, auditory, tactile, olfactory, or distasteful cues. A repellent does not *eliminate* damage by wildlife but should reduce the damage incurred or keep wildlife from causing more damage until you can implement a permanent cure. Repellents are useful in situations where you need to quickly and temporarily drive an animal from the damage site. Repellents could be used, for example, to protect a vegetable garden just long enough for the vegetables to be harvested.

Effectiveness of repellents varies depending on several factors. Many chemical repellents do not weather well and must be reapplied after a heavy dew, rain, or when a plant puts on new growth. If the damage is to vegetation, lack of preferred foods influences a repellent's effectiveness. If the wildlife population is high and under severe food stress, repellents probably will be less effective. Also, not every repellent works under every condition. If you use a chemical repellent, always follow the manufacturer's directions and label instructions before applying the chemical. Never apply repellents to any portion of a plant likely to be eaten by humans unless the label permits it.

Commercial repellents are probably more effective than home remedies, although some home remedy repellents work adequately. Examples of home remedies include dog or predator feces, human hair, soap, blood meal, dirty laundry, hot sauce, and mothballs. Home remedies can be harmful to children or nontarget wildlife in some cases, and there may be laws regulating the use of chemicals contained in some home remedies.

Scare tactics (visual and auditory repellents). Visual repellents are used to frighten an animal away from the site of damage. Examples include owl or hawk decoys; mirrors, aluminum pie tins, foil, and Mylar or plastic streamers blowing in the wind; flares, lanterns, flood or strobe lights; or special "eye" balloons.

Auditory repellents are also used to frighten an animal away from the damage site. Unnatural or loud noises can startle animals. Some noise-making devices mimic an animal's distress signal, conveying a message of distress, alarm, or imminent danger and causing the animal to flee the scene. Other auditory repellents include loud wind chimes, portable radios, predator calls, special firecrackers, propane cannons, and bird rockets. Distress calls and scaring devices are most successful when used in combination. Begin using these techniques at the first sign of a problem because it can be difficult to break an animal's behavior or movement pattern once it is established. In addition, animals become accustomed to the same sights or sounds and may move only a short distance or not at all after they have gotten used to hearing or seeing the same repellents for several days. If you use visual and auditory repellents, move the materials to a different location every day and use both types of scare tactics simultaneously. A final word of caution: many visual and auditory repellents can be as offensive to you and your neighbors as they are to the pest. Be sensitive to others, and always talk to your neighbors before or during these operations.

Tactile repellents. Special sticky repellents are designed to discourage roosting birds. You can find these nontoxic sticky substances, called polybutenes, under a variety of brand names. They can offer temporary relief for problems with larger roosting birds (starlings, pigeons), but they are messy, collect dirt, and must be reapplied often. For best results when using polybutenes, place duct tape on the surface needing protection. Then apply the repellent to the tape. This increases the effectiveness of the repellent on porous surfaces (like concrete) and makes removal easier. These repellents do not work well for small birds that can cling to minuscule spaces and avoid the chemical.

Taste or olfactory (smell) repellents. More than 100 brands of animal repellents are registered in the United States. More than 25 are made just to repel deer. Repellents that deter animals by smell alone are called *area* repellents and are usually applied on or directly adjacent to the affected plants. Examples of area repellents are bone tar oil, ammonium soaps of fatty acids, moth balls or crystals, and various home remedies like blood meal and soap that smell bad to an animal. *Contact* repellents taste bad. Examples of contact repellents are putrescent egg solids, thiram, capsaicin (hot sauce), and benzyldiethyl ammonium saccharide. Generally speaking, contact repellents are more effective than area repellents in reducing chewing or gnawing damage. The label instructions for some chemicals might permit ornamental bulbs to be dipped in them to keep burrowing animals from eating them.

Habitat Modification

Although you take great steps to create wildlife habitat, sometimes eliminating a key component of an animal's habitat can help resolve a problem. You can do this in a manner that allows you to continue to attract other wildlife to your urban green space. Habitat modification does not have to be drastic. Tie garbage cans to a solid structure so raccoons and opossums cannot get into them. Lids should be tight-fitting and tied down or weighted down to deny access to garbage. Other common-sense measures include removing dishes of pet food during the night, mowing long grass used by snakes or mice, stacking firewood away from the home and elevating it 12 to 18 inches above the ground, removing the brush pile where rabbits and chipmunks hide, trimming tree limbs that are adjacent to the house and allow squirrels to jump onto the roof, drastically trimming trees to discourage bird roosts, and planting landscape plants deer and rabbits do not like to eat.

Removal

Having an unwanted, uninvited wildlife guest removed is a wise choice in many cases. One of the most common methods homeowners and private contractors use to manage wildlife problems is to capture an animal, physically unharmed, by using a live trap and relocate the animal to the countryside. Other nonlethal methods include capturing by hand or net, snaring, and using glue boards for mice, rats, snakes, and lizards.

Translocating wildlife is not necessarily a sound approach, however, and is often a lethal solution to the problem (contrary to the belief that the animal will live to a ripe old age). If an animal is released into less than optimal habitat (as is often the case), it faces the choice of trying to live in that habitat and probably dying from a number of causes, including starvation, exposure to the weather, and predation, or moving to more suitable habitat with the increased possibility of dying from a collision with a vehicle. An animal's best chance for survival is where it already lives.

Even if an animal is translocated to appropriate habitat, mortality is often high. Studies have shown that up to 75 percent of raccoons die within three months of relocation. The primary reason is that appropriate habitat for the species is already at carrying capacity. The habitat is providing homes for as many creatures as can be supported by the available food, cover, and space. There simply might be "no more room at the inn" for a translocated animal. In even the best-case scenario, the translocated animal is at a disad-

Many homeowners prefer live trapping when dealing with problem or nuisance wildlife.

vantage in competing with members of the same species and other species for a limited supply of resources because it is unfamiliar with the surroundings.

Finally, live trapping and release do no good and can be fruitless unless you modify the habitat or remove the attractant from your property. The unoccupied territory is an open invitation to another animal to fill the void and potentially cause further damage to your property. Live trapping treats the symptom but does not solve the problem. For example, one gentleman in Madison, Wisconsin, has live-trapped and removed an average of 140 gray squirrels from his backyard every year for the past 10 years. Solving the problem requires proper planning to keep animals away from potential damage locations, exclusion or animal-proofing, good sanitation, and building maintenance.

You also can remove an animal from a site through lethal methods, including kill-type traps and toxicants or poisons. Few chemicals are registered to destroy wildlife. Those that are available must be used by someone with proper training and registration. The use of poisons is usually not a viable option for a homeowner wishing to remove problem wildlife. Shooting is also not a viable option because none of the major towns and cities in Kentucky allows firearms or guns to be discharged within city limits. For some species (moles, muskrats, beaver), the use of kill-type traps might be the most effective method of dealing with a problem. Always keep in mind that the goal of a wildlife damage program is to solve a problem, not destroy wildlife. If it is necessary to kill the problem animal(s), be humane.

Sources of Assistance

A variety of programs and agencies provide assistance or information on managing wildlife damage problems.

The Kentucky Cooperative Extension Service provides a wide range of information on prevention and control of wildlife damage. County agents and specialists receive up-to-date training on handling a variety of such situations. See the table on page 168 for a listing of educational publications on managing wildlife damage in Kentucky.

The U.S. Department of Agriculture, Animal and Plant Health Inspection Service, Animal Damage Control (USDA/APHIS/ADC) is the agency that provides most of the on-site assistance with bird damage control in Kentucky. APHIS is responsible for all major migratory bird problems, for waterfowl including Canada geese, and for some resident non-game and non-fur-bearing animal problems. APHIS personnel also provide information and advice to people who have other wildlife damage problems. Field representatives of APHIS responsible for Kentucky are located in Louisville. Other field representatives who may work in Kentucky are located in eastern, central, and western Tennessee. People who have wildlife damage problems (including those from beaver) within a county that has a cooperative agreement might be eligible for on-site assistance from APHIS personnel. Contact the USDA/APHIS/ADC office in Louisville for more information.

The primary responsibility of the Kentucky Department of Fish and Wildlife Resources is to manage and preserve wildlife and their habitat in the state. The KDFWR provides information and advice on managing wildlife populations and on preventing damage from resident wildlife species, including white-tailed deer, coyote, and beaver. The KDFWR also issues permits to kill nuisance animals when other appropriate control methods fail.

Some commercial pest control operators assist people in urban areas with managing problem wildlife species. Many pest control operators handle problems with Norway and black rats, house mice, pigeons, starlings, house sparrows, raccoons, and squirrels for a fee. These companies are listed in your local telephone directory. Commercial pest control operators must obtain a license from KDFWR for controlling vertebrate wildlife populations. This permit, along with appropriate certification and licensing through the Division of Pesticides in the Kentucky Department of Agriculture, allows the use of any chemical or device approved by the Environmental Protection Agency and the Kentucky Department of Agriculture for controlling wildlife damage.

Other sources of information and assistance include the Kentucky Department of Agriculture and the Health Department. The Kentucky Department of Agriculture is responsible for consultation and technical assistance in controlling late spring, summer, and early fall small (one or two trees) residential blackbird and starling roosts. Larger bird-roosting problems must be referred to the USDA/APHIS/ADC office in Louisville. The Health Department is responsible for problems associated with commensal rodents and situations involving public health nuisances.

To a large extent, urban wildlife owes its existence to the handiwork and generosity of man. Wildlife tends to concentrate where adequate food, shelter, and water are made available. Sometimes you are faced with hard choices and must balance your needs with the needs of the wildlife around you. When you develop habitat for one species or group of wildlife, other species may come into conflict with your goals. It is those occasional periods when wildlife is in the wrong place at the wrong time that cause homeowners aggravation. You can plan for potential problems and prevent them through good sanitation, building maintenance, and animal-proofing of your property. Of course, you cannot completely eliminate some wildlife problems. The key is to reduce the damage to a tolerable level and strive ultimately for a peaceful coexistence with your wildlife guests. Once steps have been taken to keep animals out of the house, garage, or garden, wildlife can live in harmony with you.

References

Hodge, G.R. 1991. *A Pocket Guide to the Humane Control of Wildlife in Cities and Towns.* Helena, Mont.: Falcon Press. 116 pp.

Hyngstrom, S.E., R.E. Timm, and G.E. Larson. 1994. *Prevention and Control of Wildlife Damage,* vols. 1 and 2. Lincoln: Univ. of Nebraska Cooperative Extension Service.

Native Wildflowers, Grasses, and Ferns

APPENDIX

THIS TABLE IS A LIST of attractive native Kentucky plants. Those with an asterisk (*) are difficult to propagate and the nursery may have collected them from the wild. Please ask the nursery the origins of its plants (nursery-propagated or wild-collected). Plants appear in alphabetical order by their common names. This is not an exhaustive list; rather, these are species commonly available at nurseries in the region.

KEY

Habitat and sunlight	Flower Colors	Season
F = forest (shade)	B = blue	Sp = spring
P = prairie or meadow (sun)	G = green	S = summer
A = aquatic (sun)	L = light purple/pink	F = fall
	O = orange	
	P = purple	**Other values**
Soil and water conditions	R = red	C = cut flowers
D = dry	V = violet	D = dried flowers or fruit
M = moist	W = white	F = interesting foliage
W = wet	Y = yellow	G = ground cover
		S = showy blooms
		Td = drought tolerant
		Tf = flood tolerant
		W = water garden plant

Common Name	Scientific Name	Habitat	Soil	Plant Height	Flower Color	Season	Other Values
Allegheny spurge	Pachysandra procumbens	F	M	6-10	W	Sp	
Alumroot	Heuchera americana	F	D/M	8-10	G	S	G
American lotus	Nelumbo lutea	A	W	12-48	Y	S	DFSW
Anemone							
false rue	Isopyrum biternatum	F	M	6-12	W	Sp	FG
rue	Anemonella thalictroides	F	M	4-6	W-P	Sp	S
tall	Anemone virginiana	F	M	20-30	W	S	
Arrowhead	Sagittaria latifolia	A	W	8-14	W	S	FSW
Asters							
aromatic	Aster oblongifolius	P	M	8-10	BP	F	CSTd
calico	Aster cordifolius	P	D/M	12-24	W	F	CSTd
downy	Aster pilosus	P	D	12-24	W	F	CSTd
Maryland golden	Chrysopsis mariana	P	D/M	12-24	Y	F	CSTd
New England	Aster novae-angliae	P	M	24-48	P	F	CSTd
Short's	Aster shortii	F	D/M	24-36	BP	F	CS
silky	Aster sericeus	P	D	8-18	P	F	CSTd
sky blue	Aster oolentangiensis	P	D	18-36	B	F	CSTd
smooth	Aster laevis	P	D	18-36	BW	F	CSTd
Stoke's	Stokesia asteroides	P	D/M	24-36	B	S/F	STd
Baneberry	Actaea rubra	F	M	12-18	W	S	F
white	Actaea pachypoda	F	M	12-18	W	S	F
Beardtongue							
hairy	Penstemon hirsutus	F/P	M	12-18	BV	Sp/S	
Small's	Penstemon smallii	P	M	12-18	P	Sp	CS
smooth	Penstemon digitalis	P	M	18-36	W	S	CSTd
Bee balm, red	Monarda didyma	P	M	18-36	R	S	CS
Bergamot	Monarda fistulosa	P	M	18-36	B	S	CDS
white	Monarda clinopodia	F	M	18-36	W	S	CDS
Bellflower	Campanula americana	F	M	24-60	BV	S	CS
Bellwort*							
large flowered	Uvularia grandiflora	F	M	8-12	Y	Sp	S
small flowered	Uvularia perfoliata	F	M	8-12	Y	Sp	S
bishop's-cap	Mitella diphylla	F	M	6-10	W	Sp	FG
Black cohosh	Cimicifuga racemosa	F	M	48-72	W	Sp	FS
Black-eyed Susans							
biennial	Rudbeckia hirta	P	M	18-24	Y	S	CS
brown-eyed	Rudbeckia triloba	P	M	18-36	Y	S/F	CSTd
goldenglow	Rudbeckia laciniata	P	M	24-48	Y	S/F	STf
orange-coneflower	Rudbeckia fulgida	P	M	18-36	Y	S/F	STd
Sweet Sue	Rudbeckia subtomentosa	P	M	18-36	Y	S	CSTd
Blazing stars							
button	Liatris squarrosa	P	D	12-18	P	S/F	DSTd
dwarf	Liatris cylindracea	P	D	8-12	P	F	DSTd
prairie	Liastris pycnostachya	P	M	12-36	P	S	DSTd
rough	Liatris aspera	P	D	24-48	P	F	STd
spiked	Liatris spicata	P	D	24-48	P	S/F	DSTd
Bloodroot*	Sanguinaria canadensis	F	M	4-8	W	Sp	FS
Bluebells, Virginia*	Mertensia virginica	F	M	8-12	B/L	Sp	GSTf
Blue-eyed grass*	Sisyrinchium angustifolium	P	D/M	6-18	B	Sp/S	STd
Blue sage	Salvia azurea	P	D	18-36	B	S	STd
Blue star	Amsonia tabernaemontana	F/P	W	24-40	B	S	STf
Boltonia	Boltonia asteroides	P	M/W	12-24	B/W	S	CS
Boneset	Eupatorium perfoliatum	P	M	36-60	W	S	CS

Common Name	Scientific Name	Habitat	Soil	Plant Height	Flower Color	Season	Other Values
Bundleflower	Desmanthus illinoensis	P	M/W	12-24	W	S	D
Bush clover							
round-headed	Lespedeza capitata	P	D/M	24-48	W	S	
Virginia	Lespedeza virginiana	P	D/M	24-48	L	S	
Buttercup, hairy	Ranunculus hispidus	F	M	6-12	Y	Sp	G
Butterfly pea	Clitoria mariana	F	D	vine	L	S	GS
Cactus, prickly pear	Opuntia humifusa	P	D	8-12	Y	S	FSTd
Cardinal flower	Lobelia cardinalis	F/P	M/W	24-36	R	S/F	CSTf
Cattail	Typha latifolia	A	W	36-72	GY	S/F	DWTf
Columbine	Aquilegia canadensis	F/P	M	12-36	R	Sp/S	FS
Coneflowers							
pale purple	Echinacea pallida	P	D	36-48	L	S	CDSTd
purple	Echinacea purpurea	P	M	36-48	P	S	CDS
yellow (gray)	Ratibida pinnata	P	M	36-48	Y	S	CS
Coreopsis							
eared	Coreopsis auriculata	P	M	8-12	Y	Sp	STd
lanceleaf	Coreopsis lanceolata	P	M	12-36	Y	Sp/S	CSTd
large	Coreopsis major	F	D	24-48	Y	S	STd
tall	Coreopsis tripteris	P	D	36-120	Y	S/F	CSTd
Culver's root	Veronicastrum virginicum	P	M/W	36-48	W	S	CSTf
Cup plant	Silphium perfoliatum	P	M	36-60	Y	S	CSTd
Dittany	Cunila origanoides	F	D	12-18	BL	S/F	F
Dutchman's breeches	Dicentra cucullaria	F	M	8-12	W	Sp	FS
Ferns*							
bracken	Pteridium aquilinum	F	D	18-36			
Christmas	Polystichum acrostichoides	F	M	12-18			
cinnamon	Osmunda cinnamomea	F	W/M	18-60			
fragile	Cystopteris fragilis	F	M	6-8			
glade	Athyrium pycnocarpon	F	M	18-36			
grape	Botrychium virginianum	F	M	8-12			
lady	Athyrium filix-femina	F	M	10-18			
leatherwood	Dryopteris marginalis	F	M	12-24			
maidenhair	Adiantum pedatum	F	M	8-12			
New York	Thelypteris noveboracensis	F	M	12-24			
royal	Osmunda regalis	F	M	12-18			
sensitive	Onoclea sensibilis	F/P	M/W	12-18			
spleenwort	Asplenium platyneuron	F	D/M	8-12			
walking	Camptosorus rhizophyllus	F	M	4-12			
wood	Dryopteris spinulosa	F	M	12-28			
Flowering spurge	Euphorbia corollata	P	D	12-36	W	S	CTd
Flower-of-an-hour	Talinum calcaricum	P	D	2-4	P	S	STd
Foamflower	Tiarella cordifolia	F	M	6-10	W	Sp	
Galax	Galax urceolata	F	M	6-10	W	Sp	
Gentian							
bottle	Gentiana andrewsii	P	M/W	8-12	B	S	S
soapwort	Gentiana saponaria	P	M/W	12-24	B	F	S
white	Gentiana alba	P	M	24-36	W	F	S
Geranium, wild*	Geranium maculatum	F	M	12-24	L	Sp	S
Ginger, wild*	Asarum canadense	F	M	4-8	L	Sp	FG
Ginseng	Panax quinquefolium	F	M	6-12	W	S	F

Common Name	Scientific Name	Habitat	Soil	Plant Height	Flower Color	Season	Other Values
Goatsbeard	*Aruncus dioicus*	F	M	24-48	W	S	CFS
Goatsbeard	*Pyrrhopappus carolinianus*	P	M	24-36	Y	Sp	D
Goatsrue	*Tephrosia virginiana*	F/P	D	12-24	L	S	GS
Golden club	*Orontium aquaticum*	A	W	8-12	GY	S	
Goldenrods							
grass-leaved	*Euthamia graminifolia*	P	M	24-48	Y	S/F	CTf
gray	*Solidago nemoralis*	P	M	8-30	Y	F	CSTd
rigid	*Solidago rigida*	P	D	24-48	Y	S/F	CSTd
rough	*Solidago rugosa*	P	M	24-48	Y	S/F	CSTf
showy	*Solidago speciosa*	P	M	24-36	Y	S/F	CS
zigzag	*Solidago caesia*	F/P	M	12-24	Y	S/F	CS
Goldenseal	*Hydrastis canadensis*	F	M	8-12	W	Sp	F
Grasses							
arrowfeather	*Aristida purpurascens*	P	D	24-36			
bluestem, big	*Andropogon gerardii*	P	M	48-60			
bottlebrush	*Elymus hystrix*	F/P	M	24-48			
broomsedge	*Andropogon virginicus*	P	D/M	24-36			
broomsedge, Elliot's	*Andropogon gyrans*	P	D/M	24-36			
dwarf bamboo	*Dulichium arundinaceum*	P	W	36-60			
gama grass	*Tripsacum dactyloides*	P	M/W	48-84			
Indian grass	*Sorghastrum nutans*	P	D/M	48-72			
June grass	*Koeleria macrantha*	P	D	12-24			
little bluestem	*Schizachyrium scoparium*	P	D/M	12-36			
manna grass	*Glyceria striata*	P	W	36-48			
plumegrass, silver	*Saccharum alopecuroides*	P	M/W	60-108			
prairie cordgrass	*Spartina pectinata*	P	W	36-72			
prairie dropseed	*Sporobolus compositus*	P	D/M	36-48			
prairie switchgrass	*Panicum virgatum*	P	M/W	36-60			
river oats	*Chasmanthium latifolia*	F/P	W	18-48			
ryegrass							
Virginia	*Elymus virginicus*	F/P	W	18-24			
woodland	*Elymus villosus*	F/P	D/M	18-24			
side-oats grama	*Bouteloua curtipendula*	P	D	18-24			
splitbeard bluestem	*Andropogon ternarius*	P	M	18-36			
wild cane	*Arundinaria gigantea*	F/P	W/M	60-84			
wood reed	*Cinna arundinacea*	P	W	18-48			
Gerardia	*Agalinis tenuifolia*	P	M/W	12-36	P	S/F	FS
Green and gold	*Chrysogonum virginianum*	F	M	4-6	Y	Sp/F	FGS
Green dragon	*Arisaema dracontium*	F	M/W	10-18	G	Sp/S	
Groundnut	*Apios americana*	F	W	vine	LP	S	FG
Hepatica*	*Hepatica nobilis*	F	M	6-8	W/B	Sp	FG
Hoary puccoon	*Lithospermum canescens*	P	D	6-12	Y	Sp	STd
Horsemint	*Monarda punctata*	P	M	24-36	L		
Horsetail	*Equisetum hyemale*	P	W	8-24	G		FW
Hyacinth, wild*	*Camassia scilloides*	F	M	18-36	B/W	Sp	S
Indian pink	*Spigelia marilandica*	F	M	12-24	R/Y	Sp/S	S
Indigo							
blue	*Baptisia australis*	P	M	48-60	B	S	CFS
white	*Baptisia alba*	P	M/W	48-60	W	S	CFS
Iris							
blue flag	*Iris virginica*	A	W	8-12	B/V	Sp/S	CSW
copper	*Iris fulva*	A	W	8-12	R	Sp/S	CSW

Common Name	Scientific Name	Habitat	Soil	Plant Height	Flower Color	Season	Other Values
dwarf*	Iris verna	F	D	6-8	B/V	Sp	FGS
dwarf crested*	Iris cristata	F	M	6-8	B/V	Sp	FGS
Ironweed	Vernonia gigantea	P	M/D	18-48	P	S/F	CSTd
Jack-in-the-pulpit*	Arisaema triphyllum	F	M	10-12	GP	Sp	D
Jacob's ladder*	Polemonium reptans	F	M	8-12	B	Sp	FG
Jewelweed							
pale	Impatiens pallida	F	W	24-60	Y	S/F	FTf
spotted	Impatiens capensis	F	W	24-60	O	S/F	FTf
Joe-pye weed	Eupatorium maculatum	P	M/W	36-60	P	S/F	CTf
Larkspur							
Carolina	Delphinium carolinianum	F	M	24-48	B/W	Sp	S
dwarf	Delphinium tricorne	F	M	8-18	B/W	Sp	S
Lily							
Canada	Lilium canadense	F	M	24-60	O	S	S
Michigan	Lilium michiganense	F	M/W	24-60	O	S	S
Turk's cap	Lilium superbum	F/P	M	36-48	O	S	S
wood	Lilium philadelphicum	F/P	M/D	24-36	O	S	S
Little brown jug	Hexastylis arifolia	F	D/M	4-6	W	Sp	FG
Lizard tail	Saururus cernuus	A	W	8-24	W	S	WTf
Lobelia							
blue	Lobelia siphilitica	P/F	M	8-36	B	S/F	CS
spiked	Lobelia spicata	P	D/M	8-36	B/W	S	CTd
Loosestrife, whorled	Lysimachia quadrifolia	P	D/M	12-24	Y	S	
Mallow, rose	Hibiscus moscheutos	A/P	W/M	24-48	L/W	S	WSTf
Marsh marigold	Caltha palustris	A	W	8-12	Y	S	WS
Mayapple*	Podophyllum peltatum	F	M	8-24	W	Sp/S	FG
Meadowbeauty	Rhexia mariana	P	W	12-18	L	S	STf
Meadow rue	Thalictrum dioicum	P	M	24-48	GW	S	
Meehania	Meehania cordata	F	M	4-8	B	Sp	
Milkweed							
butterfly	Asclepias tuberosa	P	D/M	8-24	O	S/F	CSTd
common	Asclepias syriaca	P	D/M	24-48	L	S	CSTd
green	Asclepias viridis	P	D/M	18-36	G	S	CSTd
purple	Asclepias purpurascens	P	D/M	18-36	P	S	CSTd
red (swamp)	Asclepias incarnata	P	M/W	18-36	L	S	CS
Mistflower	Eupatorium coelestinum	P	M/W	24	B/V	S/F	CSTf
Monkeyflower	Mimulus alatus	F	W/M	12-18	B	S/F	
Mountain mint	Pycnanthemum tenuifolium	F	D/M	12-18	W	S	CFSTd
hoary	Pycnanthemum pycnan-themoides	P	D/M	12-18	W	S	CFTd
Obedient plant	Physostegia virginiana	P	D/M	12-18	L	F	CSTd
Onion, nodding	Allium cernuum	P	D/M	12-18	L/W	S/F	CSTd
Orchids	(see note at end of table)						
Partridgeberry	Mitchella repens	F	M	1-2	W	Sp	G
Partridge pea	Chamaecrista fasiculata	P	D/M	12-24	Y	S/F	FSTd
Passionflower	Passiflora incarnata	P	M/W	vine	L/V	S	S
Pearly everlasting	Gnaphthalium obtusi-folium	P	M	24-36	W	F	D
Petunia, wild	Ruellia humilis	P	D/M	8-12	B/V	S	S

Common Name	Scientific Name	Habitat	Soil	Plant Height	Flower Color	Season	Other Values
Phacelia, purple	Phacelia bipinnatifida	F	M	12-24	B/V	Sp	FGS
Phlox							
downy	Phlox pilosa	P	D/M	8-12	L	Sp/S	CSTd
meadow	Phlox maculata	P	D/M	8-12	L/W	S/F	CS
moss	Phlox subulata	P	D	6-12	L	Sp	FGS
smooth	Phlox carolina	P	M/W	12-18	L/P	S	CS
summer	Phlox paniculata	P	M	18-48	L/P/V	S/F	CS
wild blue*	Phlox divaricata	F	M	8-12	B/V	Sp	S
Pickerel rush	Pontederia cordata	A	W	12-36	B	S	SW
Pinks							
fire	Silene virginica	F	M/D	10-18	R	Sp/S	S
round-leaved	Silene rotundifolia	F	M	10-18	R	Sp/S	S
wild	Silene caroliniana	F/P	D	8-12	L	Sp	GSTd
royal catchfly	Silene regia	P	M	24-48	R	S	CSTd
Poppy, wood	Stylophorum diphyllum	F	M	12-24	Y	Sp	S
Prairie clover							
purple	Dalea purpurea	P	M	12-18	P	S	STd
white	Dalea candida	P	D	12-36	W	S	STd
Prairie dock	Silphium terebinthinaceum	P	D	36-60	Y	S/F	CSTd
cut-leaf	Silphium pinnatifidum	P	D	36-60	Y	S/F	CS
Primrose							
evening	Oenothera biennis	P	D/M	24-60	Y	S/F	STd
showy	Oenothera speciosa	P	D/M	8-12	Y	S	STd
sundrops	Oenothera fruticosa (tetragona)	P	M	12-24	Y	S/F	STd
Quinine, wild	Parthenium integrifolium	P	M	24-48	W	S	CTd
Ragwort							
golden	Senecio aureus	F	W	12-30	Y	Sp	Tf
round-leaved	Senecio obovatus	F	D	10-28	Y	Sp	Td
Rattlesnake master	Eryngium yuccifolium	P	D	24-48	W	S	CFTd
Rose gentian	Sabatia angularis	P	D/M	12-18	P	S	STd
Rosinweed	Silphium integrifolium	P	M/W	24-48	Y	S	CSTd
Saxifrage, early	Saxifraga virginiensis	F	M	8-12	W	Sp	FG
Shooting star	Dodecatheon meadia	F	M	8-12	W	Sp	S
Snakeroot, white	Eupatorium rugosum	F	M	24-48	W	F	S
Sneezeweed	Helenium autumnale	P	M/W	18-24	Y	S/F	CTf
Solomon's seal*	Polygonatum biflorum	F	M	12-36	W	S	
false*	Smilacina racemosa	F	M	12-36	W	Sp	S
Spatterdock	Nuphar lutea spp. advena	A	W	12-36	Y	S/F	SFW
Spiderlily	Hymenocallis caroliniana	A	W	24-48	W	S/F	SFW
Spiderwort							
Ohio	Tradescantia ohiensis	P	M/W	18-36	B	S	CS
Virginia	Tradescantia virginiana	F	M	12-24	B	Sp/S	CS
Spring beauty	Claytonia virginica	F	M	2-4	W	Sp	S
St. John's-wort							
glade	Hypericum dolabriforme	P	D	8-12	Y	S	GSTd
smooth	Hypericum sphaerocarpum	P	D	12-24	Y	S	Td
Stargrass	Hypoxis hirsuta	F/P	D	4-8	Y	Sp	S
Stonecrop	Sedum ternatum	F	M	2-4	W	Sp/S	FG
pink	Sedum pulchellum	F/P	D	4-15	P	Sp/S	STd
Strawberry, wild	Fragaria virginiana	F/P	M	4-6	W	Sp	G

Common Name	Scientific Name	Habitat	Soil	Plant Height	Flower Color	Season	Other Values
Sunflowers							
downy	*Helianthus mollis*	P	D/M	36-60	Y	S/F	CSTd
narrow-leaved	*Helianthus angustifolius*	P	M/W	36-48	Y	F	CSTf
ox-eye	*Heliopsis helianthoides*	P	M	24-48	Y	S	CSTd
rough-leaved	*Helianthus strumosus*	F	D	36-60	Y	S	CS
thin-leaved	*Helianthus decapetalus*	F/P	M	24-60	Y	S	S
western	*Helianthus occidentalis*	P	D	18-24	Y	S	Td
woodland	*Helianthus microcephalus*	F	D	36-60	Y	S	S
Sweet Cicely	*Osmorhiza longistylis*	F	M	18-36	W	S	F
Sweet flag	*Acorus calamus*	A/P	W	48-60	G/Y	S	DFWTf
Thimbleflower	*Anenome virginiana*	F	D/M	24-48	W	S	Td
Tickseed sunflower	*Bidens aristosa*	P	D/M/W	18-36	Y	S/F	STdTf
Trailing arbutus	*Epigaea repens*	F	D	2-3	L	Sp	G
Trillium	(see note at end of table)						
Trout lily*							
white	*Erythronium albidum*	F	M	4	W	Sp	FGS
yellow	*Erythronium americanum*	F	M	4	Y	Sp	FGS
Turtlehead	*Chelone glabra*	F/P	W	12-18	L/W	F	CSTf
Twinleaf*	*Jeffersonia diphylla*	F	M	8-12	W	Sp	FS
Vervain							
blue	*Verbena hastata*	P	W	18-60	B/V	F	CSTf
rose	*Glandularia canadensis*	P	D	6-8	L/P	Sp/S	GSTd
Violets							
birdfoot*	*Viola pedata*	P	D	2-4	B/V	Sp	FGSTd
Canada	*Viola canadensis*	F	M	6-10	W	Sp	
common blue	*Viola sororia*	F	M	2-4	B/V	Sp	FG
spurred	*Viola rostrata*	F	M	2-4	B/V	Sp	FG
sweet white	*Viola blanda*	F	M	2-4	W .	Sp	FG
yellow	*Viola hastata*	F	M	2-4	Y	Sp	FG
Waterleaf	*Hydrophyllum canadense*	F	M	12-36	L/W	S	F
Water plantain	*Alisma subcordatum*	A	W	12-18	W	S	WS
Water primrose	*Ludwigia peploides*	A	W	4-6	Y	S/F	W
Wintergreen	*Gaultheria procumbens*	F	M	12	W	Sp	FG
Wood mint	*Blephilia ciliata*	P	D	6-12	P	Sp	DTd

Note: Few, if any, orchids or trilliums are nursery propagated. Most are collected from the wild, and numerous popu-lations of these splendid woodland wildflowers are becoming rare as a result. Please request a written guarantee when purchasing these plants from the nursery to ensure they are nursery propagated. The following trilliums are native to Kentucky: sessile *(Trillium sessile)*, snow *(T. nivale)*, recurved *(T. recurvatum)*, yellow *(T. luteum)*, painted *(T. undulatum)*, large-flowered *(T. grandiflorum)*, erect *(T. erectum)*, and bent *(T. flexipes)*. Over a dozen species of orchids are native to the state. Some of the most common are: lily-leaved twayblade *(Liparis* spp.), rattlesnake plan-tain *(Goodyera pubsecens)*, ladies-tresses *(Spiranthes* spp.), yellow lady's slipper *(Cypripedium pubscens)*, pink lady's slipper *(Cypripedium acaule)*, showy orchis *(Galearis spectabilis)*, whorled pogonia *(Isotria verticillata)*, spreading pogonia *(Cleistes divaricata)*, purple fringeless *(Platanthera peramoena)*, pale green *(Platanthera flava)*, and yellow fringed *(Platanthera cilaris)*.

Butterflies of Kentucky and Host Plants

APPENDIX

T HE FOLLOWING CHECKLIST of the butterflies of Kentucky was reported by Dr. Charles Covell, University of Louisville. It includes notes on habitat association and larval (host) plant food preferences for species that are abundant, common, or frequently observed. Brackets indicate questionable specimens or sight records for Kentucky.

KEY		
Abundance	**Habitat Type**	**Habitat Location**
A = abundant	F = woodland or forest	S = statewide
C = common	M = meadow or prairie	E = eastern Kentucky
F = frequent	C = woodland clearings	C = central Kentucky
U = uncommon	S = savanna	W = western Kentucky
R = rare	W = wetlands	
E = probably endangered or extinct		
S = stray, not native to Kentucky	An * indicates that the best opportunity for viewing is during migration.	

Common Name	Scientific Name	Abundance	Habitat	Host Plants
Silver-spotted skipper	*Epargyreus clarus*	A	F/M;S	locusts (*Robinia* spp.) tick-trefoils (*Desmodium* spp.) bush clovers (*Lespedeza* spp.) milk vetches (*Astragalus* spp.) groundnut *(Apios americana)* hog peanut *(Amphicarpaea bracteata)* trefoils (*Lotus* spp.) wild beans (*Phaseolus* spp.)
Long-tailed skipper	*Urbanus proteus*	S	M	
Golden-banded skipper	*Autochton cellus*	U	F/W;S	
Hoary edge	*Achalarus lyciades*	U	F/M/S;S	
Northern cloudy wing	*Thorybes pylades*	C	F;S	bush clovers (*Lespedeza* spp.) tick-trefoils (*Desmodium* spp.)
Southern cloudy wing	*Thorybes bathyllus*	C	F/C;S	groundnut *(Apios americana)* tick-trefoils (*Desmodium* spp.) fuzzy bean (*Strophyostyles* spp.)
Confused cloudy wing	*Thorybes confusis*	U	C;S	
Scalloped sooty wing	*Staphylus hayhurstii*	U	F;S	
Dreamy dusky wing	*Erynnis icelus*	C	F/W;S	poplars (*Populus* spp.) birches (*Betula* spp.) willows (*Salix* spp.) locusts (*Robinia* spp.)
Sleepy dusky wing	*Erynnis brizo*	A	F;S	oaks (*Quercus* spp.)
Juvenal's dusky wing	*Erynnis juvenalis*	A	F;S	oaks (*Quercus* spp.)
Horace's dusky wing	*Erynnis horatius*	C	F;S	oaks (*Quercus* spp.)
Mottled dusky wing	*Erynnis martialis*	U	F/C/S;S	
Zarucco dusky wing	*Erynnis zarucco*	R*	M;S	
Funeral dusky wing	*Erynnis funeralis*	R*	M;S	
Columbine dusky wing	*Erynnis lucilius*	R	F/C;E	
Wild indigo dusky wing	*Erynnis baptisiae*	A	S/C/M:S	false indigos (*Baptisia* spp.) milk vetch *(Astragalus canadensis)* rattlebox *(Crotalaria sagittalis)*
Grizzled skipper	*Pyrgus centaurae*	R	M;E	
Checkered skipper	*Pyrgus communis*	C	M;S	alkali mallows (*Sida* spp.) mallows (*Malva* spp.) [no common names] *(Modiola caroliniana, Anoda cristata)*

Common Name	Scientific Name	Abundance	Habitat	Host Plants
Common sooty wing	Pholisora catullus	C	M;S	Indian mallow (Abutilon theophrasti) pigweed (Amaranthus spp.)
Swarthy skipper	Nastra lherminier	U	M/W;S	
Clouded skipper	Lerema accius	U*	M/C/S;S	
Least skipperling	Ancyloxipha numitor	A	F/W;S	wild rice (Zizaniopsis miliacease)
European skipper	Thymelicus lineola	F(I)	M;C/E	
Fiery skipper	Thylephila phyleus	F	M;S	Kentucky bluegrass (Poa pratensis)
Leonard's skipper	Hesperia leonardus	F	C/F;C/E	
Cobweb skipper	Hesperia metea	U	S;S	
Indian skipper	Hesperia sassacus	E		
Peck's skipper	Polites peckius	A	M;S	Kentucky bluegrass (Poa pratensis)
Tawny-edged skipper	Polites themistocles	A	M;S	Kentucky bluegrass (Poa pratensis) panic grasses (Panicum spp.) [no common name] (Dichan-thelium clandestinum)
Crossline skipper	Polites origenes	F	M/S;S	purple top (Tridens flavus) little bluestem (Schizachyrium scoparium)
Rusty broken dash	Wallengrenia otho	R*	W/S	
Dark broken dash	Wallengrenia egeremet	A	W/F;S	panic grasses (Panicum spp.) crabgrass (Digitaria sanguinalis)
Little glassywing	Pompeius verna	U	S/M;S	
Sachem	Atalopedes campestris	A	M;S	[no common name] (Digitaria spp.) fescue grasses (Festuca spp.)
Delaware skipper	Atrytone logan	U	M;S	
Hobomok skipper	Poanes hobomok	F	F;S	panic grasses (Panicum spp.) bluegrasses (Poa spp.)
Yehl skipper	Poanes yehl	C	W;W	cane (Arundinaria spp.)
Zabulon skipper	Poanes zabulon	C	S;S	purple top grasses (Tridens spp.) love grasses (Eragrostis spp.)
Broad-winged skipper	Poanes viator	R	W;W	

Common Name	Scientific Name	Abundance	Habitat	Host Plants
Dion skipper	Euphyes dion	F	W/M;S	sedges (Carex spp.) bulrushes (Scirpus spp.)
Duke's skipper	Euphyes dukesi	R	W;W	
Eastern dun skipper	Euphyes vestris metacomet	C	W/F;S	sedges (Carex spp.)
Dusted skipper	Atrytonopsis hianna	U	M;S	
Pepper & salt skipper	Amblyscirtes hegon	U	C/S	
Textor skipper	Amblyscirtes aesculapius	U	F;S	
Roadside skipper	Amblyscirtes vialis	U	F;S	
Bells' skipper	Amblyscirtes bellis	U	F/W;W/C	
Eufala skipper	Lerodea eufala	R*	M/S	
Ocola skipper	Panoquina ocola	U*	W;S	
Pipevine swallowtail	Battus philenor	A	F;S	Dutchman's pipevine (Aristolochia spp.)
(Polydamas swallowtail)	Battus polydamas	S*	F	
Zebra swallowtail	Eurytides marcellus	C	F;S	paw paw (Asimina triloba)
Black swallowtail	Papilio polyxenes	C	F/S/M;S	[no common name] (Angelica spp.) dill (Anethum graveolens) celery (Apium graveolens) carrots (Daucus spp.) honeywort (Cryptotaenia canadensis) fennel (Foeniculum volgare)
Joan's swallowtail	Papilio joanae	R		
Giant swallowtail	Heraclides cresphontes	F	F	New Jersey tea (Ceanothus spp.) buckthorns (Rhamnus spp.) hop tree (Ptelea trifoliata)
Tiger swallowtail	Pterourus glaucus	C	F;S	tulip poplar (Liriodendron tulipifera) cherries (Prunus spp.) hornbeam (Carpinus caroliniana) spicebush (Lindera benzoin) sassafras (Sassafras albidum) hop tree (Ptelea triofoliata) ash trees (Fraxinus spp.) catalpa (Catalpa bignonioides) cottonwood (Populus deltoides)
Spicebush swallowtail	Pterourus troilus	C	F;S	sassafras (Sassafras albidum) spicebush (Lindera benzoin)

Common Name	Scientific Name	Abundance	Habitat	Host Plants
Palamedes swallowtail	Pterourus palamedes	R*	W;S	
Checkered white	Pontia protodice	U	M;S	
West Virginia white	Pieris virginiensis	C	F;E/C	bittercress (Cardamine spp.)
Cabbage butterfly	Pieris rapae	C	S	numerous spp. in mustard family (Brassicaceae)
Olympia marble	Euchloe olympia	U	C/M;E/C	
Falcate orange tip	Paramidea midea	C	S;S	bittercress (Cardamine spp.) peppergrass (Lepidium spp.) rockcress (Arabis spp.)
Clouded sulphur	Colias philodice	A	M;S	false indigos (Baptisia spp.) milk vetch (Astragalus spp.) trefoils (Lotus spp.) locusts (Robinia spp.) vetches (Vicia spp.)
Alfalfa butterfly	Colias eurytheme	A	M;S	false indigos (Baptisia spp.) milk vetch (Astragalus spp.) trefoils (Lotus spp.) locusts (Robinia spp.) vetches (Vicia spp.) bush clovers (Lespedeza spp.)
Dog face	Zerene cesonia	U	M;W	
Cloudless sulphur	Phoebis sennae	C	M;S	partridge peas (Chamaechrista spp.) sennas (Senna spp.)
(Large orange sulphur)	Phoebis agarithe	S*	F/C/S;W	
(Orange-barred sulphur)	Phoebis philea	S*	M;S	
(Lyside)	Kricogonia lyside	S*	M;S	
Sleepy orange	Eurema nicippe	F	M;S	partridge peas (Chamaechrista spp.) sennas (Senna spp.)
Dainty sulphur	Nathalis iole	U*	M;S	
Harvester	Feniseca tarquinius	U	F/W;S	
American copper	Lycaena phlaeas americana	C	M;S	dockweed (Rumex spp.)
Bronze copper	Hyllolycaena hyllus	F	M/W;C/W	dockweed (Rumex spp.)
Great purple hairstreak	Atlides halesus	R	F;S	
Coral hairstreak	Harkenclenus titus	C	F;S	cherries (Prunus spp.)
Acadian hairstreak	Satyrium acadicum	R	W	

Common Name	Scientific Name	Abundance	Habitat	Host Plants
Edward's hairstreak	*Satyrium edwardsii*	C	F;S	oaks (*Quercus* spp.)
Banded hairstreak	*Satyrium calanus*	C	F;S	box elder (*Acer negundo*) chestnut (*Castanea dentata*) hickories (*Carya* spp.) oaks (*Quercus* spp.) walnuts (*Juglans* spp.) black willow (*Salix nigra*)
Hickory hairstreak	*Satyrium caryaevorum*	U	F;E/C	
Striped hairstreak	*Satyrium liparops*	U	F/M;S	
Red-banded hairstreak	*Calycopis cecrops*	U	F;S	
Olive hairstreak	*Callophrys grynea*	C	S;S	eastern red cedar (*Juniperus virginianus*)
Brown elfin	*Callophrys augustus*	U	F/W;E	
Frosted elfin	*Callophrys irus*	R	F;E/C	
Eastern pine elfin	*Callophrys niphon*	U	F;S	
Henry's elfin	*Callophrys henrici*	C	S;S	black cherry (*Prunus serotina*) redbud (*Cercis canadensis*) blueberries (*Vaccinium* spp.) hollies (*Ilex* spp.) huckleberry (*Gaylussacia baccata*)
Northern hairstreak	*Fixsenia ontario*	U		
White-M hairstreak	*Parrhasius m-album*	R	F;S	
Gray hairstreak	*Strymon melinus*	C	M;S	pecan (*Carya illinoensis*) hawthorn (*Crateaegus marshallii*) false indigo (*Amorpha fruitcosa*) milk vetches (*Astragalus* spp.) smartweeds (*Polygonum* spp.) tick-trefoils (*Desmodium* spp.) bush clovers (*Lespedeza* spp.) wild beans (*Phaseolus* spp.) vetches (*Vicia* spp.) others
Early hairstreak	*Erora laeta*	R	F;E/C	
Marine blue	*Leptotes marina*	R*	M;W	
Eastern tailed blue	*Everes comyntas*	A	C/W	bush clovers (*Lespedeza* spp.) vetches (*Vicia* spp.) false indigos (*Baptisia* spp.) tick-trefoils (*Desmodium* spp.)

Common Name	Scientific Name	Abundance	Habitat	Host Plants
Spring azure	Celastrina argiolus	C	F;S	cherries (Prunus spp.) dogwoods (Cornus spp.) blueberries (Vaccinium spp.) New Jersey tea (Ceanothus spp.) groundnut (Apios americana) hops (Humulus lupulus) many others
Dusky azure	Celastrina ebenina	C	F;C/E	goatsbeard (Aruncus dioicus)
Appalachian blue	Celastrina neglectamajor	U	F;S	
Silvery blue	Glaucopsyche lygdamus	U	M/S;E/C	
Northern metalmark	Calephelis borealis	U	C;E/C	
Swamp metalmark	Calephelis mutica	R	W;W	
Snout butterfly	Libythaena bachmanii	C	F;S	hackberries (Celtis spp.)
Gulf fritillary	Agraulis vanillae	U*	M/S;S	
Variegated fritillary	Euptoieta claudia	C	M/S;W/S*	passionflower (Passiflora spp.) wild flax (Linum spp.) violets (Viola spp.)
Diana fritillary	Speyeria diana	C	F/E/S*	violets (Viola spp.)
Great-spangled fritillary	Speyeria cybele	A	F/M;S	violets (Viola spp.)
Aphrodite fritillary	Speyeria aphrodite	U	F/M;E/C	
Regal fritillary	Speyeria idalia	E		
Meadow fritillary	Boloria bellona	C	M;S	violets (Viola spp.)
(Silver-bordered fritillary)	Boloria selene	S	M/W;E	
Gorgone checkerspot	Charidryas gorgone	R	M;S	
Silvery checkerspot	Charidryas nycteis	C	F/M;S	black-eyed Susan (Rudbeckia laciniata) vervain (Verbesina helianthoides) sunflowers (Helianthus spp.) goldenrods (Solidago spp.) asters (Aster spp.)
Harris' checkerspot	Charidryas harrisii	S	F/C;E	
Pearl crescent	Phycoides tharos	A	M;S	asters (Aster spp.)
Tawny crescent	Phyciodes batesii	R	F;E	
Baltimore	Euphydryas phaeton	U	W;S	
Question mark	Polygonia interrogationis	C	F;S	elms (Ulmus spp.) hackberries (Celtis spp.)

Common Name	Scientific Name	Abundance	Habitat	Host Plants
Question mark, continued				nettle (*Urtica dioica*) false nettle (*Boehmeria cylindrica*)
Hop merchant	*Polygonia comma*	C	F;S	nettles (*Urtica* spp.) false nettle (*Boehmeria cylindrica*) wood nettle (*Laportea canadensis*) hops (*Humulus lupulus*) American elm (*Ulmus americana*)
Green comma	*Polygonia gaunus*	R	F/W;E	
Gray comma	*Polygonia progne*	R	F;E/W	
(Compton tortoise shell)	*Nymphalis vaualbum*	S*	F;S	
Mourning cloak	*Nymphalis antiopa*	F	F;S	ashes (*Fraxinus* spp.) elms (*Ulmus* spp.) poplars (*Populus* spp.) willows (*Salix* spp.) hackberries (*Celtis* spp.) birches (*Betula* spp.) hops (*Humulus lupulus*)
Milbert tortoise shell	*Aglais milberti*	S*	F;S	
American painted lady	*Vanessa virginiensis*	U	M;S	
Painted lady	*Vanessa cardui*	C	F/M;S	American elm (*Ulmus americana*) mallows (*Malva* spp.) thistles (*Cirsium* spp.) common sunflower (*Helianthus annuus*) nettles (*Urtica* spp.)
Red admiral	*Vanessa atalanta*	C	F/M;S	hops (*Humulus lupulus*) false nettle (*Boehmeria cylindrica*) pellitoria (*Parietaria pensylvanica*) nettles (*Urtica* spp.) wood nettles (*Laportea canadensis*)
Buckeye	*Junonia coenia*	C	M;S	blueheart (*Buchnera americana*) fog fruit (*Phyla* spp.) [no common name] (*Agalinis* spp.) speedwell (*Veronica anagallisaquatica*) [no common name] (*Linaria canadensis*) wild petunia (*Ruellia* spp.)

Common Name	Scientific Name	Abundance	Habitat	Host Plants
White peacock	Anartia jatrophae	S*	M/W;W	
Red-spotted purple	Limenitis arthemis	C	F;S	Cherries (Prunus spp.) poplars (Populus spp.) willows (Salix spp.) hop-hornbeam (Ostrya astyanax virginiana) hornbeam (Carpinus carolinana) blueberry (Vaccinium stamineum) pears (Pyrus spp.) hawthorns (Crataegus spp.) birches (Betula spp.) serviceberry (Amelanchier spp.)
Viceroy	Limenitis archippus	C	F;S	black cherry (Prunus serotina) poplars (Populus spp.) willows (Salix spp.) birches (Betula spp.) crab apples (Malus spp.) hawthorns (Crataegus spp.) serviceberry (Amelanchier spp.)
Goatweed butterfly	Anaea andria	U	F/M;S	
Hackberry butterfly	Asterocampa celtis	C	F;S	hackberry (Celtis spp.)
Tawny emperor	Asterocampa clyton	C	F;S	hackberry (Celtis spp.)
Southern pearly eye	Enodia portlandia missarkae	U	W;W/C	
Northern pearly eye	Enodia anthedon	C	F;S	reed canary grass (Phalaris arundinacea) rice cut grass (Leersia virginica)
Creole pearly eye	Enodia creola	U	W;S	
Appalachian eyed brown	Satyrodes appalachia	C	W;S	beaked rush (Rhynchospora spp.) sedges (Carex spp.)
Gemmed satyr	Cyllopsis gemma	U	W;S	
Carolina satyr	Hermeuptychia sosybius	U		
Little wood nymph	Megisto cymela	C	M/W;S	orchardgrass (Dactylis glomerata) centipede grass (Eremochloa ophiuroides)
Common wood nymph	Cercyonis pegala	C	M	purple top (Tridens flavus) big bluestem (Andropogon gerardii)
Monarch	Danaus plexippus	C	M;S	milkweeds (Asclepias spp.)
(Queen)	Danaus glippus	S*	S/M;W	

Butterflies Likely to Be Seen in Urban Environments

Silver-spotted skipper

Black swallowtail

Cabbage butterfly

Eastern tiger swallowtail

Butterflies Likely to Be Seen in Urban Environments, Continued

Clouded sulphur

Alfalfa butterfly

Eastern tailed blue

Spring azure

Butterflies Likely to Be Seen in Urban Environments, Continued

Great-spangled fritillary

Pearl crescent

Meadow fritillary

Butterflies Likely to Be Seen in Urban Environments, Continued

Question mark

Red admiral

Monarch

Native Wildflowers Attractive to Butterflies and Hummingbirds

APPENDIX

Genus	Species
Anemone	
Anemone	*lancifolia*
	quinquefolia
	virginiana
Aster	
Aster	*acuminaturs*
	concolor
	cordifolius
	divaricatus
	drummondii
	dumosus
	fragilis
	paludosus ssp. hemisphericus
	infirmus
	laevis
	lanceolatus
	lateriflorus (Ionactis linariifolius)
	linariifolius
	macrophyllus
	novae-angliae
	oblongifolius
	ontarionis
	patens var. *patens*
	var. *phlogifolius*
	paternus
	pilosus
	praealtus
	prenanthoides
	puniceus
	radula
	saxicastellii
	schreberi
	sericeus
	shortii
	solidagineus

Genus	Species
	surculosus
	tataricus
	umbellatus
	undulatus
Beardtongue	
Penstemon	*alluviorum*
	calycosus
	canescens
	digitalis
	hirsutus
	laevigatus
	pallidus
	tenuiflorus
	tubiflorus
Bee balm	
Monarda	*citriodora*
	clinopodia
	didyma
	fistulosa
	punctata
Black cohosh	
Cimicifusa	*racemosa*
Black-eyed Susan	
Rudbeckia	*fulgida* var. *fulgida*
	var. *speciosa*
	var. *umbrosa*
	grandiflora
	hirta
	laciniata
	subtomentosa
	triloba

Genus	Species	Genus	Species
Blazing star		**Goldenrod**	
Liatris	*aspera*	*Solidago*	*albopilosa*
	cylindracea		*altissima*
	microcephala		*arguta*
	pycnostachya		*bi-color*
	spheroidea		*buckleyi*
	spicata		*caesia* var. *caesia*
	squarrosa		var. *curtisii*
	squarrulosa		*canadensis*
			curtisii
Boltonia			*flaccidifolia*
Boltonia	*asteroides*		*flexicaulis*
	diffusa		*gigantea*
			gracillima
Butterfly pea			*hispida*
Clitoria	*mariana*		*juncea*
			missouriensis
Cardinal flower			*nemoralis*
Lobelia	*cardinalis*		*odora*
			patula
Coreopsis			*puberula*
Coreopsis	*auriculata*		*radula*
	lanceolata		*rigida*
	major		*roanensis*
	pubescens		*rugosa*
	tinctoria		*rupestris*
	tripteris		*shortii*
	verticillata		*simplex*
			speciosa var. *speciosa*
Culver's root			var. *erecta*
Veronicastrum	*virginicum*		*sphacelata*
			petiolaris
Evening primrose			*ulmifolia*
Oenothera	*biennis*		
	clelandii (very rare in the state)	**Iris**	
	fruticosa var. *fruiticosa*	*Iris*	*fulva*
	var. *tetragona*		*verna*
	lacinata		*versicolor*
	linifolia		
	parviflora	**Ironweed**	
	perennis	*Veronia*	*baldwinii*
	pilosella		*fasciculata*
	speciosa		*gigantea*
	triloba		*missurica*
			noveboracensis
False indigo			
Baptisia	*alba*	**Jewelweed**	
	australis	*Impatiens*	*capensis*
	bracteata var. *bracteata*		*pallida*
	var. *Leucophaea tinctoria*		
		Joe-Pye weed	
Golden aster		*Eupatorium*	*album*
Chrysopsis	*mariana*	*(Ageratina)*	*altissimum*
	pilosa		*aromatica*
			capillifolium
			coelestinum

Genus	Species	Genus	Species
Joe-Pye weed, continued	fistulosum		divaricata
	hyssopifolium		glaberrima
	incarnatum		maculata
	luciae-brauniae		paniculata
	maculatum (very rare in the state)		pilosa
	perfoliatum		stolonifera
	pilosum		subulata
	purpureum		
	rotundifolium	Pinks	
	semiserratum	Silene	caroliniana
	serotinum		ovata
	sessilifolium		regia
	steeliei		rotundifolia
			stellata
Lily			virginica
Lilium	canadense		
	michiganense	Prairie clover	
	philadelphicum	Dalea	candida
	superbum	(Petalostemum)	purpurea
Meadow pink		Prairie dock,	
Sabatia	angularis	Compass plant	
	campanulata	Silphium	integrifolium
			laciniatum
Milkweed			perfoliatum
Asclepias	amplexicaulis		pinnatifidum
	exaltata		terebinthinaceum
	hirtella		trifoliatum
	incarnata		wasiotense
	perennis		
	purpurascens	Purple coneflower	
	quadrifolia	Echinacea	pallida
	syriaca		purpurea
	tuberosa		
	variegata	Ragwort	
	verticillata	Senecio	anonymus
	viridiflora		aureus
	viridis		glabellus
			obovatus
Monkeyflower			pauperculus
Mimulus	alatus		plattensis
	ringens		vulgaris
Mountain mint		Rattlesnake master	
Pycnanthemum	tenuifolium	Eryngium	yuccifolium
Ox-eye sunflower		Rose mallow	
Heliopsis	helianthoides	Hibiscus	laevis
			moscheutos
Partridge pea			
Cassia	fasiculata	Sage	
	marilandica	Salvia	azurea
			lyrata
Phlox			nemorosa
Phlox	amoena		urticifolia
	amplifolia		
	bifida		
	carolina		

Genus	Species	Genus	Species
St. John's wort		**Tickseed sunflower**	
Hypericum	*canadense*	*Bidens*	*aristosa*
	crux-andreae		*bipinnata*
	dolabriformae		*cernua*
	drummondii		*coronata*
	frondosum		*discoidea*
	gentianoides		*frondosa*
	harperi		*laevis*
	hypericoides		*tripartita*
	lobocarpum		*vulgata*
	mutilum		
	nudiflorum	**Turtlehead**	
	perforatum	*Chelone*	*glabra*
	prolificum		*obliqua*
	pseudomaculatum		
	punctatum	**Vervain**	
	sphaerocarpum	*Verbena*	*bracteata*
			brasiliensis
Sunflower			*engelmannii (hastata x urticifolia)*
Helianthus	*angustifolius*		*hastata*
	annuus		*hybrida*
	atrorubens		*simplex*
	cinereus (mollis x occidentalis)		*stricta*
	decapetalus		*urticifolia*
	divaricatus		
	eggertii	**Vetch**	
	giganteus	*Astragalus*	*canadensis*
	glaucus (divaricatus x microcephalus)		
	grosseserratus	**Wild petunia**	
	hirsutus	*Ruellia*	*caroliniensis*
	laetiflorus (fauciflorus x tuberosus)		*humilis*
	maximiliani		*pedunculata*
	microcephalus		*strepens*
	mollis		
	occidentalis	**Wood mint**	
	silphioides	*Blephila*	*ciliata*
	strumosus		*hirsuta*
	tuberosus		
		Yellow coneflower	
		Ratibida	*pinnata*

Trees, Shrubs, and Vines for Wildlife

APPENDIX

T HIS APPENDIX PROVIDES a listing of woody plant material suitable for landscaping for wildlife. When selecting the appropriate plants from the list, keep in mind the general principles discussed in the book, particularly with reference to limiting factors. For instance, in most cases black locust can be grown throughout much of Kentucky, but silky dogwood is more limited in its area of growth. You will need to weigh this information against the numbers of species of wildlife that are attracted to a particular plant. You will also need to keep in mind color blends and how to work various colors into your landscape plan. For instance, you might want a clustering of shrubs with excellent red foliage to balance an existing green ash tree. A good selection in this case might be one of the dogwood species. Other trees that help promote biodiversity but may not be particularly attractive to wildlife include leatherwood *(Dirca palustris)*, Kentucky coffeetree *(Gymnocladus dioica)*, wild hydrangea *(Hydrangea arborescens)*, redbud *(Cercis canadensis)*, bladdernut *(Staphylea trifolia)*, sourwood *(Oxydendrum arboreum)*, and yellowwood *(Cladrastis lutea)*.

Ideal Planting Techniques

The ideal situation involves planting a balled-and-burlapped tree with a sufficiently sized root ball, recently dug, going into a noncompacted, well drained soil with 50 percent solid material and 50 percent pore space. All of the following things must be considered before trees are purchased and planted.

• Assess the site.
• Make design and site modifications.
• Choose plants that match the specific site.
• Use good transplanting techniques, as follows:

1. Aerate the surface soils by increasing the surface diameter and tapering the sides of planting holes.

2. Place the tree at the depth grown in the nursery and no deeper (look for the root collar and add or remove soil as necessary).

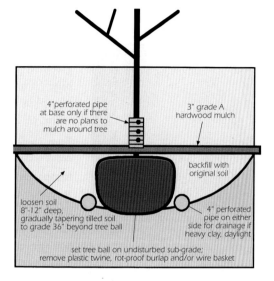

3. Replace the turf with a 2- to 3-inch layer of organic mulch around the tree base, ideally to the drip line of the tree. Grass roots compete significantly with tree roots and slow tree growth. An 8-foot circle of mulch quadruples root development of newly planted trees.

4. Be sure there is no "pimple" of excess mulch; 4 to 6 inches of mulch is *never* good; it rots the bark of the tree trunk.

5. Be sure there is no excessive saucering.

6. If mulch is not used and turf is grown up to the base of the tree, protect the trunk from lawn mower, string trimmer, or tractor with perforated pipe at the base. Check annually. Remove when the tree outgrows it.

7. Avoid using stakes; 99.9 percent of the time, stakes are unnecessary.

8. Avoid using tree wrap; it only encourages fungal and bacterial growth in the dark, humid environment under the wrap.

9. Install a 4-inch perforated pipe and connect it to a drainage area only if planting into extremely heavy clay or waterlogged soil.

Once the trees are established they will need to be pruned. For information on pruning, please ask your Cooperative Extension Agent for publication HO-45, *Pruning Landscape Trees.* For more information on growing nut trees, ask for publication ID-77, *Nut Tree Growing in Kentucky.*

Woody Plants and the Animals Attracted to Them

Large Hardwood (Deciduous) Trees

These trees are more than 30 feet tall when mature. They are listed by group.

ASH (*Fraxinus* spp.)
green *(F. pennsylvanica)*
blue *(F. quadrangulata)*
pumpkin *(F. profunda)*
white *(F. americana)*

BIRDS: red-winged blackbird, northern bobwhite, northern cardinal, cedar waxwing, wood duck, purple finch, yellow-bellied sapsucker

MAMMALS: beaver, white-footed mouse

BUTTERFLIES: Larval food for hickory hairstreak, mourning cloak, tiger swallowtail

NOTES: Ash is a medium-size tree with opposite leaf arrangement and winged seeds. Green ash has brilliant yellow fall foliage and white ash has red to maroon foliage. Ash grows best in full sunlight. Cultivars of green ash suitable for Kentucky include Bergeson, Emerald, Newport, Patmore, Summit, and Urbanite; cultivars of white ash suitable for Kentucky include Autumn Purple, Autumn Applause, Champaign County, Rosehill, and Skyline.

BEECH, AMERICAN (*Fagus grandifolia*)

BIRDS: Carolina chickadee, wood duck, purple finch, common grackle, rose-breasted grosbeak, blue jay, white-breasted nuthatch, yellow-bellied sapsucker, white-throated sparrow, tufted titmouse, downy woodpecker, hairy woodpecker, red-bellied woodpecker, red-headed woodpecker

MAMMALS: beaver, eastern chipmunk, red fox, white-footed mouse, raccoon, fox squirrel, gray squirrel

BUTTERFLIES: Larval food for early hairstreak

NOTES: Beech trees retain brown fall foliage through the winter. They have three-angled nuts that squirrels love and are shade tolerant.

BUCKEYE (*Aesculus* spp.)
Ohio *(A. glabra)*
red *(A. pavia)*
yellow, sweet *(A. flava)*

BIRDS: ruby-throated hummingbird

MAMMALS: eastern chipmunk, fox squirrel, gray squirrel

CATALPA, NORTHERN; CIGAR-TREE
(Catalpa speciosa)

BIRDS: ruby-throated hummingbird

BUTTERFLIES: Larval food for tiger swallowtail

CHERRY *(Prunus* spp.)

black *(P. serotina)*
choke *(P. virginiana)*

BIRDS: eastern bluebird, gray catbird, cedar waxwing, rock dove (pigeon), house finch, northern oriole, American robin, downy woodpecker, hairy woodpecker, pileated woodpecker, red-bellied woodpecker, red-headed woodpecker, song sparrow, mockingbird, white-crowned and white-throated sparrows, northern flicker, rose-breasted grosbeak, cardinal, wood, hermit, and gray-cheeked thrush, rufous-sided towhee, red-eyed vireo, summer and scarlet tanager, blue jay, American crow, great crested flycatcher, eastern kingbird

MAMMALS: beaver, red fox, opossum, cottontail rabbit, raccoon, striped skunk, gray and fox squirrel, eastern chipmunk, deer mouse, meadow mouse (vole), white-footed mouse

BUTTERFLIES: Larval food for tiger swallowtail, coral hairstreak, striped hairstreak, red-spotted purple, spring azure

NOTES: Cherries have white blossoms in spring, small red fruits in late summer, and yellow-orange fall foliage. They are found frequently in open areas and old fields, along fencerows, and in pastures. Cherries are among our most important wildlife food plants. The fruit can be used for wine or jelly. For more information on growing fruit trees in Kentucky, ask your county Extension agent for a copy of *Growing Fruit at Home in Kentucky,* and *Fruit Variety Sources and Reliable Information for Kentucky County Extension Agents.*

COTTONWOOD *(Populus* spp.)

Big-tooth Aspen *(P. grandidentata)*
eastern *(P. deltoides)*
swamp *(P. heterophylla)*

BIRDS: purple finch, American goldfinch, rose-breasted grosbeak

MAMMALS: beaver, cottontail rabbit, fox squirrel, vole (meadow mouse)

BUTTERFLIES: Larval food for mourning cloak, red-spotted purple, tiger swallowtail, viceroy

NOTES: Cottonwoods are fast-growing, with toothed leaves. Their seed capsule matures in late spring; each seed is attached to a tuft of white hair. The trees have brilliant yellow fall foliage.

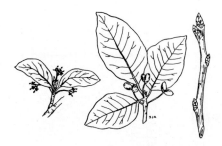

GUM (*Nyssa* spp.)

sour gum, black gum, black tupelo (*N. sylvatica*)

Tupelo gum, water tupelo (*N. aquatica*)

BIRDS: eastern bluebird, northern bobwhite, gray catbird, cedar waxwing, American crow, wood duck, purple finch, rose-breasted grosbeak, blue jay, eastern kingbird, northern mockingbird, American robin, yellow-bellied sapsucker, European starling, scarlet tanager, summer tanager, brown thrasher, gray-cheeked thrush, hermit thrush, wood thrush, tufted titmouse, hairy woodpecker, pileated woodpecker, red-bellied woodpecker, red-headed woodpecker

MAMMALS: beaver, opossum, raccoon, fox squirrel, gray squirrel

NOTES: Gum has deeply furrowed, blocky bark. Its dark blue fruits are usually found in clusters from mid-summer persisting to early winter. Its deep red and purple fall foliage is one of the first to turn color. Gum has a long taproot, making it difficult to transplant.

HACKBERRY (*Celtis* spp.)

common (*C. occidentalis*)

dwarf (*C. tennuifolia*)

sugarberry, smooth (*C. laevigata*)

BIRDS: eastern bluebird, northern bobwhite, northern cardinal, gray catbird, cedar waxwing, American crow, northern flicker, northern mockingbird, northern oriole, eastern phoebe, American robin, brown thrasher, hermit thrush, tufted titmouse, rufous-sided towhee, pileated woodpecker, red-bellied woodpecker

MAMMALS: beaver, opossum, raccoon, striped skunk, fox squirrel

BUTTERFLIES: Larval food for hackberry butterfly, question mark, mourning cloak, snout butterfly, tawny emperor

NOTES: Hackberries have gray to brown warty bark, small red fruits when ripe, and unattractive light yellow fall foliage. They are common along fencerows, roadsides, and old fields.

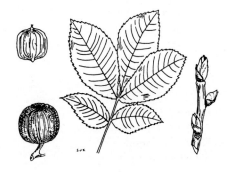

HICKORY (*Carya* spp.)

pignut (*C. glabra*)

pecan (*C. illinoinensis*)

big shagbark, big shellbark, kingnut (*C. laciniosa*)

sweet pignut, small-fruited (*C. ovalis*)

shagbark, shellbark (*C. ovata*)

mockernut, white (*C. tomentosa*)

water (*C. aquatica*)

BIRDS: blue jay, northern bobwhite, American crow, wood duck, rose-breasted grosbeak, white-breasted nuthatch, yellow-bellied sapsucker, red-bellied woodpecker

MAMMALS: eastern chipmunk, white-footed mouse, cottontail rabbit, raccoon, fox squirrel, gray squirrel

BUTTERFLIES: Larval food for banded hairstreak, hickory hairstreak

NOTES: Shagbark, pecan, big shagbark, pale, and sweet hickories have edible nuts. They are subject to disease and grow slowly. The nuts may be self-fruitful in some cases, but allowing for cross pollination is better. The varieties of shagbark hickory recommended for Kentucky include Yoder #1, Bridewater, Silvas, Wurth, Grainger, Wilcox, Porter, and Wilmoth; varieties of shellbark recommended for Kentucky include Fayette, Bradley, Chetopa, Keystone, Lindauer, Neilson, Stauffer, Stephens, and Totten; varieties of pecans recommended for Kentucky include Chickasaw, Fisher, Greenriver, Hodge, Kentucky, Major, Mohawk, Posey, and Shoshoni.

LOCUST *(Robinia* spp.*)*

black *(R. pseudoacacia)*
rose-acacia, bristly *(R. hispida* var. *rosea)*

BIRDS: northern bobwhite

MAMMALS: fox squirrel

BUTTERFLIES: Larval food for Zarucco duskywing, common sulphur, silver-spotted skipper, dreamy dusky wing

NOTES: Bristly locust is a thorny, medium-sized shrub with purple flowers.

MAGNOLIA *(Magnolia* spp.*)*

bigleaf *(M. macrophylla)*
cucumbertree *(M. acuminata)*
Fraser's *(M. fraseri)*
umbrella *(M. tripetala)*

BIRDS: northern cardinal, gray catbird, eastern kingbird, northern mockingbird, American robin, yellow-bellied sapsucker, brown thrasher, vireos, wood thrush, pileated woodpecker, red-bellied woodpecker, red-headed woodpecker

MAMMALS: white-footed mouse, gray squirrel

Notes: Magnolias have large white flowers in late spring to early summer. Cones that open in late summer release bright red seeds. Most magnolias are understory trees.

MAPLE *(Acer* spp.*)*

black *(A. nigrum)*
box elder *(A. negundo)*
red *(A. rubrum)*
silver, water *(A. saccharinum)*
striped *(A. pensylvanicum)*
sugar *(A. saccharum)*

BIRDS: northern bobwhite, northern cardinal, Carolina

continued on next page

Maple, continued

chickadee, purple finch, American goldfinch, rose-breasted grosbeak, yellow-bellied sapsucker, pine siskin, song sparrow

MAMMALS: beaver, eastern chipmunk, white-footed mouse, cottontail rabbit, fox squirrel, gray squirrel

NOTES: Maples have an opposite leaf arrangement, distinctive winged seeds called samaras, and brilliant orange to red fall foliage in sugar, black, and red maples. Maples grow best in full sun to partial shade. Cultivars of red maple suitable for Kentucky include Armstrong, Autumn Flame, Bowhall, Columnare, Edna Davis, Gerling, Karpick, Northwood, October Glory, Red Skin, and Red Sunset. Cultivars of sugar maple suitable for Kentucky include Bonfire, Caddo, Commemoration, Columnare, Green Mountain, Legacy, Steeple, and Sweet Shadow.

Oak (*Quercus* spp.)

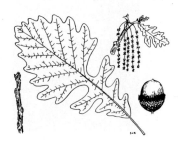

black jack *(Q. marilandica)*
bur *(Q. macrocarpa)*
chestnut, mountain chestnut, rock chestnut *(Q. prinus)*
chinquapin, yellow *(Q. muehlenbergii)*
northern red *(Q. rubra)*
overcup *(Q. lyrata)*
pin *(Q. palustris)*
post *(Q. stellata)Q. pagoda*
shingle *(Q. imbricaria)*
Shumard *(Q. shumardii)*
southern red *(Q. falcata)*
swamp chestnut, basket, cow *(Q. michauxii)*
swamp white *(Q. bicolor)*
water *(Q. nigra)*
white *(Q. alba)*
willow *(Q. phellos)*

BIRDS: downy woodpecker, hairy woodpecker, red-headed woodpecker, Carolina chickadee, tufted titmouse, northern cardinal, northern flicker, blue jay, eastern meadowlark, white-breasted nuthatch, mourning dove, hermit thrush, wood duck, mallard, northern bobwhite, rose-breasted grosbeak, brown thrasher, scarlet tanager, American crow, yellow-bellied sapsucker

MAMMALS: beaver, red fox, muskrat, opossum, cottontail rabbit, raccoon, gray and fox squirrel, eastern chipmunk, white-footed mouse

BUTTERFLIES: Larval food for Juvenal's dusky wing, Horace's duskywing, Edward's hairstreak, white-M hairstreak, banded hairstreak, sleepy dusky wing, northern hairstreak

NOTES: Oaks have lobed leaves and produce acorns. They occur in a wide range of habitats and have a wide variety of fall foliage from red to yellow to purple. White, willow, and pin oaks are relatively fast growing; white oak is difficult to transplant because of a long taproot.

Persimmon, common
(Diospyros virginiana)

BIRDS: eastern bluebird, gray catbird, cedar waxwing, blue jay, northern mockingbird, American robin, European starling, pileated woodpecker,

MAMMALS: red fox, opossum, raccoon

NOTES: The orange fruits that ripen in the fall can be eaten by humans. Persimmons have red to yellow fall foliage and are common along the edges of woodlands, old fields and fence rows. The sexes are separate, and to obtain fruit both male and female trees must be present.

Sassafras
(Sassafras albidum)

BIRDS: eastern kingbird, great crested flycatcher, northern mockingbird, gray catbird, brown thrasher, American robin, hermit thrush, Swainson's thrush, gray-cheeked thrush, veery, eastern bluebird, red-eyed vireo, white-eyed vireo, rufous-sided towhee, northern flicker, eastern phoebe

MAMMALS: beaver, fox squirrel

BUTTERFLIES: Larval food for spicebush swallowtail, palamedes swallowtail

NOTES: Sassafras leaves may be without lobes or may be two- or three-lobed. The female trees produce blue-black fruits in early summer. Their fall foliage is a brilliant red, yellow, and orange. Sassafras is common in open fields, along fence rows, and at wood edges. Tree parts are used in tea and candy, among other things. The trees are difficult to transplant because of a long taproot.

Sweet gum *(Liquidambar styraciflua)*

BIRDS: northern bobwhite, northern cardinal, Carolina chickadee, mourning dove, purple finch, American goldfinch, dark-eyed junco, mallard, yellow-bellied sapsucker, pine siskin, white-throated sparrow, rufous-sided towhee, Carolina wren

MAMMALS: eastern chipmunk, beaver, gray squirrel

NOTES: The star-shaped leaves of the sweet gum turn red to purple in autumn. The female flower forms the hard, spiny gum balls that encase the seeds. Cultivars suitable for Kentucky include Festival and Rotundiloba.

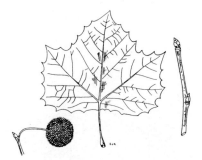

Sycamore *(Platanus occidentalis)*

BIRDS: cedar waxwing, Carolina chickadee, house finch, purple finch, American goldfinch, mallard, northern oriole, pine siskin

MAMMALS: beaver, fox squirrel

NOTES: Sycamore bark is patterned in browns and whites. The tree has shallow-lobed leaves, hanging fruits, and brown fall foliage. Large trees often become hollow and are used as nesting sites for wildlife.

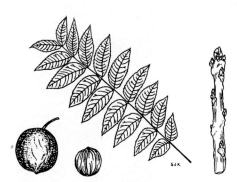

Walnut *(Juglans* **spp.)**

black *(J. nigra)*
butternut, white *(J. cinerea)*

BIRDS: red-bellied woodpecker

MAMMALS: beaver, fox squirrel, gray squirrel

BUTTERFLIES: Larval food for banded hairstreak

NOTES: Butternuts are not recommended except in the mountains at high elevations because they are susceptible to bacterial canker that results in a short-lived tree, usually less than 20 years. They are self-fruitful, although they perform better when cross pollinated. Cultivars recommended for Kentucky include Clermont, Emma K, Farrington, Myers, Sparrow, and Stabler.

Yellow poplar, tulip poplar, tulip tree *(Liriodendron tulipifera)*

BIRDS: red-winged blackbird, northern cardinal, Carolina chickadee, purple finch, American goldfinch, ruby-throated hummingbird, yellow-bellied sapsucker

MAMMALS: beaver, white-footed mouse, fox squirrel, gray squirrel

BUTTERFLIES: Larval food for spicebush swallowtail, tiger swallowtail

NOTES: Yellow poplar is Kentucky's state tree. It has lyre-shaped leaves, unremarkable yellow fall foliage, and a distinctive greenish white flower marked with orange in spring.

Evergreen Trees

Eastern hemlock *(Tsuga canadensis)*

BIRDS: Carolina chickadee, pine siskin, American robin, warblers

MAMMALS: cottontail rabbit, white-footed mouse

NOTES: Eastern hemlock is a medium to large evergreen with small cones hung from the end of branchlets. The mature cones release winged seeds. Hemlocks are common in cool, moist slopes in eastern Kentucky. They are very shade tolerant. Varieties recommended for Kentucky include Pendula or Weeping Hemlock and Sargentii.

Holly, American *(Ilex opaca)*

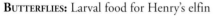

BIRDS: northern bobwhite, northern flicker, northern mockingbird, gray catbird, brown thrasher, eastern bluebird, cedar waxwing, eastern phoebe, yellow-bellied sapsucker, white-throated sparrow, gray-cheeked, hermit, olive-backed, and wood thrush, rufous-sided towhee, white-eyed vireo, pileated woodpecker, and American robin

MAMMALS: raccoon, striped skunk, fox squirrel, gray squirrel, white-footed mouse

BUTTERFLIES: Larval food for Henry's elfin

NOTES: Not a coniferous tree, American holly has glossy green leaves with spiny margins and white flowers followed by bright red fruits that persist until late winter. Cultivars suitable for Kentucky include Cecile, Chief Paduke, Indian Maiden, Julie Koehler, Judy Evans, Klein #1, Lady Alice, Maryland Dwarf, Richards, and Virginia Giant. The sexes are separate and you must plant both male and female trees to obtain fruit.

Juniper, eastern; red cedar *(Juniperus virginiana)*

BIRDS: cedar waxwing, purple finch, American robin, yellow-rumped warbler, northern flicker, northern mockingbird, eastern bluebird, northern bobwhite, Swainson's thrush, hermit thrush, tree swallow, cliff swallows, eastern kingbird, blue jay, brown thrasher, chipping sparrow, fox sparrow, European starling, yellow-bellied sapsucker, common grackle

MAMMALS: beaver, opossum, eastern chipmunk

BUTTERFLIES: Larval food for olive hairstreak

NOTES: Blue fleshy cones form the berries in autumn. Junipers are shade tolerant and are a pioneer plant, commonly in poor sites. Cultivars suitable for Kentucky include Burkii, Canaerti, and Hillspire.

Pine (*Pinus* spp.)

pitch *(P. rigida)*
Virginia, scrub *(P. virginiana)*
white *(P. strobus)*
yellow, shortleaf *(P. echinata)*

BIRDS: mourning dove, northern bobwhite, Carolina chickadee, brown creeper, house finch, northern flicker, dark-eyed junco, eastern meadowlark, white-breasted nuthatch, yellow-bellied sapsucker, brown thrasher, tufted titmouse, rufous-sided towhee, pine warbler, red-bellied woodpecker, Carolina wren, common grackle

MAMMALS: beaver, cottontail rabbit, fox squirrel, gray squirrel, eastern chipmunk, white-footed mouse

BUTTERFLIES: Larval food for eastern pine elfin

Spruce (*Picea* spp.)

Black Hills *(P. glauca)*
Colorado blue *(P. pungens)*
Norway *(P. abies)*

BIRDS: pine siskin, cedar waxwing, American robin, mourning dove, common grackle

MAMMALS: beaver, cottontail rabbit, chipmunk, white-footed mouse

NOTES: Spruce are not native to Kentucky, but they do not reproduce and can be used in the landscape for wildlife cover. A common cultivar of Black Hills spruce is Densata; cultivars of Colorado blue spruce used in Kentucky are Glauca, Hoopsii, Thompsonii, Moerheimii, Kosteri, and Fat Albert.

Small Trees or Large Shrubs

These plants are 10 to 30 feet tall.

Alder, common (*Alnus serrulata*)

BIRDS: pine siskin, mourning dove, mallard, great blue heron, northern bobwhite and American goldfinch

MAMMALS: beaver

NOTES: Alders are large shrubs with flowers that are hard, brown catkins. Common along streams and damp areas, the plants grow best in partial shade.

Birch (*Betula* spp.)

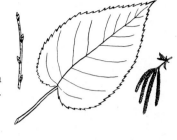

river *(B. nigra)*
sweet *(B. lenta)*
yellow *(B. lutea)*

BIRDS: dark-eyed junco, blue jay, pine siskin, tufted titmouse, Carolina chickadee, cedar waxwing, American goldfinch, purple finch, rufous-sided towhee, northern bobwhite, wood duck, northern cardinal

MAMMALS: beaver, cottontail rabbit, eastern chipmunk

BUTTERFLIES: Larval food for mourning cloak, gray comma

NOTES: Birches are small to medium-size trees that are relatively short-lived. They have attractive, flaky bark, hard, brown catkin flowers, and clear yellow fall foliage.

Black haw (*Viburnum* spp.)

arrow-wood *(V. dentatum* var. *dentatum)*
V. dentatum var. *lucidum*
arrow-wood *(V. rafinesquianum)*
black-haw *(V. prunifolium)*
Kentucky viburnum *(V. molle)*
maple-leaf *(V. acerifolium)*
possum-haw *(V. nudum* var. *nudum)*
southern *(V. rufidulum)*
withe-rod *(V. nudum* var. *cassinoides)*

BIRDS: eastern bluebird, cedar waxwing, northern cardinal, northern mockingbird, American robin, white-throated sparrow, hermit thrush, gray catbird, rose-breasted grosbeak, purple finch, red-eyed vireo, white-eyed vireo

MAMMALS: beaver, red fox, cottontail rabbit, striped skunk, fox squirrel, gray squirrel, eastern chipmunk, white-footed mouse

BUTTERFLIES: Larval food for spring azure

NOTES: Black haw is a large shrub or small tree, with dark green, glossy foliage, creamy white flowers in late spring, and clusters of dark blue fruit with white sheen in fall. It grows in full sunlight to part shade.

Buckthorn (*Rhamnus* spp.)

Carolina *(R. caroliniana)*
lance-leafed *(R. lanceolata)*

BIRDS: Gray catbird, brown thrasher, American robin, wood and hermit thrushes, cedar waxwing, northern mockingbird, pileated woodpecker, northern oriole

MAMMALS: cottontail rabbit, raccoon

NOTES: Buckthorn can be a large shrub or a small tree. It has lustrous, dark green foliage, clusters of red berries in the fall that eventually turn black, and yellow fall foliage. It grows best in full sun to part shade.

Burning bush (*Euonymus* spp.)

running strawberry bush, running euonymus *(E. obovata)*
strawberry bush, hearts-a-bursting-with-love *(E. americana)*
wahoo, burning bush *(E. atropurpurea)*

NOTES: Burning bush is a tall, tree-like shrub with branches that have two to four corky wings making them appear square. The plants have small yellow flowers in spring and purple-capped pods open in fall displaying three orange-red seeds and brilliant red fall foliage. The bush grows best in full sunlight.

Crab apple (*Malus* spp.)

M. angustifolia
M. ioensis
wild *(M. coronaria)*

BIRDS: cedar waxwing, American robin, northern mockingbird, northern bobwhite, house finch, purple finch, downy woodpecker, hairy woodpecker, red-bellied woodpecker, and red-headed woodpecker, northern flicker, gray catbird, tufted titmouse, eastern bluebird, blue jay, northern oriole, orchard oriole, common grackle, European starling, yellow-bellied sapsucker, American crow, and rufous-sided towhee

MAMMALS: red fox, groundhog, opossum, raccoon, cottontail rabbit, striped skunk, gray squirrel, fox squirrel, eastern chipmunk, deer mouse, meadow vole

BUTTERFLIES: Larval food for gray hairstreak, spring azure, red-spotted purple, viceroy, tiger swallowtail, striped hairstreak

NOTES: Crabapples are large shrubs or small trees. They often have branches bearing small spines. In early spring they have pinkish-white flowers and in the fall yellow foliage. Cedar waxwings are known to prefer the Red Jade cultivar. Cultivars suitable for Kentucky that resist diseases and insects include David, Harvest Gold, Jewelberry, Red Jade, Red Jewel, and Prairiefire.

Dogwood (*Cornus* spp.)

alternate-leaf *(C. alternifolia)*
flowering *(C. florida)*
gray *(C. racemosa)*
pale (ssp. *obliqua)*
rough-leaf *(C. drummondii)*
silky *(C. amomum* ssp. *amomum)*
stiff *(C. foemina)*

BIRDS: northern flicker, scarlet and summer tanagers, downy woodpecker, hairy woodpecker, pileated woodpecker, red-headed woodpecker, gray catbird, eastern kingbird, brown thrasher, American robin, wood thrush, hermit thrush, Swainson's thrush, veery, eastern bluebird, northern cardinal, cedar waxwing, red-eyed vireo, rose-breasted grosbeak, northern bobwhite, northern mockingbird, white-throated sparrow, song sparrow, American crow, purple finch, great-crested flycatcher, yellow-bellied sapsucker, tree swallow

Mammals: beaver, cottontail rabbit, raccoon, striped skunk, gray and fox squirrel, eastern chipmunk, white-footed mouse

Butterflies: Nectar source; larval food for spring azure

Notes: The dogwoods include small herbaceous plants and shrubs as well as small trees. They have large, showy white flowers in midspring, bright red berries in fall, and crimson autumn foliage. They area a common understory tree and are slow growing. Varieties of flowering dogwood recommended for Kentucky include Cherokee Chief, Cherokee Princess, Cloud Nine, First Lady, Pendula, Purple Glory, Rainbow, Rubra, Summertime, Sweetwater, and Welchii.

Elderberry (*Sambucus* spp.)

common *(S. canadensis)*
red-berried elder *(S. pubens)*

Birds: pileated woodpecker, red-bellied woodpecker, red-headed woodpecker, eastern kingbird, great-crested flycatcher, blue jay, northern mockingbird, gray catbird, brown thrasher, northern cardinal, eastern bluebird, American robin, gray-cheeked thrush, hermit thrush, wood thrush, Swainson's thrushes, veery, cedar waxwing, European starling, yellow-breasted chat, common grackle, rose-breasted grosbeak, northern oriole, indigo bunting, American goldfinch, rufous-sided towhee, white-throated sparrow, chipping sparrow, song sparrow, white-breasted nuthatch, yellow-bellied sapsucker, tufted titmouse, mourning dove

Mammals: cottontail rabbit, fox squirrel, gray squirrel, eastern chipmunk, white-footed mouse, groundhog

Notes: Elderberry can be a large shrub or small tree. It has white flowers from early spring to first fall frost and purple-black berries on red stems. It grows best in moist soil. The berries can be used in making jellies and wine.

Hawthorn (*Crataegus* spp.)

cockspur *(C. crus-galli)*
red haw *(C. mollis)*
Washington *(C. phaenopyrum)*

Birds: American robin, purple finch, cedar waxwing, blue jay, northern mockingbird, northern flicker, rose-breasted grosbeak, hermit thrush, fox sparrow and northern cardinal

Mammals: beaver, cottontail rabbit, raccoon, striped skunk, fox squirrel, gray squirrel

Butterflies: Larval food for gray hairstreak

Notes: Species of hawthorns are numerous, complex, and difficult to separate; there are more than two dozen species in the state. These small trees or shrubs have spines along their branches and red fruits that remain on the plant until late winter. They are common along roadsides and on old farmland.

Holly (*Ilex* spp.)

mountain winterberry *(I. montana)*
swamp holly, possum-haw *(I. decidua)*
winterberry *(I. verticillata)*

BIRDS: northern bobwhite, northern flicker, northern mocking-bird, gray catbird, brown thrasher, eastern bluebird, cedar waxwing, eastern phoebe, yellow-bellied sapsucker, white-throated sparrow, gray-cheeked thrush, hermit thrush, olive-backed thrush, wood thrush, rufous-sided towhee, white-eyed vireo, pileated woodpecker, and American robin

MAMMALS: raccoon, striped skunk, fox squirrel, gray squirrel, white-footed mouse

BUTTERFLIES: Larval food for Henry's elfin

NOTES: Cultivars of possum-haw suitable for Kentucky include Council Fire, Pocahontas, and Warren's Red; cultivars of winterberry suitable for Kentucky include Afterglow, Sunset, and Winter Red.

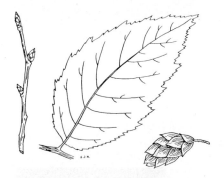

Hop-hornbeam, American (*Ostrya virginiana*)

BIRDS: northern mockingbird, rose-breasted grosbeak, northern cardinal, purple finch, downy woodpecker, and American goldfinch

MAMMALS: fox and gray squirrels, white-footed mouse

BUTTERFLIES: Larval food for mourning cloak, red-spotted purple

NOTES: Hophornbeam is a small to medium-sized tree. Its catkin flowers produce small nutlet fruits in late summer.

Mulberry, red (*Morus rubra*)

BIRDS: northern bobwhite, American crow, yellow-bellied sapsucker, eastern bluebirds, cedar waxwing, orchard oriole, northern orioles, northern cardinal, rose-breasted grosbeak, redheaded, red-bellied and hairy woodpeckers, yellow-billed cuckoo, wood thrush, eastern kingbird, northern mockingbird, scarlet tanager, red-eyed vireo, yellow warbler, American robin, gray catbird, tufted titmouse and brown thrasher, house finch, European starling

MAMMALS: beaver, opossum, raccoon, striped skunk, flying squirrel, fox and gray squirrel

BUTTERFLIES: Larval food for mourning cloak

Notes: Mulberries have heart-shaped or variably lobed leaves, red to dark purple fruits in late spring, and clear yellow fall foliage. They grow best in full sun. The fruits are edible by humans and wildlife love them. Mulberries can become invasive in some cases. The sexes are separate and you must plant male and female trees to obtain fruit. This species has been known to attract the most spectacular flocking of birds of any fruiting tree you can plant.

Pawpaw *(Asimina triloba)*

MAMMALS: Fruits are eaten by raccoons, opossums, fox and gray squirrels, red and gray fox, striped skunk.

NOTES: This is a medium-sized understory tree with large leaves. The fruits, which look like fat bananas, are edible by humans.

Plum (*Prunus* spp.)
chickasaw *(P. angustifolia)*
wild goose *(P. munsoniana)*
wild *(P. americana)*

BIRDS: cedar waxwing, house finch, northern oriole, rock dove (pigeon), American robin, eastern bluebird, downy woodpecker, pileated woodpecker, red-bellied woodpecker, red-headed woodpecker, hairy woodpeckers, gray catbird, song sparrow, mockingbird, white-crowned and white-throated sparrows, northern flicker, rose-breasted grosbeak, northern cardinal, wood, hermit thrush, gray-cheeked thrush, rufous-sided towhee, red-eyed vireo, summer tanager, scarlet tanager, blue jay, American crow, great crested flycatcher, eastern kingbird

MAMMALS: beaver, red fox, opossum, cottontail rabbit, raccoon, striped skunk, gray and fox squirrel, eastern chipmunk, deer mouse, meadow mouse (vole), white-footed mouse

NOTES: Plums have white blossoms in the spring, small red fruits in late summer, and yellow-orange foliage in the fall. The plants are found frequently in open areas and old fields, along fencerows, and in pastures. Plums are among our most important wildlife food plants. The fruit can be used for wine or jelly.

Serviceberry, Juneberry, sarvis, shadbush, shadblow (*Amelanchier* spp.)
downy *(A. aborea)*
smooth *(A. laevis)*

BIRDS: downy woodpecker, hairy woodpecker, pileated woodpecker, red-headed woodpeckers, American robin, hermit and wood thrushes, veery, cedar waxwing, northern oriole, gray catbird, northern flicker, eastern bluebird, rufous-sided towhee, Carolina chickadee, rose-breasted grosbeak, northern cardinal, blue jay, brown thrasher, eastern phoebe, mourning dove, American redstart, scarlet tanager, red-eyed vireo, eastern kingbird, house finch, northern mockingbird, red-winged blackbird, tufted titmouse

MAMMALS: beaver, red fox, groundhog, striped skunk, eastern chipmunk, white-footed mouse, fox and gray squirrels

Continued on next page

NOTES: These plants can be small trees or large shrubs. They are among the first woody plants to produce dainty white flowers in the spring. They produce purple, apple-like fruits in June and gold to red-orange foliage in the fall. Varieties are adapted to planting along ponds, rivers and streams, but will grow in full sun, partial shade, or full shade. The cultivar, Autumn Sunset, of downy serviceberry is recommended for Kentucky. Cultivars of smooth serviceberry suitable for Kentucky include Prince Charles and Cumulus.

Spicebush *(Lindera benzoin)*

BIRDS: great-crested flycatcher, eastern kingbird, Swainson's thrush, wood thrush, hermit thrush, and gray-cheeked thrushes, veery, red-eyed vireos, white-eyed vireo, white-throated sparrow

BUTTERFLIES: Larval food for spicebush swallowtail, tiger swallowtail

NOTES: Spicebush is a deciduous shrub that emits a spicy aroma when the leaves are crushed. It has red berries in late summer and a clear yellow fall foliage. It grows best in rich moist soil.

Sumac *(Rhus* spp.)

fragrant *(R. aromatica)*
smooth *(R. glabra)*
staghorn *(R. hirta)*
winged, shining *(R. copallinum)*

BIRDS: northern flicker, red-headed woodpecker, downy woodpeckers, Carolina chickadee, American robin, eastern bluebird, scarlet tanager, northern bobwhite, eastern phoebe, hermit thrush, wood thrush, Swainson's thrushes, white-eyed vireo, gray catbird, dark-eyed junco, northern cardinal, American crow, purple finch, European starling, northern mockingbird

MAMMALS: cottontail rabbit, eastern chipmunk

BUTTERFLIES: Nectar source; larval food for red-banded hairstreak

NOTES: Sumac can be a large shrub or small tree. It has wine-red panicles of fruit in late summer to fall and scarlet fall foliage. Sumac can be an invasive or aggressive plant in landscapes.

Small and Medium Shrubs

Azalea. *See under* Rhododendron and azalea

Blackberry. *See under* Raspberry, blackberry, and dewberry

Blueberry (*Vaccinium* spp.)

deerberry, squawbush *(V. stamineum)*
farkleberry *(V. arboreum)*
highbush *(V. corymbosum)*
lowbush *(V. pallidum)*
V. simulatum

BIRDS: eastern bluebird, Carolina chickadee, American robin, northern oriole, orchard oriole, tufted titmouse, northern flicker, rufous-sided towhee, eastern kingbird, gray catbird, yellow-breasted chat, blue jay, tree sparrow, white-throated sparrow, European starling, scarlet tanager, brown thrasher, cedar waxwing, veery thrush, gray-cheeked thrush, hermit thrush, wood thrush, red-bellied woodpecker, red-headed woodpecker, great crested flycatcher, northern cardinal

MAMMALS: red fox, opossum, cottontail rabbit, raccoon, striped skunk, fox squirrel, gray squirrel, eastern chipmunk, white-footed mouse

BUTTERFLIES: Larval food for brown elfin, Henry's elfin, striped hairstreak, spring azure

NOTES: Blueberries have bell-shaped, white flowers and blue-purple fruits in summer. The plants must have an acidic soil. They grow best in full sun to partial shade. For information on growing blueberries, ask your county Extension agent for a copy of *Growing Highbush Blueberries in Kentucky.*

Buttonbush *(Cephalanthus occidentalis)*

BIRDS: ruby-throated hummingbird, mallard, wood duck

MAMMALS: beaver

BUTTERFLIES: One of the top ten nectar plants for butterflies

Chokeberry (*Aronia* spp.)

black *(A. melanocarpa)*
red *(A. arbutifolia)*

BIRDS: cedar waxwing, brown thrasher, eastern bluebird, eastern meadowlark, American robin

Continued on next page

Chokeberry, continued

MAMMALS: red fox, cottontail rabbit, fox squirrel, white-footed mouse

BUTTERFLIES: Larval food for striped hairstreak

NOTES: Chokeberry is a deciduous shrub with shiny red berries that last into the winter.

Dewberry. *See under* Raspberry, blackberry, and dewberry

Filbert (American hazelnut) (*Corylus americana*)

MAMMALS: red fox, opossum, cottontail rabbit, raccoon, striped skunk, fox squirrel, gray squirrel, eastern chipmunk, white-footed mouse

NOTES: Filberts are easily propagated as seedlings. There are some named varieties, but these are generally not as hardy and often have their flowers killed during the winter.

Gooseberry (*Ribes* spp.)
Missouri (*R. missouriense*)
prickly (*R. cynosbati*)

BIRDS: gray catbird, American robin, brown thrasher, cedar waxwing

MAMMALS: red fox, raccoon, striped skunk, eastern chipmunk, deer mouse, white-footed mouse, meadow vole

BUTTERFLIES: Larval food for gray comma

NOTES: The fruits are edible by humans.

Huckleberry (*Gaylussacia* spp.)
box (*G. brachycera*)
G. baccata

BIRDS: eastern bluebird, yellow-breasted chat, Carolina chickadee, eastern kingbird, northern and orchard oriole, eastern phoebe, American robin, tree and white-throated sparrow, gray-cheeked, hermit, and wood thrush, veery, tufted titmouse, blue jay, northern mockingbird, northern cardinal, rufous-sided towhee and gray catbird

MAMMALS: red fox, opossum, cottontail rabbit, raccoon, striped skunk, fox squirrel, gray squirrel, eastern chipmunk, white-footed mouse

BUTTERFLIES: Larval food for brown elfin, Henry's elfin

NOTES: Huckleberry is a semi-evergreen shrub that flowers in late winter to early spring. Its small black fruits ripen unevenly so that fruits may be found on the plant for two to three months. The fruits are similar to blueberries and may be eaten by humans, although they contain many seeds.

Mountain laurel (*Kalmia latifolia*)

BUTTERFLIES: Nectar source

NOTES: Mountain laurel requires acid soil and looks best when grown in combination with rhododendron species. The leaves are poisonous to livestock and humans.

Raspberry, blackberry, dewberry (*Rubus* spp.)

blackberry *(R. allegheniensis)*
black raspberry *(R. occidentalis)*
dewberry *(R. flagellaris)*
flowering raspberry *(R. odoratus)*
R. pennsilvanicus
swamp dewberry *(R. hispidus)*

BIRDS: northern cardinal, yellow warbler, tufted titmouse, northern mockingbird, Carolina chickadee, downy woodpecker, hairy woodpecker, red-headed woodpecker, American robin, hermit thrush, veery thrush, wood thrush, eastern bluebird, cedar waxwing, orchard oriole, northern oriole, rose-breasted grosbeak, northern flicker, white-throated sparrow, fox sparrow, song sparrows

MAMMALS: Beaver, red fox, groundhog, striped skunk, flying squirrel, fox squirrel, gray squirrel, eastern chipmunk, whitefooted mouse

NOTES: Depending on the reference, there are more than 90 species of *Rubus* in Kentucky; they are difficult for most people to tell apart. The species listed here are the most common. Most of the species are thorny shrubs growing from 2 to 9' in height. Fruits occur in a cluster of fleshy drupelets. Roots are perennial. The plants have an orange-red fall foliage. The fruits are edible by humans except for the flowering raspberry.

Rhododendron and azalea (*Rhododendron* spp.)

flame azalea *(R. calendulaceum)*
great rhododendron *(R. maximum)*
pinxter-flower, pink azalea *(R. periclymenoides)*
purple rhododendron, mountain rosebay *(R. catawbiense)*
red azalea *(R. cumberlandense)*
rose azalea *(R. prinophyllum)*
smooth azalea *(R. arborescens)*

BIRDS: warblers, rose-breasted grosbeak, ruby-throated hummingbird
MAMMALS: white-footed mouse

continued on next page

Rhododendron and Azalea, continued

BUTTERFLIES: Nectar source; larval food for striped hairstreak, gray comma

NOTES: Rhododendrons are evergreen and azaleas are deciduous shrubs. Both plants have brilliant colored flowers from late spring to early summer and oblong fruits. They are frequently understory shrubs and need acidic soil and soil amendments if grown outside the Cumberland Plateau region.

Rose (*Rosa* spp.)

carolina *(R. carolina)*
climbing *(R setigera)*
swamp *(R. palustris)*

BIRDS: cedar waxwing, wood thrush, northern cardinal, American robin, eastern bluebird, northern mockingbird, rose-breasted grosbeak, northern bobwhite, American goldfinch, vireos, Carolina chickadee

MAMMALS: beaver, cottontail rabbit, striped skunk, white-footed mouse

BUTTERFLIES: Nectar source

NOTES: Roses are upright, trailing, or climbing shrubs with thorny stems and red berries.

Vines

Bittersweet (*Celastrus scandens*)

BIRDS: eastern bluebird, northern mockingbird, wood thrush, American robin, fox sparrow, yellow-rumped warbler, cedar waxwing,

MAMMALS: cottontail rabbit, gray squirrel, fox squirrel

NOTES: The berries are commonly used for ornamental purposes in the fall.

Cross vine (*Bignonia capreolata*)

BIRDS: ruby-throated hummingbird

Grape (*Vitis* spp.)

Bailey's *(V. cinerea* var. *baileyana)*
catbird *(V. palmata)*
fox *(V. labrusca)*
frost *(V. vulpina)*
graybark, sweet winter *(V. cinerea* var. *cinerea)*
muscadine *(V. rotifolia)*
riverbank *(V. riparia)*
summer *(V. aestivalis)*

BIRDS: northern bobwhite, northern cardinal, house finch, purple finch, American robin, blue jay, gray catbird, American crow, northern flicker, great crested flycatcher, dark eyed junco, eastern kingbird, northern oriole, orchard oriole, yellow-bellied sapsucker, fox sparrow, European starling, summer tanager, scarlet tanager, brown thrasher, gray-cheeked thrush, hermit thrush, wood thrush, olive-backed thrush, pine warbler, pileated woodpecker, red-bellied woodpecker, red-headed woodpecker, rufous-sided towhee

MAMMALS: Red fox, opossum, cottontail rabbit, raccoon, striped skunk, gray squirrel, fox squirrel

NOTES: Grapes have heart-shaped leaves, small flowers in long clusters, and purple berries. They are common in many habitats but can be harmful to trees as they can grow up a tree and shade it out with broad leaves. Many cultivated species and varieties are available at nurseries.

Greenbrier (*Smilax* spp.)

bristly *(S. bona-nox)*
greenbrier *(S. rotifolia)*
hispid *(S. tamnoides)*
sawbrier, catbrier *(S. glauca)*

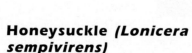

BIRDS: Red-bellied woodpecker, pileated woodpecker, American crow, northern mockingbird, gray catbird, brown thrasher, American robin, hermit thrush, Swainson's thrush, gray-cheeked thrush, eastern bluebird, white-throated sparrow, fox sparrow, northern cardinal

MAMMALS: beaver, opossum, raccoon, gray squirrel, fox squirrel

NOTES: The thorny stems of greenbrier can be hazardous. It is difficult to find at nurseries and difficult to transplant because of a long taproot.

Honeysuckle *(Lonicera sempivirens)*

BIRDS: ruby-throated hummingbird

Old man's beard, virgin's bower *(Clematis virginica)*

BIRDS: ruby-throated hummingbird

BUTTERFLIES: Nectar source

NOTES: The plant has small white flowers; after flowering, the seed pod takes on the appearance of a long, silky beard.

Passionflower *(Passiflora* spp.)

P. incarnata

P. lutea

BIRDS: ruby-throated hummingbird

BUTTERFLIES: Nectar source

NOTES: The blossoms are spectacular.

Trumpet vine; trumpet-creeper *(Campsis radicans)*

BIRDS: ruby-throated hummingbird

NOTES: Trumpet vine is a vigorous, woody, deciduous climbing vine with orange and scarlet flowers. It is a good ornamental but can escape and become invasive.

Virginia creeper *(Parthenocissus quinquefolia)*

BIRDS: eastern kingbird, great crested flycatcher, white-breasted nuthatch, house finch, purple finch, northern flicker, red-bellied woodpecker, pileated woodpecker, and red-headed woodpecker, tufted titmouse, eastern bluebird, American robin, wood thrush, hermit thrush, and Swainson's thrush, northern mockingbird, brown thrasher, yellow-bellied sapsucker, yellow-rumped warbler, red-eyed vireo, scarlet tanager, European starling, fox sparrow, American crow, Carolina chickadee

MAMMALS: red fox, striped skunk, cottontail rabbit

NOTES: Virginia creeper has small white flowers in early summer, small grape-like berries in the fall, and crimson fall foliage. Be careful where you plant it because it can escape and become invasive.

References

Strang, John, Mary Witt, Terry Jones, and Jerry Brown. 1990. *Growing Fruit at Home in Kentucky.* HO-64. 30 pp.

Strang, John, Terry Jones, and Jerald Brown. 1996. *Fruit Variety Sources and Reliable Information for Kentucky County Extension Agents.* POM 96-1. 25 pp.

Strang, John, Terry Jones, and Jerald Brown. 1989. *Growing Highbush Blueberries in Kentucky.* HO-60. 7 pp.

Strang, John, et al. 1989. *Nut Tree Growing in Kentucky.* ID-77. 19 pp.

Witt, Mary, William McNeill, and William Fountain. 1991. *Pruning Landscape Trees.* HO-45. 11 pp.

Sources of Native Plants, Seeds, and Accessories

Native Plants and Seeds

Inclusion in the following list of nurseries does not indicate endorsement or recommendation by the Cooperative Extension Service. Every attempt has been made to include all native plant nurseries in this region; any omission is the result of simple oversight and was not intentional. Most of the nurseries offer cultivars, domesticated plants, and invasive exotics in addition to native species. Please check to ensure the plants are native to your region of Kentucky. When purchasing seed, it is best to buy certified seed, which will indicate the amount of pure live seed (PLS) of native grasses. It is generally recommended that you use plants or seeds that originate no more than 200 miles south, 100 miles north, or 250 miles east or west of your specific location.

Kentucky Nurseries

J&M Seed Distributors
P.O. Box 133
London 40741
(606) 864-9668
Tree seeds, seedlings

Jane's Jungle
Sawridge Creek Road
Monterey 40359
(502) 484-2578
Wetland seeds and plants

Kentucky Division of Forestry
627 Comanche Trail
Frankfort 40601
(502) 564-4496
Tree seedlings in bundles of 100

Michler's Florist and Greenhouse
417 E. Maxwell
Lexington, KY 40502
Wildflowers, shrubs

Nolin River Nut Tree Nursery
797 Port Wooden Road
Upton 42784
(502) 369-8551
Tree seedlings and grafted varieties of native nut trees

Nurtured Gardens Nursery
Lower Licking Road
Morehead 40351
(606) 784-GROW
Native trees and shrubs, some containers, some balled and burlaped

Shooting Star Nursery
444 Bates Road
Frankfort 40601
(502) 223-1679
Native grasses, wildflowers, vines, shrubs, wetland plants

Springhouse Gardens
6041 Harrodsburg Rd.
Nicholasville, KY 40356
Wildflowers, trees, shrubs

Stinson Rhododendron Nursery
10400 Florian Road
Louisville 40223

Producers in Other States

Appalachian Wildflower
    Nursery
Rt. 1, Box 275A
Reedsville, PA 17084
Wildflowers

Applied Ecological Services
Steve Apfelbaum, Tom Aranow
Rt. 3, Smith Road
P.O. Box 256
Brodhead, WI 53520
*Prairie, woodland, wetland
plants*

Baker's Tree Nursery
13895 Garfield Road
Salem, OH 44460
Tree and shrub seedlings

Beebe Crownvetch Farm
R.D. 4, Box 226
Towanda, PA 18848
Native grasses

Beersheba Wildflower Garden
P.O. Box 551
Stone Door Road
Beersheba Springs, TN 37305
Wildflowers

Ben Pace Nursery
Rt. 1, Box 925
Pine Mountain, GA 31822
*Wildflowers, rhododendrons,
and azaleas*

Bluestem Prairie Nursery
Rt. 2, Box 92
Hillsboro, IL 62049
Wildflowers, native grasses

Bluestem Seed Company
R.R. 3, Box 32
Grant City, MO 64456
Native grasses

Boehlke's Woodland Gardens
W140 N10829
Country Aire Road
Germantown, WI 53022
Woodland ferns and perennials

Botanico
P.O. Box 922
McMinnville, TN 37110
Tree seedlings

Buddies Nursery
P.O. Box 14
Birdsboro, PA 19508
Rhododendrons and azaleas

Camellia Forest
125 Carolina Forest Road
Chapel Hill, NC 27516
Rhododendrons and azaleas

Cantrell Nursery Co.
Smithville, TN 37166
Tree seedlings

Cartwright Nursery Co.
11861 E. Shelby Drive
Colliesville, TN 38017
Tree seedlings

Classic Groundcovers, Inc.
Rt. 3, Belmont Road
Athens, GA 30605
Wildflowers

Coastal Gardens
Rt. 10, Socastee Boulevard
    4611
Myrtle Beach, SC 29577
Wildflowers, native grasses

The Cummins Garden
22 Robertsville Road
Marlboro, NJ 07746
Rhododendrons and azaleas

The Dabney Nursery
5576 Hacks Cross Road
Memphis, TN 38125
Tree seedlings

Dello Nursery
11034 Highway 64
Arlington, TN 38002
Wildflowers, tree seedlings

Delta View Nursery
Rt. 1, Box 28
Leland, MS 38756
Tree seedlings, wetland plants

Dixon Gallery and Garden
4339 Park Avenue
Memphis, TN 38117
Wildflowers

Environmental Concern, Inc.
210 W. Chew Ave., P.O. Box P
St. Michaels, MD 21663

Ernst Crownvetch Farms
R.D. 5, Box 806
Meadville, PA 16335
Wildflowers, native grasses

Forrest Keeling Nursery
Box 135
Elsberry, MO 63343
Tree seedlings

Game Food Nurseries
P.O. Box V
4488 Highway 116
Omro, WI 54963
*Wildlife specialty seeds, wetland
plants*

Garden Place
6780 Heisley Road
P.O. Box 388
Mentor, OH 44061-0388
Native grasses, wildflower plants

Gardens of the Blue Ridge
P.O. Box 10
Pineola, NC 28662
Woodland plants

Girard Nurseries
Box 428
Geneva, OH 44041
Tree seedlings, rhododendrons and azaleas

Hamilton Seeds
HCR Rt. 9, Box 138
Elk Creek, MO 65464
Native grasses, wildflowers

Harvest Farms
P.O. Box 278
Morrison, TN 37357
Tree seedlings

Hauser's Superior View Farm
Rt. 1, Box 199
Bayfield, WI 54814
Wildflowers

Hidden Springs Nursery
Rt. 14, Box 159
Cookeville, TN 38501
Tree seedlings

Hillhouse Nursery
90 Kresson-Gibbsboro Road
R.D. 1
Voorhees, NJ 08043

Hillis Nursery Co.
Rt. 2, Box 142
McMinnville, TN 37110
Wildflowers, tree seedlings

Hi Mountain Farm
Rt. 2
Galena, MO 65656
Wildflowers

Huffman's Native Plants
P.O. Box 39
Otto, NC 28763
Rhododendrons and azaleas

Intermont Nursery
4305 Old Bluefield Road
Princeton, WV 24740
Native shrubs

J&J Seed Company
Rt. 3
Gallatin, MO 64640
Native grasses

Jim Plyler's Natural Land
scapes
354 N. Jennersville Road
West Grove, PA 19390
Azaleas

Kathy Clinebell
R.R. 2, Box 176
Wyoming, IL 61491
Wildflowers

Kettle Moraine Natural Land-
scaping
W996 Birchwood Drive
Campbellsport, WI 53010
Prairie and woodland plants

Lafayette Home Nursery, Inc.
R.R. 1, Box 1A
Lafayette, IL 61449
Native grasses, wildflowers

Lamtree Farm
Rt. 1, Box 162
Warrensville, NC 29693
Rhododendrons and azaleas

Lichterman Nature Center
5992 Quince Road
Memphis, TN 38119
Native grasses, wildflowers

Little Valley Farm
Rt 3, Box 544
Snead Creek Road
Spring Garden, WI 53588
Tree seedlings, shrubs, wildflowers

L.L. Olds Seed Company
2901 Packers Avenue
P.O. Box 7790
Madison, WI 53791
Wildflowers

Longview Gardens
11801 E. Bannister Road
Kansas City, MO 64138
Wildflower plants, tree seedlings

Mangelsdorf Seed Co.
P.O. Box 327
St. Louis, MO 63166
Wildlife specialty seeds, native grasses, wildflowers

Massie, Glen E.
Illinois Forest Products Co.
P.O. Box 194, R.R. 1
Beardstown, IL 62618
Tree seeds

Mellinger's Nursery, Inc.
2310 W. South Range Road
North Lima, OH 44452-9731
Wildflowers, tree seedlings

Midwest Wildflowers
Box 64
Rockton, IL 61072
Wildflowers

Milaeger's Gardens
4838 Douglas Avenue
Racine, WI 53402
Native grasses and wildflowers

Missouri Wildflowers Nursery
Rt. 2, Box 373
Jefferson City, MO 65109-9805
Native grasses, wildflowers, shrubs

Montrose Nursery
P.O. Box 957
Hillsborough, NC 27278
Wildflowers, rhododendrons and azaleas

Mountain Ornamental Nursery
P.O. Box 83
Altamont, TN 37301
Wildflowers, tree seedlings

Munchkin Nursery
323 Woodside Drive
Depauw, IN 47115-9039
Woodland wildflowers (no mail order)

Musser's Forests Inc.
P.O. Box S-90
Indiana, PA 15701
Tree seedlings

N&N Nursery
208 Oak Street
Poynette, WI 53955
Wetland species

Native Gardens
Rt. 1, Box 494
Greenback, TN 37742
Wildflowers, tree seedlings

The Natural Garden
38W443 Highway 64
St. Charles, IL 60174
Wildflowers, native grasses, wetland species

Nature's Nursery
6125 Mathewson Road
Mazomanie, WI 53560
Prairie, woodland, and wetland species

Nepco Lake Nursery
Port Edwards, WI 54469
Tree seedlings

Niche Gardens
111 Dawson Road, Dept. VN
Chapel Hill, NC 27278
Wildflowers, rhododendrons and azaleas

Norwood Farms
P.O. Drawer 438
McBee, SC 29101
Native grasses

The Ohio Seed Company
P.O. Box 87
127 Jackson Street
West Jefferson, OH 43162
Wildflowers, tree seeds

Park Seed Co.
P.O. Box 46
Greenwood, SC 29648-0046
Wildflowers

The Planter's Palette
28 W. 521 Roosevelt Road
Winfield, IL 60190
Woodland plants

Possibility Place Nursery
R.R. 1, Box 235B
Monroe, IL 60449
Tree seedlings

Prairie Future Seed Co.
P.O. Box 644
Menominee Falls, WI 53052
Native prairie seeds

Prairie Nursery
P.O. Box 365
Westfield, WI 53964
Native grasses, wildflowers

Prairie Ridge Nursery
9738 Overland Road
Rt. 2
Mt. Horeb, WI 53572
Native grasses, wildflowers

Prairie Seed Source
P.O. Box 83
North Lake, WI 54064-0083
Native prairie species

Purple Prairie
R.R. 2, Box 176
Wyoming, IL 61491
Wildflowers, native grasses

Reeseville Ridge Nursery
P.O. Box 171
309 S. Main Street
Reeseville, WI 53579
Tree and shrub seedlings

Rhodes Nursery
Rt. 2 Box 24B
Neshkoros, WI 53805
Woodland, wetland, and prairie plants

Richard Owen Nursery
2300 East Lincoln
Bloomington, IL 61701
Tree seedlings, wildflowers

Ridgecrest Nursery
Highway 64E
Rt. 3, Box 241
Wynne, AR 72396
Tree seedlings, wildflowers

Rivendell Botanic Garden
P.O. Box 17
Beardstown, IL 62618-0017
Prairie plants

Robert's Tree Farm
305 Edgewood Drive
Beckley, WV 25801
Native shrubs

Roslyn Nursery
211 Burrs Lane
Dix Hills, NY 11746

Royal Seeds, Inc.
1212 W. 8th Street
Kansas City, MO 64101
Native grasses, wildflowers, tree seeds

Royal Seeds, Inc.
1011 West Miller
Jefferson City, MO 64101
Native grasses, wildflowers, tree seeds

Savage Farm Nursery
P.O. Box 125-S N.
McMinnville, TN 37110
Wildflowers, tree seedlings

Schramm, Peter
Native Plant Materials
766 Bateman Street
Galesburg, IL 61401
Tree seedlings, prairie plants

Scott Brothers Nursery
P.O. Box 581
McMinnville, TN 37110
Wildflowers

Second Creek Nursery
Rt. 3, Box 312-B
Natchez, MS 39120
Tree seedlings, wetland plants

Sharp Brothers Seed Company
P.O. Box 665
Clinton, MO 64735
Native grasses

Shephard Farms, Inc.
R.R. 1
Clifton Hill, MO 65244
Native grasses

Southwest Wisconsin Prairie
   Enthusiasts
4192 Sleepy Hollow Trail
Boscobel, WI 53805
Native prairie seeds

Springbrook Gardens, Inc.
P.O. Box 388
6776 Heisley Road
Mentor, OH 44061
Wildflowers

Spring Hill Nurseries
110 West Elm Street
Tipp City, OH 45371
Tree seedlings, wildflowers

Sunlight Gardens, Inc.
174 Golden Lane
Andersonville, TN 37705
Wildflower plants

Sunshine Seeds Inc.
Wyoming, IL 61491
Native grasses, wildflowers

Tanglewood Nursery
1920 Kirby Parkway, #201
Memphis, TN 38138
Tree seedlings

The Three Laurels
Marshall, NC 28753
Woodland plants

Transplant Nursery
Parkertown Road
Lavonia, GA 30553
Rhododendrons and azaleas

Trees by Touliatos
2020 E. Brooks Road
Memphis, TN 38138
Wildflowers, tree seedlings

Triangle Nursery
Rt. 2, Box 204
McMinnville, TN 37110
Wildflowers, tree seedlings

Vick's Wildgardens
P.O. Box 115
Gladwyne, PA 19035
Wildflowers

Warren County Nursery, Inc.
Rt. 2, Box 204
McMinnville, TN 37110
Tree and shrub seedlings

Waynesboro Nurseries
P.O. Box 987
Waynesboro, VA 22980
Tree seedlings

Weaver Seed Inc.
P.O. Box 25087
Winston-Salem, NC 27114
Native seeds and plants

We-Du Nurseries
Rt. 5, Box 724
Marion, NC 28752
Wildflowers, rhododendrons, and azaleas

Wehr Nature Center
9701 W. College Avenue
Franklin, WI 53132
Wildflowers

Wherry Nurseries
P.O. Box 148
Beckley, WV 25801
Native shrubs

Willow Springs Nursery
R.D. 2
Indiana, PA 15701
Tree seedlings

Windbeam Way Nursery
Box 69
Flatwoods, WV 26621
Native shrubs

Woodland Acres Nursery
Rt. 2
Crivitz, WI 54114
Woodland plants

Woodlanders, Inc.
1128 Colleton Avenue
Aiken, SC 29801
Wildflowers

Water Gardening Supplies and Plants

Kentucky Retailers

In addition to the retail businesses that sell plants or materials, numerous pet stores also carry water gardening supplies.

Ambrosia
1314 S. Virginia Street
Hopkinsville 42240

Ashley's Woods
2390 Highway 90
Bronston 42518

Bee's Garden
626 Broadway Street
Brandenburg 40108

Blackburn's Greenhouses
P.O. Box 128
Stanville 41659

Bluegrass Gardens
626 Westport Road
Elizabethtown 42701

Boone Gardiner Garden Center
16411 Shelbyville Road
Louisville 40245

Caldwell County Forest
118 West Main
Princeton 42445

Cardinal Ridge Garden Center
2119 S. Dixie Boulevard
Radcliff 40160

Clear Creek Construction
1343 Fords Mill Road
Versailles 40383

Colonial Garden Center
4432 Nicholasville Road
Lexington 40503

Countryside Lawn & Landscape
316 S. Highway 27
Somerset 42501

Cox's Variety & Garden
570 River Ridge Plaza
Brandenburg 40108

Evergreen Grocery
1450 Chelsa Drive
Madisonville 42431

Florida Garden Center
1725 Guthrie Avenue
Paducah 42003

Frank Otte Nursery
5025 Shelbyville Road
St. Matthews 40207

Garden Center
1100 Burlew Boulevard
Owensboro 42303

Joseph Greenhouse & Gardens
626 W. Lexington Avenue
Winchester 40391

Highland Garden Center
2227 Alexandria Pike
Newport 41076

Hillenmeyer Nursery
2370 Sandersville Road
Lexington 40511

Hoffman's Inc.
R.R. 3, Box 16
Murray 42071

Holly Nursery & Garden
  Center
R.R. 3
Calvert City 42029

Indian Hills Garden & Craft
P.O. Box 611
Hopkinsville 42241

James Sanders Nursery
4123 Schneidman Road
Paducah 42003

Joe's Lawn & Garden
5103 Elizabethtown Road
Clarkson 42726

Kentucky American Seeds, Inc.
P.O. Box 1104
Hopkinsville 42241

Lose Brothers Nursery/Garden
4530 Poplar Level Road
Louisville 40213

Michler's Florist & Greenhouse
417 E. Maxwell
Lexington 40508

Mink's Nursery & Garden
Center
808 S. Dixie Street
London 40741

Mount Eden Greenhouse
2976 Van Buren Road
Mt. Eden 40046

Nelson's Garden Center
4788 Alexandria Pike
Alexandria 41001

Plant Potters Florist
225 Southland Drive
Lexington 40502

Red Hen Nursery
3895 Ironworks Pike
Georgetown 40324

Roberts Landscaping & Garden
3201 New Columbia Road
Campbellsville 42718

Rolling Hills Nursery
407 N. 12th Street
Murray 42071

Southern States Cooperatives
2 S. Jefferson Street
Alexandria 41001

205 E. Railroad Street
Clay 42404

1607 Irvine Road
Richmond 40475

941 N. Highway 27
Somerset 42501

Stan Humphries Nursery &
Garden
9708 Old Brownsboro Road
Louisville 40241

Stonegate Gardens
1318 Lebanon Road
Danville 40423

Suburban Florist & Garden
Center
2750 Outer N. Main Street
Madisonville 42431

TLC Landscaping & Nursery
131 Lutheran Church Road
Bardstown 40004

Tropical Breeze Aquarium &
Pets
1925 Triplett Street
Owensboro 42303

Wahl's Landscape Contractor
901 S. 21st Street
Paducah 42003

Wallitsch Nursery
2608 Hikes Lane
Louisville 40218

Mail Order Companies

The following companies sell water-gardening supplies through the mail. For more thorough information on water gardening mail order companies, you may purchase *Aquaculture Magazine's Buyers Guide*, from *Aquaculture Magazine*, P.O. Box 2329, Asheville, NC 28802.

Aquacide Company
P.O. Box 10748
1627 9th Street
White Bear Lake, MN 55110-
0748

Aquascapes Unlimited
P.O. Box 364
Perkasie, PA 18944

Carolina Water Gardens
821 Lake Boone Trail
Raleigh, NC 27607

City Gardens
451 W. Lincoln
Madison Heights, MI 48071

Country Wetlands Nursery
and Consulting
S. 75 W. 20755 Field Drive
Muskego, WI 53150

Lehman Hardware & Appli-
ances, Inc.
P.O. Box 41
4779 Kidron Road
Kidron, OH 44636-0041

Lilypons Water Gardens
P.O. Box 10
6800 Lilypons Road
Buckeystown, MD 21717-0010

Lilypons Water Gardens
839 FM 1489
P.O. Box 188
Brookshire, TX 77423

Maryland Aquatic Nurseries
3427 N. Furnace Road
Jarrettsville, MD 21084

Nitron Industries, Inc.
P.O. Box 1447
4605 Johnson Road
Fayetteville, AR 72702

Paradise Water Gardens
14 May Street
Whitman, MA 02382

Patio Garden Ponds
7919 S. Shields Boulevard
Oklahoma City, OK 73149

Patio Ponds, Inc.
2756 Lycoming Crk. Road
Williamsport, PA 17701

Pond Doctor
H.C. 65, Box 265
Kingston, AR 72742

Resource Conservation Technology
2633 N. Calvert Street
Baltimore, MD 21218

Stigall Water Gardens
7306 Main Street
Kansas City, MO 64114

Tilley's Nursery/The Water
Works
111 Fairmont Street
Coopersburg, PA 18036

Trees by Touliatos
2020 Brooks Road
Memphis, TN 38116

Waterford Gardens
74 E. Allendale Road
Saddle River, NJ 07458

Wicklein's Water Gardens
P.O. Box 9780
1820 Gromwell Ridge Road
Baldwin, MD 21013

William Tricker, Inc.
7125 Tanglewood Drive
Independence, OH 44131

Windy Oaks Daylillies &
Aquatics
W. 377 S. 10677 Betts Road
Eagle, WI 53119

Bird-feeding and Watering Supplies

Kentucky Retailers

Garden's Alive and Wild Bird
Crossing
3329 Tates Creek Rd.
Lexington, 40502

Wild Birds Unlimited
153 Patchen Drive # 39
Lexington 40517

1969 S. Hurstborne Lane
Louisville 40220

Woodland Habitat
1103 Cecelia Avenue
Park Hills 41011

National Mail Order Companies

Avian Aquatics
6 Point Circle
Lewes, DE 19958

Audubon Workshop, Inc.
1501 Paddock Drive
Northbrook, IL 60062

Bird N' Hand, Inc.
73 Sawyer Passway
Fitchbird, MA 10420

Birds-I-View
P.O. Box 190
Mt. Juliet, TN 37122

Coveside Conservation Products
H.C. 33, Box 462
Five Islands, ME 04548

The Crow's Nest
Cornell Lab of Ornithology
159 Sapsucker Woods Road
Ithaca, NY 14850

Duncraft
Penacook, NH 03303-9020

Wells L. Bishop Co., Inc.
464 Pratt Street
Meriden, CT 06450

Wild Bird Suppliers
4815 Oak Street
Crystal Lake, IL 60014

Artificial Nesting Structures

APPENDIX

ARTIFICIAL NEST BOXES are an important wildlife management technique used to enhance the nesting habitat for wildlife that require large, old, hollow trees. Nest boxes are used by a variety of bird, mammal, reptile, and amphibian species found in Kentucky:

Amphibians and Reptiles

gray tree frog
green tree frog
broadheaded skink

five-lined skink
rat snake

Birds

eastern bluebird
Carolina chickadee
wood duck
house finch
northern flicker
great crested flycatcher
American kestrel
purple martin
white-breasted nuthatch
barred owl
common barn owl
eastern screech owl
eastern phoebe

American robin
house sparrow
European starling
barn swallow
tree swallow
tufted titmouse
downy woodpecker
pileated woodpecker
red-bellied woodpecker
red-headed woodpecker
Bewick's wren
Carolina wren
house wren

Mammals

big brown bat
little brown bat
deer mouse
golden mouse
white-footed mouse

Virginia opossum
eastern gray squirrel
fox squirrel
southern flying squirrel
eastern woodrat

Recommended Dimensions for Bird Nest Boxes*

Bird	Entrance Hole		Floor Dimensions (Box interior)	Total Height of Box
	Diameter	Height above floor		
Bluebird, eastern	1 1/8	6-7	4 x 4	11-12
Chickadee, Carolina	1 1/2	6-7	4 x 4 to 5 x 5	9-12
Duck, wood	3 x 4	16-18	10 x 10 to 12 x 12	24-25
Finch, purple	1 1/4-2	5-7	4 x 4 to 5 x 5	9-12
Flicker, northern	2-3	10-20	6 x 6 to 8 x 8	14-24
Flycatcher, great-crested	11/2-4	6-7	5 x 5 to 6 x 6	9-12
Kestrel, American	3	10-12	8 x 8 to 9 x 9	14-16
Martin, purple	2-2 1/2	1	6 x 6	6
Nuthatch, white-breasted	1 1/4-1 1/2	6-7	4 x 4 to 5 x 5	9-12
Owl, barn	6-8	4	16 w x 22 d	16
Owl, barred	6-8	14-18	13 x 13 to 14 x 14	22-28
Owl, screech	2 1/2-4	10-12	6 x 6 to 8 x 8	15-18
Titmouse, tufted	1 1/4-1 1/2	6-7	4 x 4 to 5 x 5	9-12
Warbler, prothonotary	1 1/4-1 1/2	5-7	4 x 4 to 5 x 5	9-12
Woodpecker, downy	1 1/4-1 1/2	8-12	3 x 3 to 4 x 4	10-14
Woodpecker, hairy	1 3/4-2 3/4	10-12	5 x 5 to 6 x 6	14-16
Woodpecker, red-bellied	1 3/4-2 3/4	10-14	5 x 5 to 6 x 6	14-16
Woodpecker, red-headed	1 3/4-2 3/4	10-14	5 x 5 to 6 x 6	14-16
Wren, Carolina	1 1/2	6-7	4 x 4 to 5 x 5	9-12
Wren, house	1-1 1/2	6-7	4 x 4 to 5 x 5	9-12

*Note: All dimensions are in inches.

Building and placing nest boxes for these animals is a popular pastime and hobby for many Kentuckians interested in wildlife.

This appendix includes designs for twelve different nesting boxes. It is important that nest boxes be built according to exact specifications and that they be placed in the appropriate habitat. If not, they can quickly become house sparrow "slums." The above table lists the appropriate dimensions for building various boxes.

General Instructions for Building Nest Boxes

1. Make the boxes specific for each species of wildlife you are trying to attract. This is important because various wildlife require different size boxes and entrance holes. Be sure to place the box at the correct height and in the appropriate habitat for each species you are trying to attract.

2. Most boxes will need to be checked and cleaned at least once a year. To make this servicing job easier, be sure that one side of the box is hinged. This can

be accomplished by attaching rust-proof hinges or placing a nail in the same location on each side of the door at the bottom and no nail at the top. At the end of the nesting season leave the door to the nest box open. This will discourage mice from using the box. Mice might defend the box against returning songbirds. They can even kill and eat the returning birds.

3. Be sure to provide drain holes in the bottom of every house. Provide adequate ventilation in the house by drilling several holes near the top of the house or by leaving a tiny space between the roof and sides of the house. *Do not place a perch on any box because only house sparrows and starlings use a perch.*

4. Use well-seasoned hardwood lumber and galvanized nails if possible. Woods that are particularly good include cypress, redwood, western cedar, and

Figure 1

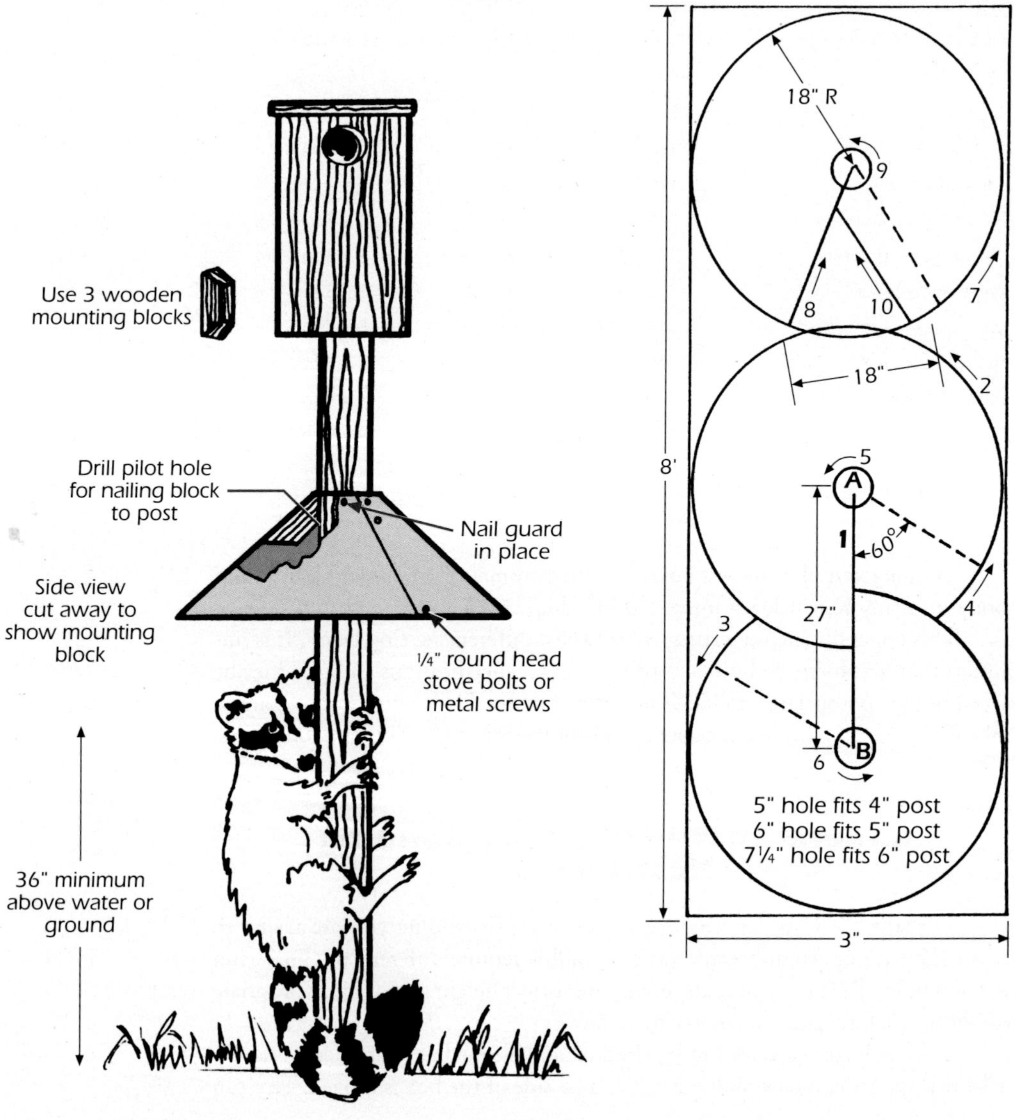

Use 3 wooden mounting blocks

Drill pilot hole for nailing block to post

Nail guard in place

Side view cut away to show mounting block

¼" round head stove bolts or metal screws

36" minimum above water or ground

18" R

18"

5" hole fits 4" post
6" hole fits 5" post
7¼" hole fits 6" post

eastern hemlock. Other species such as pine or fir will work but will deteriorate faster. *With some exceptions* (see information on purple martins and bats) *do not paint or treat boxes with a wood preservative.* They should be allowed to weather naturally. Painted or treated boxes may last longer, but these materials may make the box too warm or may give off toxic vapors. If you use hardwood lumber, be sure to drill pilot holes for the nails so the wood will not split.

5. All nest boxes (except wren houses) should be firmly attached to a post, tree, or building depending on the species. The best place for many boxes is on a post. All nest boxes should be protected by a predator guard. Do not nail a nest box to a living tree. Either wire the box so it is firmly attached, or use a lag screw and washer so the screw can be loosened as the tree ages.

6. With the exception of purple martin and wood duck boxes, houses should be spaced according to the territorial needs of each species. For example, bluebird houses should be placed about 75 to 100 yards apart. Wood duck boxes should be clustered, and martins require an "apartment house" style of nest box.

7. If house sparrows or European starlings begin nesting in the box, remove their nest and eggs. These species are not protected by state or federal law. You may have to remove nests and eggs six or seven times before the birds abandon the site. You can minimize sparrow use by trapping them with an elevator-type sparrow trap. (This trap is available from several commercial vendors. Contact the Kentucky Department of Fish and Wildlife Resources or the Extension wildlife specialist at the University of Kentucky for information on sparrow traps.)

Tree Squirrel

1. Construct the box following the plans outlined in figure 2 on page 246. Use rough-sawed 1" cypress, redwood, western cedar, or hemlock lumber.

2. Place the completed box in older oak or hickory trees that are at least 10" or more in diameter and at least 20' tall (taller trees are preferred). The boxes should be placed 20 to 30' up the tree no later than December 1.

3. Place the boxes in woodlands where there is abundant food and where natural den trees average no more than one per acre.

4. Distribute the boxes in woodlands at a rate of 1 to 4 per acre depending on the number of natural cavities present.

5. Attach the den box on the tree with #9 wire or nails so the opening is away from the prevailing winds and adjacent to the tree.

6. Place two to three inches of wood chips, shavings, or tree leaves in the bottom for nesting material.

7. Clean the box every two years.

Figure 2

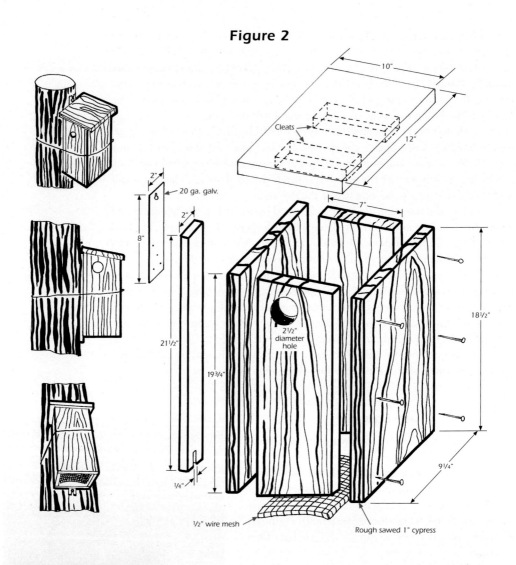

Cleats

10"

12"

7"

2"

20 ga. galv.

2"

8"

21½"

19¾"

¼"

18½"

2½"
diameter
hole

9¼"

½" wire mesh

Rough sawed 1" cypress

American Kestrel, Eastern Screech Owl, Flying Squirrel

1. Construct the box following the plans outlined in figure 3. The best wood to use is western cedar, cypress, redwood, or hemlock. You can also use any commercial lumber or plywood if these woods are not available.

2a. To attract kestrels, place the completed box 10 to 15' above ground in relatively open country. Ideal locations include in an orchard or on an interstate or parkway road sign. The grassed median of a four-lane highway provides ideal habitat for kestrels. These boxes are also predator-proof because raccoons, cats, and snakes cannot climb the steel posts that support the sign. If you plan on placing a nest box on a public right-of-way, get permission from the Kentucky Department of Transportation or other highway management agency. The entrance hole should be placed to the south or west.

2b. Boxes used for screech owls should be placed in open woodland terrain (the preferred location is on the edge of a woods next to a field or wetland). Place the box as high on the tree as physically possible.

2c. Flying squirrel nest boxes should be placed at least 10' high in trees located in hardwood forests. Attach a predator guard, a sheet of tin or aluminum wrapped around the tree, several feet below the nest box.

3. Install new boxes about half a mile from each other. Clean old boxes and install new boxes in January and February before kestrels, screech owls, or flying squirrels begin nesting.

4. Place one to two inches of wood chips or shavings in the bottom of the box.

5. Check the boxes every one to two weeks to remove house sparrow or European starling nests and eggs. These species are not protected by law and can easily take over a nest box. Because the entrance hole diameter is about 3", persistent starling and house sparrow control is necessary.

Figure 3

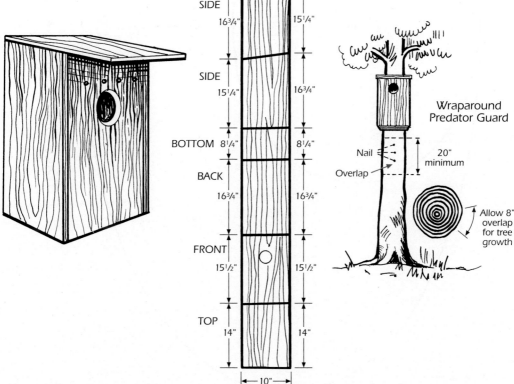

SIDE 16¾" 15¼"
SIDE 15¼" 16¾"
BOTTOM 8¼" 8¼"
BACK 16¾" 16¾"
FRONT 15½" 15½"
TOP 14" 14"
10"

Wraparound Predator Guard

Nail
Overlap
20" minimum
Allow 8" overlap for tree growth

Figure 4

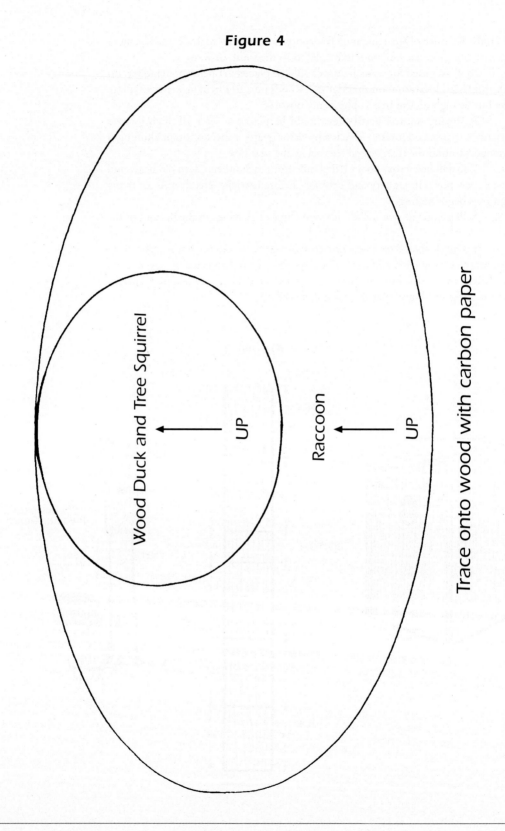

Wood Duck and Tree Squirrel

UP →

Raccoon

UP →

Trace onto wood with carbon paper

Wood Duck, Raccoon, and Tree Squirrel

1. There are numerous designs for this type of nesting box including a top cleat (sliding), top hinge, side pivot, and side hinge design.

2. Use the template in figure 4 as a guide (trace it onto the wood using carbon paper) to cut the necessary size entrance hole for either wood ducks or raccoons. Cut the hole in the front piece so that the center of the hole is 5" from the top of the board. If you are making a nesting box for squirrels, cut the hole on a side panel rather than the front panel.

3. Construct the nest box following the plans outlined in figure 5. Use seasoned redwood, cypress, or western cedar lumber. The boxes will weather naturally. Use hot-dipped or ringed galvanized 8-penny or 10-penny nails. To avoid splitting the wood, drill pilot holes before nailing together. Remember to drill four drain holes in the floor. Place a 3" to 4" strip of 1/4" hardware cloth inside the box under the entrance hole to act as a ladder when the young ducklings leave the box.

4. Add three to four inches of wood chips or shavings to the bottom of the box. This is important because female wood ducks do not bring nesting material to the cavity.

5a. For wood ducks, place the completed boxes in small groups of two to four per acre *over water*. Attach the boxes to posts or dead standing timber about 6 to 8' above the water's surface. Because wood ducks are not strongly territorial, several boxes can be placed close to one another. Often, wood duck boxes have been widely scattered throughout woodland areas close to water. It is difficult and inefficient to maintain and service these boxes.

5b. If a wood duck nest box must be placed in a tree close to water, attach it more than 20' high in the tree with the entrance hole facing the water. Boxes should be placed in trees 10 to 30 yards from the water's edge. Remove any overhanging tree limbs close to the box to make the entrance more visible to wood ducks while preventing easy access for predators.

5c. For raccoons and squirrels, place the completed box in a live or dead tree that measures at least 12" in diam-

Figure 5

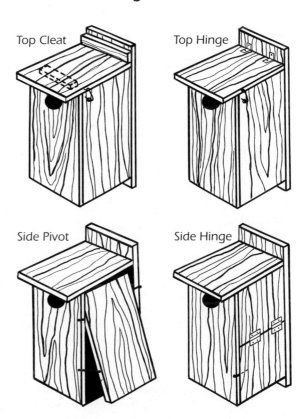

Top Cleat

Top Hinge

Side Pivot

Side Hinge

Figure 6

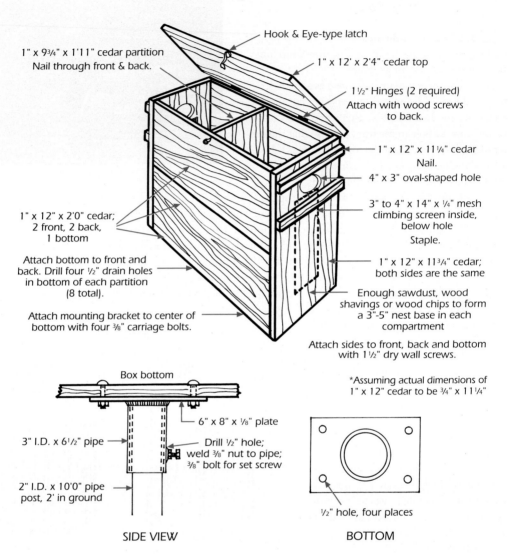

Hook & Eye-type latch

1" x 9¾" x 1'11" cedar partition
Nail through front & back.

1" x 12' x 2'4" cedar top

1½" Hinges (2 required)
Attach with wood screws
to back.

1" x 12" x 11¼" cedar
Nail.

4" x 3" oval-shaped hole

3" to 4" x 14" x ¼" mesh
climbing screen inside,
below hole
Staple.

1" x 12" x 2'0" cedar;
2 front, 2 back,
1 bottom

1" x 12" x 11¾" cedar;
both sides are the same

Attach bottom to front and
back. Drill four ½" drain holes
in bottom of each partition
(8 total).

Enough sawdust, wood
shavings or wood chips to form
a 3"-5" nest base in each
compartment

Attach mounting bracket to center of
bottom with four ⅜" carriage bolts.

Attach sides to front, back and bottom
with 1½" dry wall screws.

Box bottom

*Assuming actual dimensions of
1" x 12" cedar to be ¾" x 11¼"

6" x 8" x ⅛" plate

3" I.D. x 6½" pipe

Drill ½" hole;
weld ⅜" nut to pipe;
⅜" bolt for set screw

2" I.D. x 10'0" pipe
post, 2' in ground

½" hole, four places

SIDE VIEW

BOTTOM

eter. The boxes should be placed at least 10 to 20' high with the entrance hole facing to the south or east. Raccoon boxes should be placed close to a permanent source of water. See the section on squirrel nest boxes for information on the placement of these boxes.

6. Check and clean the boxes and install new boxes every year before March 1. Replace the inside material if necessary. On wood duck boxes, be sure the lid fits tightly and is wired shut to prevent raccoons from entering the box.

7. Install predator guards to deter raccoons and other animals from eating and destroying the eggs and nest. Predator guards are essential and should be placed beneath all wood duck nest boxes. One way to discourage predators is to place a sheet of tin around trees several feet below the box. For boxes placed over

water, a cone-shaped metal guard (figure 1, page 244) protects nest boxes from predators. The predator guards should be built of 26- to 32-gauge aluminum or galvanized sheet metal. The cone-shaped guard should be held together with #6 sheet metal screws, 1/4" round-headed stove bolts, or pop rivets and attached to the post with 1-1/2" roofing nails. The cone-shaped predator guard should be placed 36" above the water's surface.

8. The double compartment wood duck nest box is similar in design and construction to the single-compartment box. You can build a double compartment wood duck nest box following the plans outlined in figure 6. The box can be built from one piece of 1" lumber 12" wide and 18' long. Follow the instructions for placement, maintenance, and predator guards described in the previous paragraphs.

Mourning Dove

1. Construct the nesting cone from 1/4" or 1/2" hardware cloth following plans outlined in figure 7. You can also build a nesting cone of composition asphalt shingles (black side up).

2. Place the cone 6' to 10' in a tree with considerable open space available around the cone. Good choices for placing

Figure 7

1. Cut out a 12" square piece of hardware cloth.

2. Trim to form a circle.

3. Cut out "piece of pie" as shown.

4. Close pie cut by overlapping cut edges about 3".

5. Side view of cone ready for nailing in tree.

6. Options for attaching in tree.

a nesting cone include urban or suburban areas or in trees along the edge of woodlands or other forested areas.

3. Make sure the cone is placed in a somewhat shaded area that is not blocked by numerous twigs or limbs so the dove can move about freely. Attach it to the tree with roofing nails, staples, or wire and bend the edges down slightly after it is in place.

Figure 8

Door

Pivot Nail

1 1/2" wood screw
with washer

8 1/4"

5 3/4"

LEFT ROOF

6 3/8"

RIGHT ROOF

4 5/8"

3/8" vent
holes

BACK

4 5/8"

4 5/8"

1" to 1 1/8"
diameter

4 1/4"

FRONT

4 5/8"

4"

3/4"

℄ pivot
nails

7/8" drain
holes

DOOR

4"

4"

BOTTOM

House Wren

1. Construct the nesting box following plans outlined in figure 8.

2. Wren houses should be placed 5' to 10' above ground. They can be located under the eave of a building or in a tree. This is the only bird house that can be hung from wire on a tree.

3. Do not put a perch on the house because it will encourage house sparrows to use the box.

4. If you wish to attract chickadees and nuthatches, enlarge the entrance to 1-1/4".

5. After the family of wrens leaves the house, clean it out immediately so another batch of young can be raised.

White-breasted Nuthatch, Carolina Chickadee, Tufted Titmouse, Prothonotary Warbler, Deer Mouse, White-footed Mouse

1. Construct the nest following plans outlined in figure 9. The entrance hole size should be:
- 1" for chickadee, white-breasted nuthatch, and prothonotary warbler
- 1-1/4" for tufted titmouse and mice

2. Nest boxes for chickadees, white-breasted nuthatches, and tufted titmice should be placed along a tree trunk 5' to 15' above ground on trees located in smaller woodlots, along the edge of forest habitats, and close to woodland openings.

Figure 9

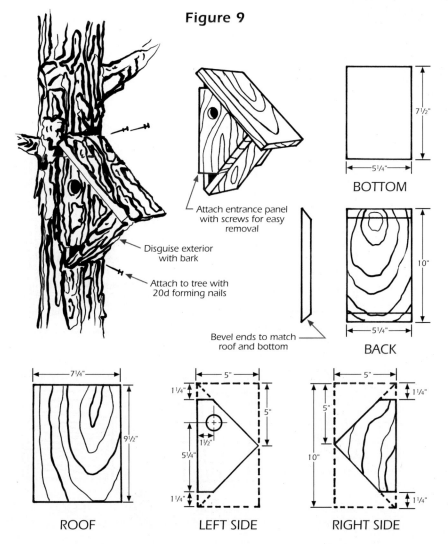

Attach entrance panel with screws for easy removal

Disguise exterior with bark

Attach to tree with 20d forming nails

Bevel ends to match roof and bottom

BOTTOM — 7½", 5¼"

BACK — 10", 5¼"

ROOF — 7¼", 9½"

LEFT SIDE — 5", 5", 1¼", 1½", 5¼", 1¼"

RIGHT SIDE — 5", 5", 10", 1¼", 1¼"

Nest boxes for prothonotary warblers should be placed 4 to 8' above ground on a tree trunk located in bottomland hardwood forests or along rivers or streams.

Nest boxes for white-footed and deer mice should be mounted 3 to 4' above ground on posts. The mice also use these boxes during the winter; therefore, the entrance should face to the south or southeast.

3. Place about an inch of coarse sawdust in the bottom of the nest box designed for Carolina chickadees.

Nest Shelf for Robin, Barn Swallow, House Finch, and Eastern Phoebe

1. Construct the nesting shelf following plans provided in figure 10.

2. Place the nesting shelf 6' to 10' above ground on a tree trunk or the side of a building to attract robins. After the robins have raised a brood of young, remove the old nest because robins build a new nest (made of grass and mud) each year.

3. Place the nesting shelf under the eaves of the house to attract barn swallows, house finches, or eastern phoebes. The house should be near a permanent body of water (lake) to attract phoebes.

Figure 10

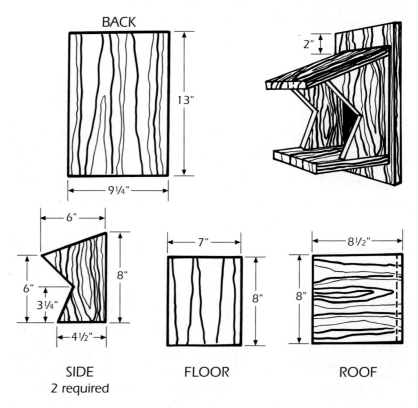

BACK

13"

9¼"

SIDE
2 required

6"

8"

6"

3¼"

4½"

FLOOR

7"

8"

ROOF

8½"

8"

4. A small wooden strip placed across the front of the nesting shelf may help attract house finches and keep the nest from being destroyed by high winds.

5. If barn swallows already have a nest where it is undesirable, wait until after the first set of young have fledged and destroy the mud nest. Staple a piece of plastic over the area where the nest was located. This will prevent the swallows from getting the mud to stick. Place a nesting shelf in a desirable location 10 to 20' from the site of the original nest. This will allow you to enjoy the benefits of the swallows (their insect-eating capabilities) without their being a nuisance.

Purple Martin

Building a purple martin house is an ambitious project. Because martin house design is intricate and the construction of the box is time-consuming, there are numerous companies that sell martin houses, and it may be more feasible to purchase a preconstructed house if you do not have the expertise or time to build one yourself. Even if you purchase a ready-made house, the following instructions will help you attract martins to your property. Martins may be difficult to attract; however, there are a few tricks you can use to put the odds of attracting the birds in your favor.

If you purchase a preconstructed house, look for the following details:

- proper ventilation,
- at least six compartments (each compartment must measure at least 6" x 6"),
- 2-1/4" diameter entrance holes, and
- holes with bottoms that are 1" above the floor.

If you construct the martin house yourself, follow the plans in figures 11 and 12 on pages 258 and 259.

1. Make sure the individual compartments measure 6" by 6". Rooms that are smaller than this discourage martins and encourage house sparrows. Make sure the entrance holes are no smaller than 2-1/4" in diameter. Rectangular entrance holes 2" wide by 3" high are also acceptable.

2. *Provide adequate house ventilation.* Drill vent holes in the attic and between compartments. There should also be an open air shaft in the center compartment venting through an opening in the attic to allow for good air movement.

3. Paint the outside of the house *white.* Do not paint or treat the wood on any of the interior surfaces. Do not stain or paint the house dark colors because it will become too hot for the birds. Attic insulation (1" styrofoam or newspaper sandwiched between corrugated cardboard) can be placed in the attic. You may shingle or place lightweight roofing paper on the roof, but this is not necessary. If you place roofing paper on the roof, paint it with aluminum paint before painting it white.

4. *Make sure the house is placed in the proper location.* Martins arrive in Kentucky sometime around mid- to late March or April (see map, page 257). As soon as you see the first martins (scouts) arriving, erect the house. If you have kept

The following ideas may help you attract martins to a house: provide a 1' to 2' area of water-soaked bare dirt close to the house to serve as a watering area.

- Place crushed egg shells on a bare spot near the martin house. This will serve as a source of calcium for the birds.
- Place a handful of sawdust in each compartment in the spring.
- Spread a small amount of high-quality hay or alfalfa close to the martin house. This will serve as a source of nesting material for the birds.
- Create a backyard butterfly, hummingbird, and insect flower garden to provide food for the birds.
- Locate the house adjacent to a lake, wetland, marsh, river, or pond.
- Mow the lawn close to the ground in the area surrounding the nest box. Martins are sensitive to predators and dislike dense, thick vegetation under the house.

covers on the holes to keep out sparrows and starlings, remove the covers at this time. The house should be located in the open, at least 50' away from trees or a building. It should be erected within 100' of the primary human residence for viewing. The house should be 12' to 18' above ground. Martin houses should be mounted so they can be cleaned out on a regular basis. You can use a commercially available telescoping pole, a hinged post, or a solid post.

5. *Keep the martin houses clean.* Each year the houses must be cleaned immediately after the martins leave. Once the house has been cleaned, it should be taken down, because house sparrows and martins do not mix. The entrances must be covered to prevent house sparrows or starlings from living in the house. *Do not let the sparrows or starlings become established in the house.* During the spring and summer months, if house sparrows or starlings are using the house, martins will not use it. If house sparrows or starlings move into the house, their nests, eggs, and young should be removed and destroyed. These species are not protected. If both martins and other species are living in the same house, remove unwanted nests in mid-afternoon when the martins are out feeding.

For understanding more about attracting purple martins, I recommend *Enjoying Purple Martins More: The Martin Landlord's Handbook,* by R.A. Wolinski.

James R. Hill III, from the Purple Martin Conservation Association in Edinboro University of Pennsylvania writes there are twelve reasons people lose purple martin colonies. Those reasons are:

1. Nest raiding by predators. It takes just one or two visits from a hawk, owl, snake, raccoon, or opossum for the entire colony to abandon the site, often never returning.

2. Trees and shrubs encroaching or growing taller and closer to the house.

3. Prolonged severe weather that could include droughts, excessive heat (days over 100° F), prolonged cold or snow, ice, or heavy winds.

4. Competition from house sparrows and European starlings for nesting spaces; these birds will also kill young and adult martins and throw their eggs from the nest.

5. Infestations of blackflies, blowflies, nest mites, and mosquitoes.

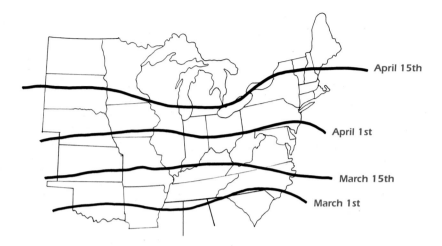

April 15th

April 1st

March 15th

March 1st

6. "Losing" martins to another nest site if your site becomes unsuitable, encroached by trees, and so on.

7. Not providing enough housing. Although a 12-hole martin house is enough to start a colony, it will not ensure survival of the colony. Multiple houses of more than 24 holes should be made available for nesting.

8. Inadvertent or unwise use of pesticides.

9. Failure to open the nesting holes on time. (Kentuckians should plan on opening their boxes by March 15 or when the scouts have arrived.)

10. Not properly orienting the house after cleaning.

11. Change of housing from season to season. You should not replace a housing unit from one year to the next unless the unit is exactly the same and oriented in the same direction.

12. Death of the caretaker of the colony.

More information about attracting martins can be obtained by contacting: The Purple Martin Conservation Association, Edinboro University of Pennsylvania, Edinboro, PA 16444, or by calling (814) 734-4420.

Materials for a two-story martin house

1 sheet 4' x 8' exterior type 1/4" plywood
1 sheet 2' x 4' exterior plywood (with face grain in 2' direction)
1 piece 2" x 2" x 6" pine or spruce 0for chimney
1 piece 1" x 2" x 14' pine or spruce
1 piece 1" x 1" x 8' pine or spruce
1 piece 4" x 8" aluminum or copper window screen wire cloth staples
2" or 2-1/4" nails (galvanized or aluminum preferred)
1" wire nails (galvanized or aluminum preferred) or 3/4" #6 flat head
    screws (rust-resistant)
resorcinol glue (waterproof)
1 each 1/4" x 24" or 30" thread rod with 2 nuts and
2 washers

Figure 11

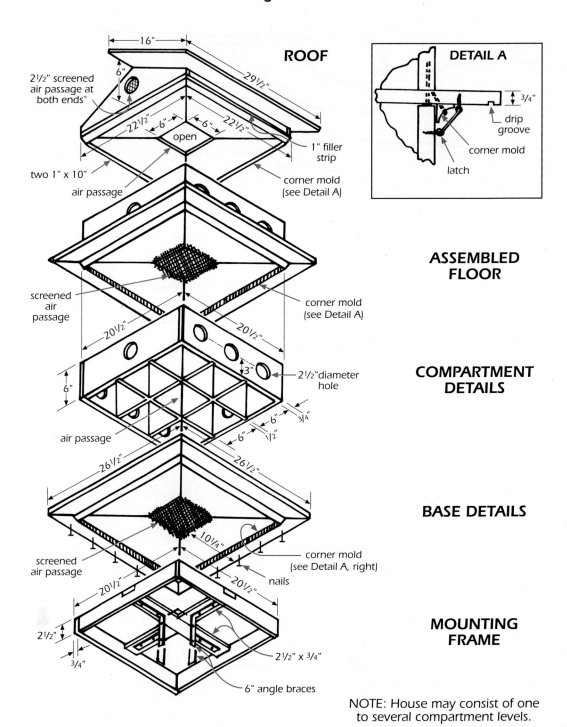

ROOF

16"

2½" screened air passage at both ends"

6"

29½"

22½" 6" 6" 22½"

open

1" filler strip

two 1" x 10" air passage

corner mold (see Detail A)

DETAIL A

¾"

drip groove

corner mold

latch

ASSEMBLED FLOOR

screened air passage

corner mold (see Detail A)

20½" 20½"

COMPARTMENT DETAILS

6"

3"

2½" diameter hole

air passage

6" ¾"

6" ½"

26½" 26½"

BASE DETAILS

screened air passage

10¼"

corner mold (see Detail A, right)

nails

20½" 20½"

MOUNTING FRAME

2½"

¾"

2½" x ¾"

6" angle braces

NOTE: House may consist of one to several compartment levels.

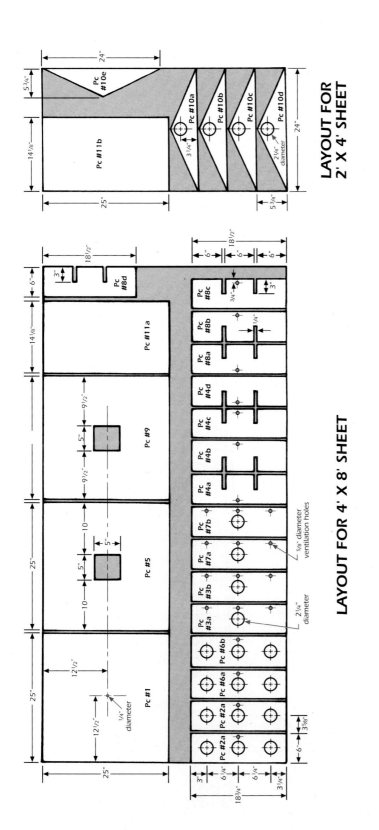

LAYOUT FOR 2' X 4' SHEET

LAYOUT FOR 4' X 8' SHEET

Figure 12

Eastern Bluebird

Bluebirds are not selective about the type of box they use and there are numerous effective designs. In general the birds probably prefer a round-hole design box to a rectangular opening. If house sparrows are a problem, the Kentucky-style box is recommended over other designs. For more complete information on bluebirds, I highly recommend *Bluebirds and Their Survival* by W.H. Davis and P. Roca, and *The Bluebird: How You Can Help Its Fight for Survival* by Lawrence Zeleny.

1. Construct one of the nesting boxes described in figures 13b to 13f on the following pages.

2. Mount the box on fence posts, metal posts, utility poles, buildings, or fences 3' to 5' above the ground. The best site is a metal post. The next choice is a wooden post. Fences are excellent if the box side is located away from domestic livestock.

3. Place a predator guard under the box as in figure 13a, below.

4. Select appropriate habitat to place the box. Bluebirds will not nest in urban habitats. The best location is near suitable habitat where insects abound and there is a mixture of scattered trees and open grassland. Open fields, roadsides, cemeteries, golf courses, and pastures are all excellent habitat. You may have to place several boxes in good locations to attract one pair of birds.

Figure 13a

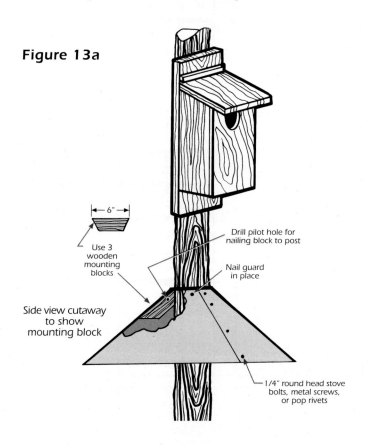

← 6" →

Use 3 wooden mounting blocks

Side view cutaway to show mounting block

Drill pilot hole for nailing block to post

Nail guard in place

1/4" round head stove bolts, metal screws, or pop rivets

5. Place the boxes 75 to 100 yards or more apart. Boxes can be erected at any time, but you'll have the best chance of getting tenants if you put the boxes up by the end of February when the bluebirds begin searching for nesting locations.

6. If house sparrows or starlings evict the bluebirds, quickly erect another box nearby. Bluebirds will not return to boxes sparrows have taken over, but they will quickly find an empty box in the vicinity. The eviction is a minor setback to the bluebirds if another box is available.

7. Inspect, clean, and repair nest boxes periodically. By late February each year, clean boxes of debris, open drains, and make any structural repairs. During the nesting season, frequent inspection may be required to prevent starlings or house sparrows from using nest boxes. Leave old nesting material in the box in the winter to provide insulation for birds taking refuge in the boxes on cold nights.

Figure 13b

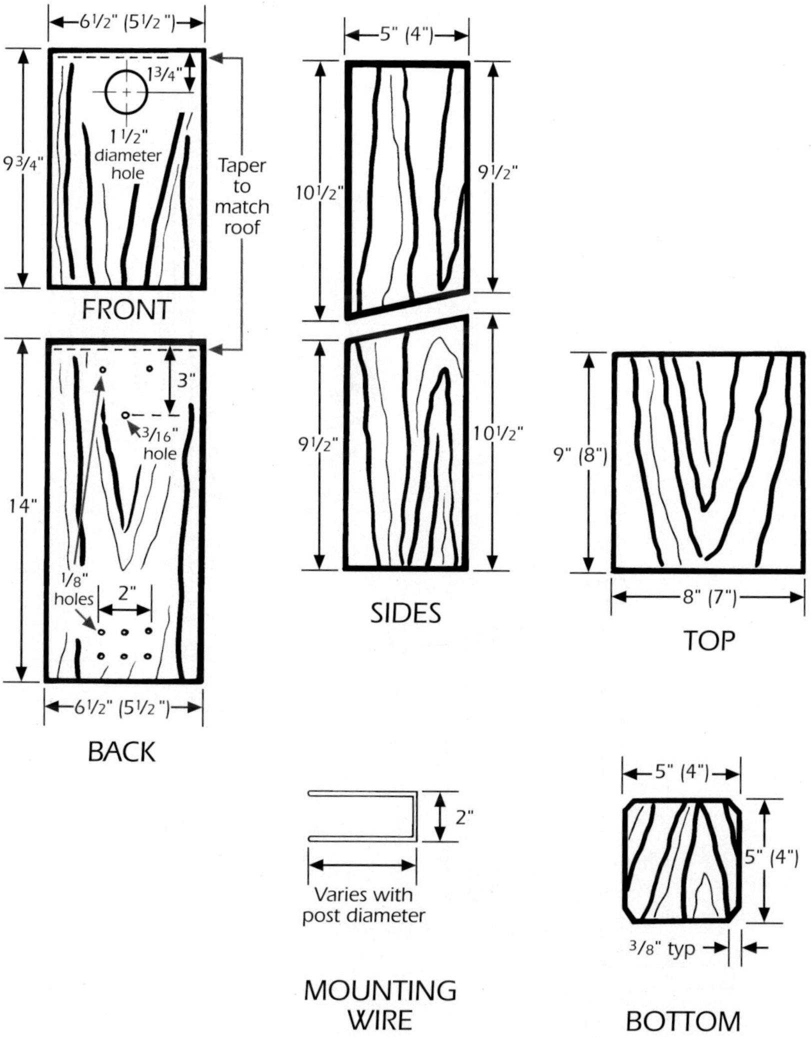

FRONT

BACK

SIDES

TOP

MOUNTING WIRE

BOTTOM

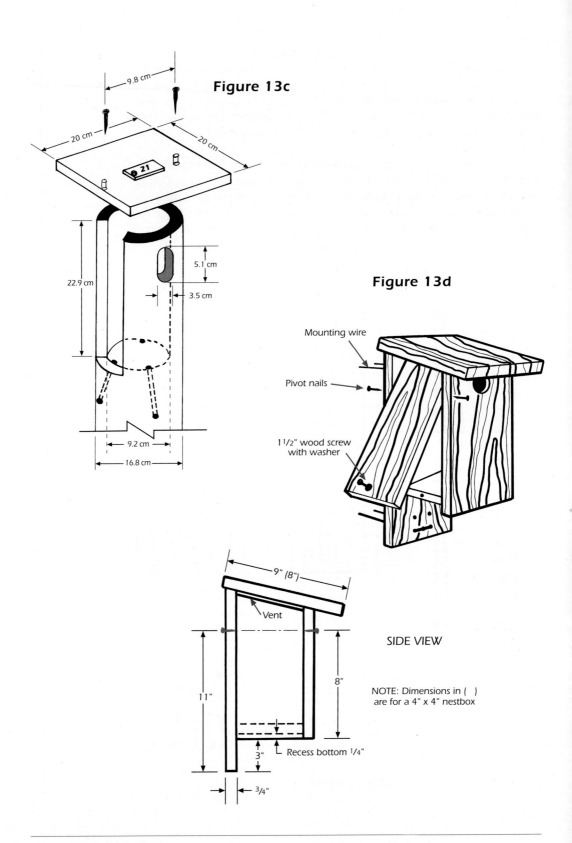

Figure 13c

9.8 cm

20 cm

20 cm

22.9 cm

5.1 cm

3.5 cm

9.2 cm

16.8 cm

Figure 13d

Mounting wire

Pivot nails

1¹/₂" wood screw
with washer

9" (8")

Vent

SIDE VIEW

8"

NOTE: Dimensions in ( )
are for a 4" x 4" nestbox

11"

3"

Recess bottom ¹/₄"

³/₄"

Figure 13e

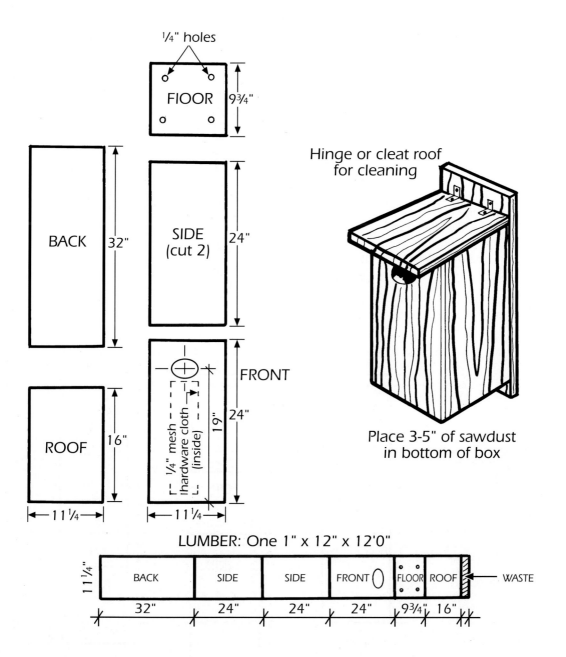

¼" holes

FlOOR 9¾"

BACK 32"

SIDE (cut 2) 24"

ROOF 16"

FRONT

¼" mesh hardware cloth (inside)

19" 24"

11¼" 11¼"

Hinge or cleat roof for cleaning

Place 3-5" of sawdust in bottom of box

LUMBER: One 1" x 12" x 12'0"

11¼"

BACK	SIDE	SIDE	FRONT ◯	FLOOR	ROOF	WASTE
32"	24"	24"	24"	9¾"	16"	

Figure 13f

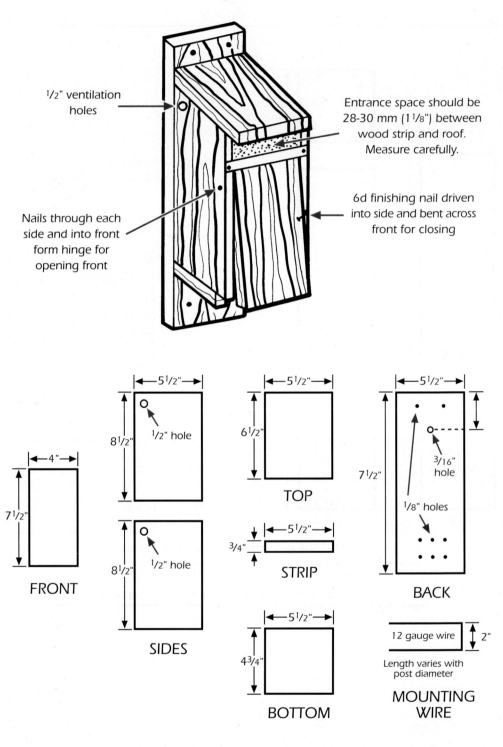

½" ventilation holes

Entrance space should be 28-30 mm (1⅛") between wood strip and roof. Measure carefully.

6d finishing nail driven into side and bent across front for closing

Nails through each side and into front form hinge for opening front

FRONT
4"
7½"

SIDES
5½"
8½" ½" hole
8½" ½" hole

TOP
5½"
6½"

STRIP
5½"
¾"

BOTTOM
5½"
4¾"

BACK
5½"
7½"
3/16" hole
⅛" holes

MOUNTING WIRE
12 gauge wire 2"
Length varies with post diameter

Bats

Bats are interesting and useful animals. People often fail to realize that bats benefit humans. One benefit is their ability to consume large numbers of insects. A single little brown bat may eat 500 to 600 mosquito-sized insects an hour. That's more than 3,000 insects a night! Another benefit provided by bats includes pollination and dispersal of seed for many tropical plants. The local grocery store would not be the same without products that depend on bats for their survival. Wild stocks of bananas, avocados, dates, figs, peaches, mangoes, cloves, cashews, and agave are all pollinated by bats.

Bats have also contributed to medical research in birth control and artificial insemination techniques, navigational aids for the blind, vaccines and drugs, and new low-temperature surgical techniques.

The red, hoary, and silver-haired bats help to maintain forest by feeding on forest pests such as tent caterpillar moths. These bats are important for maintaining ecosystem health. Without bats, we would suffer great economic losses, and our quality of life would be reduced.

Few animals are as misunderstood as bats. They are the subject of myths, misunderstandings, and folklore that make them among the most feared animals in Kentucky. Bats are relentlessly persecuted wherever they are found. The presence of a bat in a house probably causes more alarm than does any other wildlife species. This intense fear is probably more dangerous that the bats themselves. People have broken arms and legs in frenzied escapes, almost drowned falling off boat docks as bats swoop for mosquitoes, or become inadvertently poisoned or otherwise injured when fumigating a house. These fears are unwarranted. Contrary to what you may have heard, most bats are not rabid; bat droppings in buildings are usually not a source of histoplasmosis; bats are not filthy and will not infest homes with dangerous parasites; bats are not aggressive and will not attack people or pets; and Kentucky bats do not feed on blood.

Why worry about conserving bats? Bat populations in Kentucky and America are declining at a rapid rate. Fifty-seven percent of Kentucky's bat fauna is listed as rare, threatened, or endangered. More than half of America's 43 bat species are in the same status. Bat populations have been declining in the United States and Kentucky for more than 20 years. One method homeowners can use to keep bats out of their attics and still benefit from the bats' control of insects is to erect a bat house or box.

Research in recent years has provided a wealth of information on developing bat boxes that work. The concept of a bat box originated in Europe, but as little as 15 percent of early bat boxes were occupied by bats. Boxes of newer designs have increased the occupancy rate to as high as 74 to 88 percent. For more information on constructing bat houses, I recommend *The Bat House Builders Handbook* by M.D. Tuttle and D.L. Hensley.

Figure 14

Dimensions:

A	Roof	16½" x 11¼"
B	Front	18¾" x 9¼"
C	Back	27" x 9¼"
D	Ceiling	9¾" x 9¼"
E	Partition	9¼" x 8"
F	Partition	9¼" 14"
G	Sides	11¼" wide, 27" back, 18¾" front

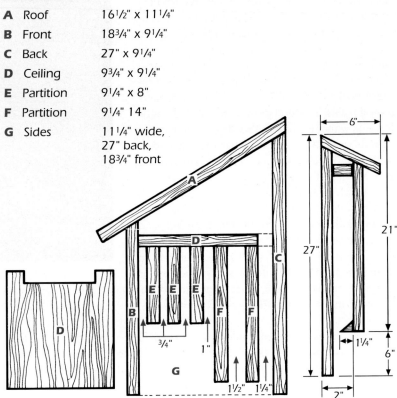

The three most important considerations when constructing a bat house are size, interior construction, and temperature control.

1. Generally speaking, larger houses are better. Boxes should be at least 7" deep, 24" wide, and 12 to 24" tall.

2. Divide the box into individual roosting chambers using interior baffles. The crevices should measure 3/4" to 1-1/2" deep.

3. All interior surfaces must be roughened with saw cuts.

4. Finally, all boxes should be stained dark brown or black and have black roofing paper tacked to the upper portions of the box, while ventilation slits should be cut into the lower sides and front.

5. Placement is also important in attracting bats to boxes. The box should be placed so it receives a minimum of 7 hours of full sunlight. The boxes can be placed on a building or a post. Do not mount the boxes in trees. The best location is near a pond, marsh, wetland, or river. Do not place the box in an area that is heavily trafficked by people or where droppings from the box will pose a problem.

6. The boxes should be placed at least 10 to 15' above ground.

7. If you are moving bats from the attic of a house, gather a cup of droppings from the attic, mix with water to make a slurry, and pour this mixture into the bat box.

References

Davis, Wayne H., and Philippe Roca. 1995. *Bluebirds and Their Survival.* Lexington: Univ. Press of Kentucky.

Tuttle, M.D., and D.L. Hensley. 1993. *The Bat House Builders Handbook.* Austin: Univ. of Texas Press.

Wolinski, R.A. 1995. *Enjoying Purple Martins More: The Martin Landlord's Handbook.* [Place?:] Bird Watcher's Digest Press.

Zeleny, Lawrence. 1976. *The Bluebird: How You Can Help Its Fight for Survival.* Bloomington: Indiana Univ. Press.

Index

Page numbers followed by **f** indicate figures or captions. Those followed by **t** indicate tables. Scientific names are indexed only when there is no common name for a species.

adelgid, balsam wooly, 71
Adler, Bill, Jr., 159
admirals: red, 96, 108, 200t, 205f; white, 108
aeration, of water gardens, 136
aesthetic appeal, of natural landscaping, 21-22
Agalinis spp. [no common name], 200t
agave, 5
alder, common, 220, 220f
alfalfa butterfly, 197t, 203f
algae control, 128-29, 137
alumroot, 187t
amphibians: fish and, 123; salamanders, 118, 123; toads, 38f, 123; water for attracting, 116, 118, 119. *See also* frogs
anemone, 187t, 206t; false rue, 187t; meadow rue, 190t; rue, 187t; tall, 187t
Angelica spp. [no common name], 196t
anglewings, 96
annual wildflowers, list of, 82
Anoda cristata [no common name], 194t
apple trees: as butterfly host, 96; as moth host, 113t. *See also* crab apple trees
arbutus, trailing, 192t
arrowfeather, 189t
arrowhead, 134f; cultivation information, 187t; in water gardens, 133t; water requirements, 5
arrow-wood. *See* black haw
Ashland Oil Headquarters, 116-17
ash trees: animals attracted by, 212;

as butterfly host, 196t, 200t, 212; cultivars for Kentucky, 212; description of, 212, 212f; as moth host, 112t, 113t; white, 113t, 212
aspen, big-tooth, 213. *See also* cottonwood
aspergillosis, 162
asters, 100f; as butterfly host, 96, 99, 199t; cultivation information, 187t; desirability of, 82; maturation time, 83; as nectar source, 101t, 102t, 113, 206t, 207t
—species/types: aromatic, 187t; calico, 187t; downy, 187t; golden, 207t; Maryland golden, 187t; New England, 102t, 187t; Short's, 187t; silky, 102t, 187t; sky blue, 102t, 187t; smooth, 187t; Stoke's, 187t
auditory repellents, 180-81
avian pox, 162
azaleas. *See* rhododendrons and azaleas
azures: dusky, 199t; spring, 199t, 203t, 213, 221, 222, 227

bacon fat, 149
balsam wooly adelgid, 71
Baltimore (butterfly), 199t
bamboo, dwarf, 189t
banded birds, 164
baneberry, 187t; white, 187t
bare-root stock, 81
base map, 54
bass, 123
basswood, 112t, 113t
bats: description of, 18f, 266, 266f;

houses for, 18, 45, 265-66; impact of land use on, 8; for insect control, 18; pesticides and, 17; pest problems with, 174, 175-76; water for attracting, 118
—species/types: big brown, 18, 18f, 174; little brown, 18, 174
beans, 194t, 198t; fuzzy, 194t; wild, 194t, 198t
beardtongue, 187t, 206t; hairy, 187t; Small's, 187t; smooth, 187t
Beargrass Creek, 11
beaver: pest problems with, 183; trees/shrubs for attracting, 212-14, 216-21, 223-27, 229, 230; vines for attracting, 231
bee balm, 187t, 206t; red, 187t
beech, American: animals attracted by, 212; birds that nest in, 44; description of, 212, 212f; as moth host, 112t
beefsteak, 70
bellflower, 187t
bellwort, 187t; bishop's-cap, 187t; large flowered, 187t; small flowered, 187t
bergamot, 102t, 187t; white, 187t; wild, 102t, 103f
biodiversity, natural landscaping for protecting, 23. *See also* diversity
biofilters, 129, 130-31
birches: animals attracted by, 221; as butterfly host, 194t, 200t, 201t, 221; description of, 221, 221f; as moth host, 112t, 113t; river, 5, 221
Bird Banding Laboratory, 164
birdbaths, 38, 119, 121